A LOVE AFFAIR WITH BIRDS

A Love Affair with Birds

THE LIFE OF THOMAS SADLER ROBERTS

Sue Leaf

University of Minnesota Press

Minneapolis · London

The University of Minnesota Press gratefully acknowledges financial assistance provided for the publication of this book from the James Ford Bell Foundation.

Published by the University of Minnesota Press
111 Third Avenue South, Suite 290
Minneapolis, MN 55401-2520
http://www.upress.umn.edu

A Cataloging-in-Publication record for this book is available from the Library of Congress.

ISBN 978-0-8166-7564-7 (hc)
ISBN 978-0-8166-7565-4 (pb)

Printed in the United States of America on acid-free paper

The University of Minnesota is an equal-opportunity educator and employer.

28 27 26 25 24 23 22 21   10 9 8 7 6 5 4 3 2 1

For my "Dr. Tom"

To him who in the love of Nature holds
Communion with her visible forms, she speaks
A various language
      — *William Cullen Bryant, "Thanatopsis"*

Contents

Acknowledgments

A book like this, drawn almost entirely from letters and journals, does not get written without tremendous support from librarians and archivists. I owe much to the late Penelope Krosch, head archivist at the University of Minnesota Archives, who labored for years transcribing Thomas Sadler Roberts's journals and published her efforts in *Shotgun and Stethoscope* in 1991. Penny also cataloged the voluminous collection of letters and memorabilia that Roberts, a packrat, accumulated over his lifetime. Her work made this book possible.

Thanks are due, too, to Lois Hendrickson, assistant curator at the Wangensteen Historical Library of Biology and Medicine at the University of Minnesota, for her broad knowledge of university and Minneapolis medical history and of Krosch's work, and for her enthusiastic interest in this project. University archivists Erik Moore and Erin George were unflaggingly helpful in retrieving material, often on short notice. Staff at the Minnesota Historical Society were also cheerful in retrieving material about Roberts time and again as I rechecked facts and quotes.

Don Luce, curator of art at the University of Minnesota's Bell Museum of Natural History, offered invaluable help over the course of the project, giving me access to wonderful photographs taken by Roberts, scanning numerous images, and offering insight into Lee and Florence Jaques and the inner workings of the Bell Museum. He read early chapters of the manuscript, and both he and John Moriarty, the natural resources specialist at the Ramsey County Parks system, who read the final draft, have been most supportive. My thanks to them.

Diane Buganski of the Goodhue County Historical Society helped bring Mabel Densmore to life. Vonda Kelly of the Bloomington Historical Society helped find information on the Long Meadow Gun Club.

I interviewed a number of people who knew *of* Roberts, but only two who had direct memories of him. Bob Binger of White Bear Lake, Minnesota, was one of Roberts's bird students. Thomas Robert Breckenridge, oldest child of Walter Breckenridge, had childhood memories of a very old Roberts. Tom and his sister, Barbara Breckenridge Franklin, gave me insight into their father. Lucy Bell Hartwell, granddaughter of James Ford Bell, shared her memories of her grandfather with me.

Tom Holman, a board member of the Hennepin History Museum and formerly of the Minneapolis Heritage Preservation Commission, helped identify one of Roberts's photographs merely labeled "Old Tiger in front of Ninth Street house" and placed it in Minneapolis. He also provided expertise on the historical city.

Roberts's last residence, at 2303 Pleasant Avenue, still stands. Owner Mark Dolski and resident Nancy Ahmad were incredibly gracious to a stranger who contacted them out of the blue and asked for a tour of their house.

Tony Hertzel of the Minnesota Ornithologists' Union provided information about the Thomas Sadler Roberts Award.

The far-flung Roberts clan has been helpful, inspirational, and enthusiastic partners in this endeavor. Nancy C. Roberts, granddaughter-in-law to Roberts, provided dates, stories, and family photographs when I visited her home in Panama City, Florida. She also read the first completed draft of the manuscript and made sharp-eyed edits. Carl Roberts, great-grandson, who resembles Roberts to a remarkable degree, scanned photographs. Both Nancy and Carl showed Floridian hospitality by hosting a Gulf shrimp boil, where I met other great-grandchildren Doug, Cathy, and Helen. Great-granddaughter Shelley Roberts also provided photographs and good conversation. Lane Phillips, another great-grandchild, and his sisters Jane and Catharine have been very generous with family photographs and memories. Lane has been my local family contact in Minnesota.

My editor, Todd Orjala at the University of Minnesota Press, encouraged me early on in the project and granted a deadline that both gave me enough time for thorough research and yet made sure this did not consume the remainder of my life. Novice biographer that I was, I relied wholly on his judgment. Kristian Tvedten, editorial assistant at the Press, was prompt and authoritative on the many nuts and bolts I encountered in the process of transforming my research into a book.

My faithful, talented writing group, the core of which has been together for fifteen years, read every single chapter. If they told me a passage was boring, I rewrote. If they wanted more detail, I fleshed it out. They frequently did quick reads of material when I needed a second set of eyes. Past and present members include Judy Helgen, Patti Isaacs, Gayla Marty, Susan Narayan, and Pam Schmid. They were critical to the writing of this book.

My children, Andy, Katie, John, and Christina Leaf, know more about Roberts and about Minnesota birds than they ever wanted to. My thanks to them for tolerating their mother's obsession.

Finally, my husband, Tom Leaf, was my first reader for all the chapters, provided advice on medical aspects in the manuscript, and learned to ask, "What year are we talking about here?" whenever I launched into another story as if it happened that day. He has cheerfully tolerated my interest in another man for five long years. Penny Krosch said the same of her husband. Roberts does attract the ladies.

Introduction

Thirty-five years ago, when I was a zoology graduate student, I was quartered on the third floor of the Bell Museum of Natural History on the University of Minnesota campus. My desk and those of my fellow graduate students were nestled among the cabinets containing the "scientific collection": study skins of birds and mammals that had accumulated over the years. This was the working museum. Hidden from the public eye, directly over the Touch and See room, our little rabbit warren of office space nurtured would-be biologists amid the fur, feathers, and bones of once-living animals.

Down the hall from the scientific collections was a small natural history library. In the age before the Internet brought nearly limitless information to a laptop, this library was invaluable. If I needed to know, say, the range of the Chestnut-sided Warbler or wanted to read a recent article in *Science* that people were talking about, I wandered down to the library. The most-used material was at hand just inside the door, but beyond were several rows of shelves that harbored thousands of books, leather-bound and lettered in gilt. The titles covered a wealth of natural history topics, and some were quite old. I frequently wished I had the time to browse through their ranks, to linger and breathe in the enticing scent of yellowed paper and embossed covers, to relish the creak of a book's spine as the apricot-colored pages were turned.

I did not know it then, but this was the personal library of Thomas Sadler Roberts, a Minneapolis physician, the man responsible for breathing life into Minnesota's natural history museum. Over the span of seventy years, Roberts methodically collected representative birds that lived, bred, or migrated through the state, spearheaded the effort to assemble the same type of collection of the mammals of Minnesota, and then oversaw the formation of a public museum that would bring the beauty and wonder of the state's natural history to its citizens.

I also did not know, merely because I did not look, that on a shelf in the little natural history library were small volumes even more valuable than the attractive assemblage of natural history books. These were the bird journals of Roberts, begun in 1874 when he was sixteen years old, living in his home-town of Minneapolis, a small community on the Mississippi near the Falls of St. Anthony. Many people, apparently, knew those journals were there; few bothered to take them off the shelf and read through the entries. Roberts's spiky, sometimes illegible handwriting may have dissuaded would-be readers. Eventually, these bird journals found their way to the university archives, where a meticulous and perseverant archivist transcribed them and laid bare the natural world that Roberts experienced as a teenager, the world in which he fell in love with birds.

Reading through Roberts's journals today, one enters a world that is both familiar and unknown. In this world, Minneapolis's neighborhoods extend only to a glacial moraine called "the Bluffs," where the Walker Art Center now stands; water pools in marshes and lakes, runs in creeks, and spills over rock ledges. In the sparse oak woods surrounding the town, Passenger Pigeons nest in colonies and whip-poor-wills sing on summer nights. Where the trees thin into prairie patches, Horned Larks arrive early, and prairie chickens perform courtship dances.

How does a love affair start? What drives a passion? Roberts himself had trouble answering these questions. When he was asked in later life about his boyhood interest in birds, his answer was hazy. He attributed it to a penchant for collecting things, but that begs the question, why birds and not butterflies? Or rocks? Or, even, tin soldiers? He came to believe, though, that naturalists are generally born and not made, that some people unaccountably resonate to the heartbeat of nature.

I include myself among those who hear the heartbeat, though I make no claims of the prowess Roberts acquired. I clearly remember the birds of my childhood—the Western Meadowlark with its sweet, flutelike song that woke me most June mornings, the pewee that plaintively sang in the white pines at our family cabin, the loon that called at dusk from the lake. At age nineteen I began a Life List. Many of the most common birds were of such intimate acquaintance that I listed them merely as "Roseville." Date of first sighting: unknown.

But the ability to hear the heartbeat needs to be nurtured. For my seventh birthday, my mother gave me a slim little bird guide by Chester Reed, a classic that was first published in 1906. I pondered the pictures endlessly.

Even today, a glimpse of Reed's "American Goldfinch" calls forth a flood of associations of my grade school years, when this little beauty was Minnesota's state bird.

Here, too, was a point of contact with Roberts, though of course I did not know it. He delighted in introducing those around him to the avian world, and this was a book he recommended when asked about identification guides. He loved to share his passion for birds with those around him, and so his secretaries, his nurses, his cribbage partners, his patients, his students, his children and grandchildren all became conversant with robins and chickadees, Mourning Doves and Blue Jays. Many became reliable birders, and their observant records became valuable information about the avifauna of Minnesota.

Roberts was raised in a world in which the fortunate—and he was among the fortunate—had an obligation to contribute to the shaping of society, and he felt this obligation keenly. He arrived in Minnesota as a young boy, when the state itself was only nine years old. In his teens, he dreamed of ways he could foster a love of nature in Minnesota's people, and the dream never faltered. He came of age in a state that was giddy with the wealth of natural resources at its disposal, and ruthless in its plundering of them. Undeterred in the wake of habitat destruction and declining bird populations, Roberts had a natural buoyancy that propelled him forward. Under its head of steam, he wrote the definitive, two-volume *The Birds of Minnesota,* formed bird clubs, spoke to schoolchildren, delivered radio talks, and personally escorted museum attendees to various exhibits until the final few months of his long, active life.

Great love affairs seldom vanish without a trace, but his legacy to us is in many ways diffuse. The little natural history library in the Bell Museum has long been disbanded, the volumes that Roberts accumulated so thoughtfully scattered here and there in the university's greater library system. But other vestiges remain.

A surprising number of nature lovers in Minnesota can trace a lineage to Roberts, whether they realize it or not. When at work on this book, I was startled one day to recognize the face of my undergraduate ecology professor Ward Tanner (with hair on a head I had only seen bald) in the bird class photo of 1940. Many, many people remember school field trips to the Bell Museum of Natural History—Roberts was the guiding force behind most of the dramatic dioramas in the museum. *The Birds of Minnesota* can sometimes be found in used bookstores throughout the state. I found my copy in a tiny, rural shop on the top shelf of the "Minnesota" section. I promptly went home and told my husband it was the only thing I wanted for Christmas that year.

Let us not forget the breathing spaces of the untrammeled places that have come under protection—places that are now national wildlife refuges or nature preserves, land that was often saved upon his recommendation.

The bird-watchers in Minnesota who know of Roberts tend to claim him as one of their own and dismiss his medical career as a misguided decision that he eventually rectified when he closed his practice and devoted the remainder of his life to ornithology. But in the course of researching this book, I have come to disagree. Roberts was dedicated to his medical career and devoted especially to those patients he had brought into the world, whom he thought of as "his babies." He felt honored to witness the intimate events in human life—birth and death, sickness and health. Decades after assuming care of the University of Minnesota's natural history museum, he demurred at the label of "ornithologist" and referred to himself as a retired physician.

There is a link between these two seemingly disparate occupations, and indeed in all of his efforts, beginning in youth: Roberts was a healer, a crafter of wholeness. A kind man, he drew upon the expansion of scientific knowledge to nurture the young, comfort the sick, and protect the vulnerable—and later in life, those in the last category most often possessed feathers! This compassion—laced with humor and shrewd commentary—appears on the pages of *The Birds of Minnesota* in his vignettes of the birds, in the letters from his patients stored in the university archives, and even, in terse scribbles, in his little pocket diaries, which in later years he kept tucked in his shirt pocket.

So often I have wished that I could resurrect him, reform his ashes, and animate his bones. In this book, I have tried to do the next best thing and raise him up on its pages. I was aided in this by the numerous journals, letters, bird lists, and field notes that Roberts kept over his long life. In places in this book where he seems to spring to life, I have drawn on photographs, his own journal accounts, and his sightings of birds as documentation to recreate these scenes. If I have done my job, he can be found here. If he comes to meet you as you read, perhaps you, too, will discover the beauty of the bird world, the losses it has incurred, and what we—the inheritors of his legacy—must do to put it back together.

CHAPTER 1

A Fledgling Start

> As a general proposition, it is a dangerous experiment
> to introduce a foreign species of any kind.
>
> — *The Birds of Minnesota,* 1: 419

The *Key City* slowly wound its way past the banks of the Mississippi River after a night of torrential rain. The river's water levels were already high and would rise higher with the night's deluge. The month of June 1867 had been uncommonly wet.

It was a fine morning, clear and blue, as if the world had been reborn after the tempestuous lashing. The steamboat's travelers, having weathered the storm, breakfasted in the dining room. Among those on board enjoying their breakfast was a family of four from Philadelphia: John Roberts, his wife, Elizabeth, and their sons, Thomas and Walter, ages nine and four. A third child remained behind in the care of relatives.[1] The Robertses had been in transit six days, traveling by rail and stopping nightly in small-town hotels and in Chicago at the Tremont, one of the finest in the bustling city.

The night on the *Key City* was the last leg of the journey. No railroad bridges yet spanned the wide Mississippi. Visitors from the East Coast traveling west of the river usually engaged a packet service, which offered a combination of rail and paddleboat tickets. With its several tiers and wedding cake profile, the *Key City* was considered a gem among paddleboats plying the river that decade. The Robertses had boarded at Dubuque, Iowa, and were headed upriver to St. Paul, Minnesota, the final navigational port on the river.

With the steamboat moving at a leisurely speed of fifteen miles per hour, passengers on the deck observed the limestone bluffs rising above the river's floodplain. The heavy rain had rinsed the trees and vines studding the banks of the river, giving a freshness to the tender green hues of June. Birdsong hung reedy and sweet on the morning air. The sky was crystalline.

Nearing St. Paul, the steamer glided past a series of small hills on its starboard side. Naked and stark, the Indian burial mounds gave a mute testimony to the native Dakota who had so recently lived on the river. Newcomers to the state must have puzzled over their meaning. The *Key City* blew its whistle to signal her approach to the city and minutes later arrived at the lower levee.

If a camera eye had captured the Robertses as they gathered up belongings and disembarked the *Key City*, it would have recorded a slight, bearded blond man, painfully slender; accompanied by two young boys, also blond, with sensitive faces; and a plump, pretty, dark-haired woman, well-dressed in traveling clothes.

None of the Robertses had ever been this far west. But they came to Minnesota on the thin hope of restored health for John, who in his forties was wasting away from consumption. That was the term in popular parlance for pulmonary tuberculosis, a good word to convey the eating away of the body's vitality, a sapping of energy, a disease that ravaged the lungs, causing its victims to cough up blood, lose weight, and sink into a listless existence until a nearly inevitable death. This seemed to be the fate that awaited John. He arrived in Minnesota weighing only 115 pounds.[2]

It would be many years before medicine could identify the tuberculosis bacterium, and almost a century before a cure would be had. In John Roberts's time, the consumptive was often advised to seek fresh, dry air and sunshine. Though John sometimes discounted his doctors' advice, he had chosen to heed this injunction. He had much to live for. He also had the good fortune to be able to devote his days to the endeavor. Buoyed by successful real estate ventures with his brother in Philadelphia, he would be financially independent for the remainder of his life.

In later years, Thomas never commented on how much his parents had told their children about John's health. But he had a particularly strong bond with his father. He could not have misinterpreted the spells of coughing that wracked his father's frail form, John's days of listlessness, the bright blotches of red on a clean white handkerchief.

That the family relinquished Pennsylvania for frontier Minnesota underscored the desperation of the trip. The Roberts family had made their home in the environs of Philadelphia for almost two hundred years. The Welsh ancestral immigrant, Thomas Roberts, a Quaker, had accompanied

William Penn on his second trip to his colony in 1699. In the intervening years, the Robertses had acquired a substantial farm in Germantown, on the outskirts of Philadelphia. It was there that John and Elizabeth's oldest child, Thomas Sadler, had been born. The former Elizabeth Sadler, known to intimates as "Lizzie," was also rooted in the East, with family in Havre-de-Grace, Maryland. In coming to Minnesota, John and Lizzie and their boys had left behind parents, siblings, and numerous cousins.

As they made their way from the Lower Landing up the hill to the Merchants Hotel, the Roberts family had opportunity to observe their surroundings. The contrast to long-established Philadelphia, with bricked streets and graceful elms, was stark. Minnesota had been a state for a mere nine years. White settlement had begun less than twenty years before, with the attainment of territorial status in 1849. Immigrants from northern Europe and Yankees from the East flooded the capital city, erecting helter-skelter a mélange of frame buildings, houses, barns, and rough pioneer stores.

The bloody summer of 1862, only five years in the past, had dealt a serious setback to European settlement of Minnesota. While most of the nation had been focused on an ugly Civil War, fighting between homesteaders and the native Dakota had broken out in the south-central part of the state. Hundreds of people from both sides had died, and large numbers of settlers, shaken by the carnage, had pulled up roots and left for the East Coast. If the Roberts family had journeyed up the Mississippi only fifteen years earlier, they would have seen thriving Dakota villages at Winona, Red Wing, and South St. Paul. After the bloodshed, however, the federal government had forcibly removed the Dakota from their homeland. Still, settlers in the hinterlands remained jittery.

Not so in St. Paul, which was secure in its status as an urban area. Released from the fiscal restraints imposed by the Civil War, the city now boomed. Its population had rocketed from four thousand to twenty thousand people in a mere fifteen years. The city was the young state's largest, its only port, and its capital. Still, its appearance was rough. Nearly all the streets were unpaved and rutted and, after a night of rain, muddy. Multistoried brick structures hunkered next to squat, rude shanties. Here and there, a church steeple rose above the downtown. The large, domed capitol off by itself, north of downtown on Tenth and Cedar, dominated the horizon. As they had in Chicago, the Robertses took accommodation at St. Paul's finest hotel, the Merchants, but oh, what a contrast! The hotel had undergone a series of additions, until in 1867 it was a conglomerate of brick, lumber, and logs with a hundred rooms. The original tamarack log building remained under clapboard siding. The hodgepodge of a hotel was indicative of the city as a whole. To an eye accustomed to lovely Philadelphia, St. Paul must have seemed gawky and uncomely.

First impressions were not auspicious. Later that day, John would admit in his journal that although he found the city to be a "thriving place" on a walk about town, it was "not near so large as I had expected from the representation that had been given me."[3]

The good weather the Robertses had met upon arrival remained with them. The next day dawned clear and bright, and the family made plans to do some sightseeing. Two attractions that lay to the west of St. Paul were well known to East Coast visitors: the Falls of St. Anthony—the largest cataract on the Mississippi River—and the Falls of Minnehaha, made famous by the publication in 1855 of Henry Wadsworth Longfellow's popular poem *The Song of Hiawatha*.

The Robertses joined a couple from Dubuque that they had met on the steamer and took the train to St. Anthony, twelve miles away. "Riding the cars" they called it. At St. Anthony, the party rented a horse and carriage and drove over the suspension bridge into the smaller community of Minneapolis for the first time.

By 1867, the banks of the Mississippi were already lined with mills of all kinds, using the waterpower to saw logs, grind grain, and spin wool into yarn. St. Anthony Falls itself was marred by a dam that diverted the river above the falls to chutes on either bank, leaving the central limestone bedrock exposed. Only in times of high water did the mighty Mississippi spill over the dam, restoring the falls as a genuine cataract.[4] It was this sight, however, that the Roberts expedition likely saw on their first trip to Minneapolis. The storm they had experienced on their trip up from Dubuque was only one of many that month that had raised river levels to their highest in eight years.[5]

A well-traveled road led from Minneapolis south to Minnehaha Falls. Here, too, the falls were white with swollen flow, tumbling over the limestone and crashing in sprays of water rising from the stream below. A small footbridge crossed the creek at the base of the falls, where adventuresome tourists could experience the torrent of water rushing underfoot. There were even wooden park benches resting on a wooden platform on the south bank of the creek. Already, evidence of numerous visitors could be seen in the compacted earth and exposed tree roots on the creek bank.

Still, a trip to the Falls of Minnehaha was a venture that took the sightseer beyond the established town, and even beyond the cultivated acres, into the remnant of oak savanna that flourished between the Mississippi and Minnesota Rivers. The area bordered the Fort Snelling Reserve, which was closed to development. Prairie plants—big bluestem and Indian grass—grew amid scattered bur oaks. Early observers had commented on the savanna's beauty. One tried to domesticate the landscape: "the clumps of oak on the prairies seen at a distance, resemble an orchard; and the leaves rustling in the wind and showing their underside give them the beauty of blossoms."[6] Imagine the native Philadelphians, accustomed to the gentle, cultivated farms of Pennsylvania, seeing this wild land for the first time. Did it seem sparse and lacking in trees? Open and inviting? Untamed and in need of some pruning?

All in all, the junket to Minneapolis and St. Anthony was considered a success. "Pleasant," John pronounced it, back home that evening, "though rather a long [trip] being between 25 and 30 miles."[7]

Having made the obligatory pilgrimage to major tourist sites, the Robertses now settled into daily life in St. Paul. They moved from the hotel to a boarding-house on Tenth Street with a shady front yard. Acting on his resolve to spend a great share of time in fresh air, John embarked on daily outings. Sometimes he hiked, often with Thomas and Walter; sometimes he rented a horse and went riding. On occasion, the whole family ventured out together.

Other outings were simple walks about town. From these, John came to the conclusion that St. Paul was only a "middling" town, with generally poor streets, but within a fortnight, he conceded that he liked the town "better than I did at first."[8] The weather was a source of dissatisfaction. It was rainy, it was windy, storms were violent, and conditions changed unpredictably. Even in late June, people made fires in stoves and fireplaces to keep warm on chilly mornings and evenings.[9]

Lake Como was a favorite destination of St. Paulites. A road ran directly from the city out to the lake. One day, Thomas and Walter went fishing with

John, who had rented a two-seater carriage and horse. Soon, however, dark blue storm clouds loomed on the western horizon, and before they could make it home, they were caught in a downpour.

The newcomers were regularly drenched that summer. "[We came] home with thunder and lightning and heavy winds and rain," John reported on July 2. "It comes to shower here very suddenly nearly every day."[10]

About a week and a half after their arrival in St. Paul, John and Lizzie again rode the cars to Minneapolis, this time to explore the town. They dined at the elegant Nicollet House, the major downtown hotel. Situated on Hennepin and Washington Avenues, its five-storied, cream-colored brick presence dominated Bridge Square, the commons at the foot of the suspension bridge crossing the river to the city of St. Anthony. The Nicollet was known for its excellent food and for the elegant furnishings—Belgian carpets, lace curtains, and tapestries—uncommon in Minnesota in 1867.[11] It sported a little observation cupola on its roof. A visitor to the cupola could look down Hennepin Avenue to the three-storied Pence Opera House, seating one thousand, which had celebrated its grand opening four days before.

But the view from the Nicollet must have been anything but refined on the day of the Robertses' visit. It had rained nearly every day for the past ten; the muddy unpaved streets were undoubtedly frightful. Sidewalks were constructed of boards. Many of the buildings, both commercial and residential, were of unpainted wood. Hennepin Avenue, in the business district near the foot of the bridge, consisted primarily of two-storied false-fronted buildings, so that the main thoroughfare resembled a western frontier town—which, in 1867, it was.

Despite John's feeling unwell all day, the outing was pleasant. "I like the appearance of Minneapolis much better than St. Paul," he wrote in his journal.[12] So much better, in fact, that two weeks later, Thomas accompanied his father on a return trip to Minneapolis to look at houses to buy. And a week after that, the elder Robertses again went house hunting, this time to examine a house and lot on Hennepin Avenue selling for $3,000. That price was the upper end of the housing market in the emerging city. The *Minneapolis Morning Tribune* carried listings for houses ranging in price from $1,200 to $2,000.[13] The place proved not to be what they were looking for, but that same day they made arrangements at a Minneapolis boardinghouse and prepared to move to the younger, smaller town.

Why would people from old, established Philadelphia choose little Minneapolis over the capital city, St. Paul? The two, though hardly twin in 1867, were beginning to distinguish themselves. St. Paul's seventeen-year-old newspaper, the *Pioneer,* carried national and international news and printed waterfront activity—the arrivals and departures of paddleboats, which came into the port with passengers and freight. Minneapolis's *Morning Tribune,* only weeks old in June 1867, also had outstate correspondents and news coming over the telegraph wires, but it highlighted East Coast market activity, how grain, wool, cattle, and "produce"—butter, eggs, flour, pork, and candles—were selling. Neither city had a sewer system or water works yet, but discussion was under way in each city's council. St. Paul's capitol building was gaslit, but Minneapolis could not make such a claim.

"Minneapolis is not near so large a place as St. Paul but has a much finer location," John explained on the pages of his journal. He had just returned from taking Thomas and Walter to see a roaring St. Anthony Falls, again full with floodwater. "[The falls] present at this time a beautiful appearance as the River is very high from the late heavy rains. . . . Minneapolis . . . is quite nice in character."[14]

Perhaps the Roberts family gravitated toward the smaller city precisely because it was less populated. John spent long hours every day on walks or rides out into the countryside. In Minneapolis, it was much easier to get out of town. The city was developed only to "the Bluffs," a narrow glacial moraine that local residents also called "the Devil's Backbone." Even a good portion of the platted area was open woods, with a marshy lake at the foot of the bluffs. Hennepin Avenue cut through the bluffs and led up to the lakes and open country, past farms and shallow duck ponds. Remnant oak woods and rolling farmland surrounded Lakes Calhoun and Harriet, and southeast of these was the savanna of Fort Snelling's reserve. In 1867, Minnehaha Creek formed the reserve's northern boundary.

The suspension bridge between Minneapolis and St. Anthony gave a wanderer access to the other side of the river and to open land to the north and east, all the way to Lakes Josephine and Johanna and the surrounding oak woods. There were many more places to explore in Minneapolis.

In August, the incessant rains of June and July gave way to ninety-degree heat. The Roberts family, now settled in Minneapolis, made daily trips of discovery around town. A new railroad track proved to be a terrific place to hunt for agates. At the end of August, a local woods produced an abundance of hazelnuts, which the whole family gathered to enjoy in the winter. The lakes provided opportunities to fish—Cedar Lake and Lake Calhoun were favorite spots—but John never seemed to catch many fish.

In his journal, John recorded his health status and his physical activity. "I did not feel well and raised some little blood through the day. I rather overdid myself yesterday [on] my hot trip to St. Paul," he wrote on August 7, 1867, the day after he had ridden the cars to the capital city on an errand for a friend.[15] Coughing up blood was an alarming event, and John underlined the words whenever he recorded an occurrence. Despite frequently feeling ill, John investigated the various milling activities on the river, attended a trial of a bigamist at the courthouse, went to a lecture on the Second Coming, and made an expedition to Lake Minnetonka to fish.

The journals also give evidence of an active, inquisitive mind. He and Lizzie tried out a number of the local churches that first summer. Lizzie, of English descent, had been raised Episcopalian, but they found St. Paul's Episcopal congregation too formal and perhaps a trifle pretentious: "the congregation [was] exceedingly fashionable, the ladies having trains to their dresses *two feet long*."[16] In Minneapolis, they visited the Congregationalists, the Presbyterians ("I can't say that I was very well pleased with the sermon"), the Universalists ("I have never visited a church of that kind"), and the Young Men's Bible Club ("was not much impressed").[17] John, still a Quaker in adulthood, discovered a Friends Society, the only one in Minnesota. Its meetinghouse was on the corner of Hennepin Avenue and Eighth Street. That summer, he took Thomas and Walter to Sunday school.

In mid-August, Thomas accompanied his father on a trip up the Minnesota River to Mankato. They went by rail to Belle Plaine, the halfway point between St. Paul and Mankato, where they had dinner ("a very poor savor"). Father and son then boarded a paddleboat for the overnight journey upriver to Mankato. With Thomas tucked in bed, John went on deck to watch the high bluffs of the Minnesota River drift by in the moonlight of a warm summer night. "I never saw a more beautiful sight than our ride up the river," he later wrote.[18]

They arrived in Mankato in time for breakfast, got settled in a hotel, made a social call, and then rented a carriage. Their destination was Minneopa Falls on the Blue Earth River, a lovely double cascade that plunged forty feet into a shaded gorge, "which we found almost equal to Minnehaha." They liked Mankato, too, describing it as "quite a lively place," a center of both trade and industry.[19]

After a night in the hotel, they retraced their steps. In the daylight, John found the Minnesota had lost its moonlight appeal and was, in truth, "the most crooked stream that I ever saw and quite difficult to navigate from its sharp turns and many obstructions."[20] Nonetheless, they were back in Belle Plaine by midafternoon and in Minneapolis in time for supper.

As September drew to a close, John and Lizzie received word that his brother had rented out their home in Philadelphia for six months. "We have concluded to remain away from home all winter if all goes well," he wrote in his journal.[21] The phrase "if all goes well" was a tacit acknowledgment that he might very well take a turn for the worse. His health was not noticeably improved. He was painfully thin—109 pounds, occasionally coughing up blood—and frequently had energy only to lounge around the house. "But," he noted, "I may have been worse if I had remained at home."[22]

The decision made to stay the winter, it became necessary to enroll Thomas in school. One school building served all of Minneapolis. Washington School, a three-story limestone structure on the east side of Third Avenue South between Fourth and Fifth Streets, was new in fall 1867. It replaced a building that had been destroyed by fire two years before. Washington housed the elementary grades on the lower levels and the high school on the floors above.[23] Public school was a first for Thomas; in Philadelphia, he had attended a Quaker school.

In October, John's older brother, Thomas Jefferson Roberts, and his wife, Cornelia, arrived for a visit and presumably brought John and Lizzie's middle child, Emma, to rejoin the family. The Minneapolis Robertses entertained their company with day trips to all the tourist attractions: St. Paul's statehouse, the Falls of St. Anthony and Minnehaha, Fort Snelling, and Lake Calhoun. On several days, John, his brother, and "little Thomas" went out duck hunting at Lake Calhoun, but it was a difficult undertaking without a dog. The birds were wary and distant.

Two weeks later, the Philadelphia Robertses left for home. Snow was already on the ground, and Thanksgiving was coming. After Thanksgiving, Minneapolis experienced a cold snap. The temperature dropped below zero, and the days were frigid and bright. John took his sons out to the woods west of town to track rabbits but found none. "I do not think there are rabbits in this part of the country," he surmised, perhaps a bit hastily, on his first time out in the snowy woods. Nonetheless, it was a lovely time spent in the crystalline air. "I felt very well," he concluded, "and do not mind the cold at all."[24]

CHAPTER 2

Acquiring an Eagle Eye

> [The Broad-winged Hawk nestlings] were all very
> restless and spent most of the time tramping about
> the nest, now up on the edge peering over, now round
> and round, clambering over one another.
>
> — *The Birds of Minnesota*, 1: 322

Thomas Roberts burst through the doors of Minneapolis High School and into the watery sunshine. The first of April! Spring at last! The sixteen-year-old had been taking note of the early signs of the changing weather for a month, not in anticipation of the baseball season like most boys—he took scant interest in organized sports—but because they heralded the return of migratory birds to Minnesota.

He surveyed the activity on Third Avenue and saw that his father waited for him, reins in hand, with the family horse and buggy. Though Thomas lived only eight blocks from school, it was not uncommon for his father to take the family dog and meet him when the school day ended. When Thomas glimpsed the familiar silhouette of the Robertses' buggy, he knew they were in for a few hours of leisurely driving about the countryside, on the lookout for whatever birds they could find before the setting sun drew their explorations to a close. Seeing the open buggy today, however, gave Thomas's heart an extra lift. It was the first time it had been out this spring, replacing the sleigh of the previous months.

The winter of 1873–74 had been cold and snowy. As April opened, snow still blanketed the ground. Thomas and Walter had been skating only three days before on Bassett's Creek just west of town, which remained frozen solid. In fact, the worst storm of the winter had come on a Friday evening only several weeks before, blasting Minneapolis with a fury, knocking out telegraph wires, and leaving more than a foot and a half of snow. There was a report in the *Minneapolis Tribune* of a sleighing party that had left

Minneapolis for an event in nearby Richfield shortly before the storm hit. The force of the driving snow had blinded the partygoers and obscured the road. They had wandered for an hour on the open prairie before chancing upon the road leading back to town.[1]

But this afternoon, the sun shone, and the prospect of another blizzard seemed remote. Thomas and his father headed south on the road to Lake Calhoun to see how the land had endured the long winter.

Hennepin Avenue was the old territorial road running from the Falls of St. Anthony and downtown, through the bluffs and up to the high country of lakes and farmland south of the city. As father and son followed Hennepin out of town, they crossed over a stream issuing from Johnson Lake and meandering westward into a wetland nestled in a marshy meadow. Thomas and Walter sometimes fished for bass and northern pike in the stream. It was within walking distance of home.

The horse strained at its traces as Hennepin climbed "the Bluffs," the thick vegetation on either side of the road still bearing tightly closed buds. The land then leveled, and open prairie spread around them. Off to the east, a sizable lake, which they called Powderhorn because of its shape, was still iced over, as were the many small duck ponds scattered over the landscape.[2] Two or three farmhouses dotted the countryside. Some of the land was under cultivation. The road wound about the eastern shores of Lake of the Isles and Lake Calhoun. The Robertses took note of the stream connecting the two lakes. It was a good place to see ducks during spring and fall migration, but there were none to record today. The creek was not open.

As the horse patiently picked its way along the rough road, Thomas and his father took stock of the snowdrifts, which remained as high as the fences in some places, and the rapidly diminishing snowpack on the open expanse of fields. They spied a pair of hawks they could not identify and a large, white owl.[3] Over the exposed patches of brown, wet earth, father and son noted a number of dun-colored birds, rising and falling with trills of weak twitters. Thomas called them "shore larks"—today, we know them as Horned Larks—and the Robertses thought the birds were uncommonly early in their migration north.

The next day, Thomas asked his father's friend Mr. Tiffany about the larks. Tiffany, big and bluff, with a bushy mustache and a goatee, co-owned the Arctic Flouring Company of Minneapolis with William Dunwoody, another friend of his father's. Both men were East Coast natives transplanted to Minnesota, like the Roberts family, and frequent companions of John Roberts on his daily nature outings. Dunwoody was a neighbor and in his early thirties, the perfect age to be a role model for an impressionable young man, but it was his partner, W. L. Tiffany, who was interested in birds. Thomas gravitated toward Tiffany, later describing him as a "thorough out-of-door man," and Tiffany, in turn, took a special interest in the teen's budding fascination with birds. The two spent time together each Sunday to chat about Thomas's adventures the week before. Tiffany had gained his knowledge firsthand as an avid waterfowl hunter who had spent his younger days tramping along the New Jersey shore, immersed in that region's rich bird life. Tiffany introduced Thomas to the young city's most prominent avian enthusiast, Philo Hatch, a homeopathic physician in St. Anthony, on the east side of the river.

Thomas found Tiffany interesting and stimulating in other ways. The mill owner was well read and widely traveled and rubbed elbows with literary and artistic types. In the young and ambitious town of Minneapolis, this East Coast bon vivant was considered "a bit odd."[4]

But the real reason to call on Tiffany that day was not to discuss shore larks—it was to see if he could identify a bird Thomas and Walter had shot in the afternoon.[5] Thomas had bagged the gray and white, robin-sized bird in the tamarack swamp that grew in a low area at the foot of the Bluffs (near the present-day Minneapolis Sculpture Garden). The boys had never encountered this bird before.

Thomas had handled a shotgun since an early age. He was accustomed to accompanying his father on outings when John shot birds for sport and for identification, using a muzzle-loading gun. Shooting birds, any birds, was a common practice among amateur and professional ornithologists alike in the days before strict regulation of hunting. Throughout the United States, the killing of birds for recreation was widespread. Birds of all kinds were abundant, and human populations were small and clustered in towns and cities. Much of the land remained in its native vegetation, so habitat was plentiful. In 1874, few people even knew the term *extinction*. The Robertses reflected the attitudes of most naturalists of the age.

But another, more practical reason for shooting birds was to identify them. No one had binoculars with which to view the small, constantly active avians, flitting high above in the trees or hiding in the long grass at the far side of a marsh. The nearest approximation to binoculars available for use at the time were opera glasses—which a few bird-watchers, mostly women, were only just beginning to train on the birds outside their windows.

Tiffany knew at once that the boys' gray and white bird was a Northern Shrike, a "butcher bird," so called because it preys on other songbirds, impaling their carcasses on the thorns of shrubs, like a miniature meat cutter hanging sides of beef. Shrikes were not uncommon residents of the area, but Tiffany was surprised that the boys had found it in early April. He thought they usually did not arrive until May or June.

Thomas made one more stop with the butcher bird. The next Saturday, when he was off school, he and his father went to Howling's Curiosity Shop in St. Anthony to see William Howling, a taxidermist. The shop, crammed with all manner of attraction, was an irresistible draw to a young boy, and Thomas dropped by often to poke about. Howling frequently had unusual birds on display. That Saturday, he showed the Robertses a pair of Evening Grosbeaks that had been shot in January and eight Bohemian "Chatters" that Howling himself had taken in his own yard earlier in the week.[6]

When he was an old man, Thomas would view his Quaker upbringing as peaceable and gentle. Family life kept on an even keel. No one lost their temper, and he and his siblings seldom resorted to rowdiness. Both parents wrote daily journals at certain times in their lives, in which their jottings revealed them to be thoughtful and reflective. They, in turn, produced a son both introspective and kind. Years later, his sister, Emma, would recall that her older brother frequently surprised her by opening the school door and standing aside to let her pass.[7]

At his father's urging, Thomas recorded the April 1 outing to Lake Calhoun and the shooting of the butcher bird in a journal that he began on March 1, 1874. His interest in birds, kindled some time on the brink of his teens, had been growing. At age sixteen and established in the high school, he was on his way to manhood. Perhaps it seemed to father and son that Thomas's passion for birds now begged for more intentional study.

He did not write in the journal every day, making entries only when there was something to report: "April 10—I saw a Robin for the first time today. Papa saw a Robin and one Blackbird." Or out by Lake Calhoun: "[I] saw three loons, a flock of Snow Buntings, two of which we shot and a flock of about *fifty Robins*."[8]

Frequently, he did not know what kind of bird he had observed. "While on the way to school in the afternoon I saw a large bird resembling a hawk flying over at a considerable height. . . . The whole of the wings and that portion of the body lying between the shoulders and the rump appeared to be dark brown and all the head, neck and tail a pure white . . . the wings were very large."[9]

The Robertses owned a house at the corner of Utah Street (today's First Avenue North) and Eighth Street. The large Victorian home with a bay window and a porch wrapping around nestled in a residential neighborhood, one that still had remnants of prairie and rail fencing enclosing undeveloped lots. The Robertses had a barn, which stabled the family horse, and a garden, which provided vegetables for the table, including rhubarb, which the former East Coasters called "pie plant." Several big bur oaks shaded the yard, and a few fruit trees, apple and plum, had been planted after the original savanna had been domesticated into a yard. Neighbors' houses were generally frame, two-storied dwellings with steep roofs and porches, reminiscent of New England.

Soon after the Robertses settled into the neighborhood, a growing family with children moved in a few blocks away. The Charles A. Bovey family already had four children, and two more would be added. The oldest, Caroline, was exactly Emma's age, and the two struck up a friendship. The next two, Will and Charles, were closer in age to Walter than to Thomas, but all the children attended school together. The neighborhood was full of children; the Boveys would remain lifetime friends of the Robertses.

From that neighborhood carved out of wild land, it was a walk of five or six blocks east on Hennepin to the commercial district of Minneapolis. The heart of the business district lay at the foot of the suspension bridge over the Mississippi River in a central commons known as Bridge Square. Native bur oaks shaded the square,[10] and it was the site of the hay and wood markets, where heads of households came to contract for deliveries when supplies ran low. Small businesses lined Hennepin and Nicollet Avenues. At their confluence stood City Hall, a building that also housed the *Minneapolis Tribune,* one of several newspapers recording events in the young city.

Looking back late in life, Thomas described the Minneapolis of his childhood as "little more than a village."[11] Even so, the thriving, bustling community of 1874—which already had a waterworks, a sewer system, and limited gas lighting at least on some blocks and in some buildings—was an astonishing change from what had existed on that patch of earth a mere twenty-five years prior. An 1849 photo of what would become Bridge Square showed only the first frame house in the "city," belonging to John Stevens, and in front of it, an encampment of twenty Dakota tepees, their white conical forms already ghostly under the unblinking eye of the camera.[12]

The spring of 1874 continued as chilly as the winter that had preceded it. The cold weather affected the bird migration, and in mid-April, Thomas recorded an amazing sight:

> April 15—Today for the first time, I have noticed a great number of small birds which seem to be in everybody's yard and in fact in almost every large tree. Upon shooting one and taking it to Mr. Tiffany I found it to be a Yellow-rumped Warbler.... These birds first attracted Papa's and my attention by their constant chirping and twittering and by their restlessness as they were scarcely ever still for any length of time but were constantly jumping from one twig to another and flying from tree to tree.[13]

The spring migration of Yellow-rumped Warblers—those early harbingers of the larger migration of warblers to come in May—had been hung up, probably due to inclement weather, and all the birds had descended on Minneapolis in one great rush.

Many people who are keenly attuned to nature can later recall a deep, almost mystical experience from their youth that stays with them a lifetime. For Thomas, that moment was the migration of the yellow-rumps in 1874. Sixty years later, he wrote the following in *The Birds of Minnesota*:

> The beginner in bird-study has many wonderful disclosures and many thrilling experiences, never to be duplicated and never to be forgotten. When on a chilly fifteenth of April in 1874 the writer, a boy of sixteen, appreciated for the first time the arrival of the

Yellow-rumps—and they came that year all at once in a vast horde—
feelings of wonder and delight were aroused that have never been
repeated. Whenever this warbler is encountered in numbers, there
still is brought up from memory a vivid picture of the then village-like
Minneapolis, filled with myriads of restless, twittering little birds, gay
in their blue, black and white, set off by four showy, golden patches. It
seemed certain that this could never have happened before.[14]

The cool April of 1874 turned into a warmer May. Minneapolis's high
school prepared to graduate five students.[15] Thomas, an underclassman,
studied for the end-of-the-year exams. He was a conscientious student,
consistently at the top of his class.

On the cusp of summer, Thomas, his father, and Walter planned an excursion northeast out of Minneapolis to Lake Johanna in neighboring Ramsey
County. The intervening country was farmland, but a large portion of the
lake's shoreline was protected by remnant oak savanna that had matured into
oak woods. In late May, the bur oak leaves would still be small, and nests,
visible. The Robertses wanted to look for nests, but the main attraction was
the Passenger Pigeon colony occupying the oaks:

> May 30—Papa, Walter and myself went up over near Lake Johanna
> to look for pigeons and hunt birds' nests. The pigeons were quite
> plenty and we also [saw] a number of large flocks flying. We got
> fourteen, the largest bag for us so far. We were not very successful in
> finding nests. We hunted considerable for the nests of the Bartram
> Sandpiper and the Short-tailed Tern but could find neither.[16]

Passenger Pigeons were tasty fare, but being small, a number of birds were
needed to make a meal. Thomas did not record in his journal whether this
outing was a junket for game, but the pigeons most likely were served for
dinner at the Robertses' table.

Although he did not know it then, Thomas was witnessing the last days
of the Passenger Pigeon in Minnesota. In Minneapolis, he had seen the fa-
bled migrations. Early American ornithologists had vividly described flocks
of pigeons so large that they darkened the sky for days. Thomas did not see
flocks of that epic proportion, but he would later write that "the birds flew in

close formation, those in advance bunched together forming a dark, wedge-shaped mass outlined against the sky . . . the flight was very rapid and direct, and these great masses of clean-cut birds swept along with all the power and majesty of an advancing army," adding, "There is nothing like it in the bird-life of our country today."[17] On some migrations, the flight was directly over Minneapolis, the flock flying high. Other years, they flew in and "swarmed into the oak woodlands to rest awhile and feed on acorns."[18] The days of the migration through the city were called "Pigeon Days," and the migrants attracted widespread attention.

The extinction of the Passenger Pigeon remains one of the most lamentable events in the natural history of North America. Ask twenty-first-century bird-watchers what they most regret about the diminishment of avian fauna on this continent, and they will likely mention the demise of the Passenger Pigeon. The large scale of its presence is somehow most representative of the lush abundance of wildlife of presettlement America. The migratory flocks were incomprehensible in size. Early ornithologist Alexander Wilson estimated one flock to number over two *billion* birds.[19] Some think they comprised between 25 to 40 percent of the birds of presettlement North America.[20]

The pigeons' nesting and behavioral habits made them easy targets. They tended to nest in large colonies—as they did at Lake Johanna—and in such numbers that they were known to break the sturdy branches of the oaks in which they nested. Despite their tremendous population size, however, their reproductive rate was low, producing only one chick a year, and once their numbers began dropping, the population could not quickly restore itself. Pigeons were slaughtered, for food and for sport, in immense numbers in a few short decades in the mid-nineteenth century.

The jottings in Thomas's 1874 journal are some of the earliest Minnesota records of pigeon breeding activity, but by that year, the species was already waning. Large spring migrations through Minneapolis were noted by him and others through the 1870s, but by the 1880s, only small flocks and single birds were seen. The last Passenger Pigeon in North America died in captivity in Cincinnati in 1914. The last nesting record of the bird in Minnesota was in 1895.[21]

In June, with school out, Thomas pursued his interests without the constraints of classes, exams, theme papers, and required readings. He and

Walter, a frequent companion, though he was only eleven, searched for nests nearly every day.

It was a short hike from their home on Eighth Street to the Bluffs. Hennepin Avenue snaked up the moraine through a narrow, densely wooded ravine tangled with Virginia creeper and bittersweet. When they were younger, Thomas and Walter had been both thrilled and apprehensive as they scrambled their way to the top. They had imagined panthers and wolves, and maybe even Indians, hiding in the understory.[22]

Atop the Bluffs was an abandoned slaughterhouse surrounded by pasture, and in this field the boys found a meadowlark's nest with two nestlings and a nest of a Killdeer with four mottled eggs, all duly noted in the bird journal.[23] The bluff tops served as grazing land for families that kept a cow. A neighbor boy, Charles Bovey, would later recall how he would daily lead the family cow—and Mr. Dunwoody's—to the pasture as part of routine chores.[24]

Early in the summer, Thomas met a visitor from Astoria, New York, a young man a few years older than he, Franklin Benner. The son of a New York lawyer, Benner was an avid amateur ornithologist possessing knowledge and skill that in the ensuing months and years he passed on to Thomas. That summer he taught him the method of putting up a study skin, a necessary skill for a serious collector. It was not something Thomas could easily have picked up on his own. It entailed removing the viscera of the dead bird with as little damage to the plumage as possible and replacing it with cotton batting, positioning the limbs in a prescribed way, and sewing it up without losing feathers, so that the specimen could be measured and examined scientifically.

Benner was in Minnesota to collect bird skins, eggs and nests, and also plants and flowers of the state. In Benner, Thomas recognized a kindred spirit, and within a week after meeting him, the two went looking for eggs. Thomas led the newcomer to a grove of trees in back of St. Anthony, where they located a tree cavity with a Northern Flicker's nest containing nestlings; a Red-winged Blackbird's nest with five eggs, which Benner took; and the nest of an Orchard Oriole high in a red oak. They cajoled a little boy to climb up and retrieve it. The nest contained five white eggs marked with brown and black blotches. Benner took these also and the nest as well.[25]

Exhibiting the restlessness of teens, Thomas, Benner, and Thomas's school pals Harry Neiler and Clarence Herrick planned a camping trip to Lake

Minnetonka west of Minneapolis at the end of June. Clarence, lanky and earnest, had known Thomas since grade school. The son of a Baptist minister, Clarence had a keen mind interested in science. Harry, son of a local banker, was also one of the bright boys of the class and an amusing companion. Although a train line ran to Excelsior, the young men instead piled their gear into the Robertses' wagon, pulled by the Herrick horse.

The trip took five hours. At Excelsior, they shifted their equipment to a rental boat and rowed to a campsite. They set up a heavy canvas tent—no screening, of course—and that night the mosquitoes were horrendous. No one, except Benner, slept much. Nonetheless, they were up bright and early, fished for breakfast, and then headed for Crane Island. While on the water, the party caught sight of a mature Bald Eagle on the wing, and Thomas located its nest atop an ancient white oak on the adjacent shore:

> We went ashore and after considerable work Clarence Herrick succeeded in climbing up to the nest but it was so large and projected so far out at the sides that he could in no way see into it. We at last concluded that it would be best for him to try and work a hole up through the nest. After more than an hour's work he succeeded in knocking the entire nest out of the top of the tree. Down with the nest came two young eagles nearly ready to leave the nest.[26]

The boys took the birds, abandoned their plans for Crane Island, and headed back to camp in the rowboat. Late in the afternoon, they rowed into Excelsior to get salt and ice to preserve the fish they had caught. When they returned to the campsite, they discovered one of the eagles had escaped. This was not wholly regrettable. The young eagles had screamed during the long afternoon, and all four boys had been kept occupied catching fish to feed the eaglets' voracious appetites, while the parent birds clamored and circled overhead.

After a second sleepless night filled with the whine of mosquitoes, the boys brought the remaining eaglet to Excelsior and traded it to the boatman in lieu of the rental fee. The four boys brought home fifty fish, about seventy-five pounds worth, and an excellent story of magnificent birds.

A short ten years later, however, these once-common majestic birds were increasingly scarce in Minnesota. A rueful, much older Thomas, writing in

The Birds of Minnesota, recalled the adventure with regret, surmising that the group of "thoughtless boys" had "possibly hasten[ed] the end" of Lake Minnetonka's eagles.[27]

Traversing with horse and buggy the open patchwork of savanna and prairie that spread out between Minneapolis and Fort Snelling, the Robertses came to know intimately its seasonal rhythms. On a section of prairie south of the city, at the present-day intersection of East Twenty-Ninth Street, Minnehaha Avenue, and Lake Street (where a Target store now stands), the Robertses witnessed a great cloud of migrating golden plovers spring and fall as they made their way to their ultimate destination. Thomas would later compare their flight to that of the Passenger Pigeon, both species suddenly appearing in incomprehensible numbers, in a compact flock, winging strongly and purposefully.[28] But whereas the pigeons congregated in the woods, the plovers sought out the prairie for rest and restoration.

Because the flock circled around and around in closed ranks, even when shot at, the birds were an easy target, and tens of thousands were killed in a season. Looking back, Thomas could recall "the numerous hunters... seemingly wholly indifferent to the devastation."[29] But unlike the wild pigeons, which nested near human settlement and thus could be killed throughout the summer, golden plovers only passed through on their way to their Arctic nesting grounds. So, while their numbers were decimated within two decades while Thomas was still a young man, the species eventually made something of a comeback, under stiff protection.

A favorite haunt of Thomas and his father was in the far northeast corner of Minneapolis in what is now the Waite Park neighborhood. The area was a remnant of native prairie with a small, shallow wetland—Sandy Lake— that attracted large numbers of shorebirds.[30] In 1874, Sandy Lake was "out in the country," its shores lush with little bluestem, hidden gems of colorful flowers, and subtly patterned, ground-nesting birds, like the doe-eyed Upland Sandpiper, which the Robertses knew as "Bartram's." Sandy Lake was a delectable destination:

July 27—Papa, Walter and I went up to Sandy Lake and shot 21 Bartram's Sandpipers or Field Plover. These were the first that we had shot this year and we left it most too late as they had already began to flock up. There were a great many around Sandy Lake. We also shot one pigeon.[31]

The Upland Sandpiper was a game bird, good to eat. This outing was for hunting, not a scientific collection trip. But the birds were small, and many were necessary to make a meal. The Robertses went back for more:

> July 31—Papa, J. Campbell, Walter and I went up to Sandy Lake to look for Plover (Field) and we succeeded in getting 21. There were a good many there but they were very wild. I saw a boy there who said that "Me and my Dad killed forty eight last Sunday morning."[32]

And they went back for still more:

> August 6—Papa, Walter and self went up by Sandy Lake to look for Field Plover . . . altogether we got fifteen, which makes 66 that Papa and I have killed and 85 including what F. Benner and J. Campbell have killed while in company with us.[33]

Upland Sandpipers were extremely common in the fields and prairie remnants surrounding Minneapolis in 1874. Their distinctive, plaintive whistle filled the air in early summer. Leggy and graceful, the birds were unafraid of people and approachable, so large numbers were easy to shoot in one afternoon. These qualities spelled disaster for the bird, the legacy of which we live with today, when spotting an Upland Sandpiper is a rare pleasure. But how could a sixteen-year-old know this, surrounded as he was by such abundance? Thomas later wrote, "To recite the history of the Upland Plover in Minnesota is to tell a sad tale of the wanton destruction of a valuable and once abundant bird that resulted in its almost complete extermination. Sixty years ago it was present all through the summer everywhere in open country in countless thousands. Now it is a question of whether the remnant left can be saved even with careful protection."[34]

Reading through the entries of Thomas's early bird journal, it is easy to get the impression that the young man shot everything he saw. A closer scrutiny reveals that he was more discriminating, shooting birds of one species but not of another, depending, perhaps, on what his collection lacked. He frequently took half the eggs of a nest and left the others to hatch, and he prepared skins for most of the birds he shot. Such collections were a common practice of the serious bird-watcher. John James Audubon shot every bird he painted when compiling *The Birds of America*, and even today, some ornithologists with special collecting permits will shoot a bird to obtain positive identification.

Thomas kept meticulous records, noting the species, sex, and age; date on which the specimen was collected; and where and by whom. His teenage records were complete enough that some of these early specimens still remain in the University of Minnesota's bird collection a century later. Having the skin in hand was and still is verification that his youthful records were accurate.

As the summer waned and the buttery yellows of goldenrod washed the meadows around Minneapolis, Thomas and his friend Harry Neiler embarked on a final trip before classes began. Their destination was Hutchinson, a small community west of Minneapolis; their aim was game hunting. The excursion was eighty miles by horse and wagon—an indication of how much freedom John and Lizzie Roberts allowed their sixteen-year-old.

The trip began badly. One of the horses, on loan from Dunwoody and perhaps unfamiliar with the boys, balked on the Bluffs. Thomas and Harry tried coaxing the animal forward, but instead the recalcitrant creature backed up and broke the wagon yoke. The teens decided not to deal with a difficult horse, and Harry rode it back to town to exchange it for the Neiler horse, while Thomas took the other horse to fetch another yoke.

Under way once more by noon, they arrived in Carver by sundown, the first stop on their itinerary. Carver, they found, was "full of teams, drunken men, cattle, etc." having hosted a fair that day.[35] Undaunted, Thomas and Harry located "the best hotel in the place" and stayed the night. They got an early start the next morning and headed due west, through the woods, to Glencoe, a prairie town and county seat. Glencoe had a "first-rate hotel," but they were aiming for Hutchinson, so they stayed there only a night. On day three, they headed out on "a good prairie road" to Hutchinson, on the Hassan River, "a little larger than Bassett's Creek," which later was recognized as a branch of the Crow.

Hutchinson was a small farming community that had been involved in the U.S.-Dakota War twelve years before. Beleaguered Dakota on reservations in south-central Minnesota had launched a series of attacks on white settlements, killing hundreds of residents and causing survivors to abandon homesteads and flee the region permanently. Hutchinson had in the ten years following the bloody conflict recovered some of its numbers and resumed normal life. Even so, the boys were disappointed in it. Although the town's population size was many times smaller than that of Minneapolis, the boys found "the game scarcer than around Minneapolis." Thomas thought this was due to overhunting: "Every man and boy in town was a hunter and went hunting nearly every day."

Their hopes for a successful hunting trip thwarted, Thomas and Harry left the next day and headed east on a little-traveled road through an intact portion of the Big Woods to Watertown, spent the night, and arrived home the day after, ahead of schedule. Recounting the trip in a letter to Benner, Thomas struck an ambivalent tone, sometimes disgusted—at the balky horse, the size of Hutchinson, the lack of game—but was unable to disguise his sense that it had been a jolly good adventure, nonetheless. He summed up the trip this way: "We had a flying trip and killed altogether ten (10) Pheasants, three (3) Teal duck and one mud hen . . . [but] I never went on a trip that I saw so little game of any kind."

As the nights grew longer and cooler and the maples and elms along the Mississippi flamed scarlet and gold, classes at the high school resumed. The bur oaks in town and out in the countryside gradually became burnished with rusts and coppers, and Thomas's entries in his bird journal were scanty, as he immersed himself in the rigors and social events of the school year. Benner had returned to New York at summer's end, and the two began a correspondence that would continue for decades.

"Dear Benner," Thomas wrote on October 18, 1874, "I believe that it is your turn to write to me but I wish to tell you that I have not yet sent those eggs as I have been waiting for two reasons. One of which is that I have not been able to see Herrick to find out the date on which he collected the Shrike's egg he gave me to send to you, and the other is I have been waiting for a hawk to dry that I intend sending you." The two young men exchanged bird skins ("If you want any Snow Birds, write soon.") and eggs. They informed each other of recent sightings ("I have seen several flocks of Bonaparte's

Gulls lately."), and they kept lists—of course—of what they had seen.[36] In some respects, their collector's passion resembled that of boys of a different generation, collecting and trading baseball cards.

Winter arrived in early November. Johnson's Lake (known today as Loring Lake) froze first, the temperature plummeted to zero, and Thomas reported the skating was "good." Within a week, Lake of the Isles iced over, and loons and late-migrating ducks could be found on the larger Lakes Harriet and Calhoun, which remained open.

On Thanksgiving Day, the Roberts males went deer hunting in the oak woods beyond Calhoun. The object of this excursion was strictly venison— Thomas did not mention a single bird when recounting the tale in his journal. Conditions were perfect: light snow had fallen Wednesday, and the deer could be tracked. The Robertses soon came across the delicate indentations of hooves freshly marking the road. They followed them all morning, but the deer remained out of range.

Around lunchtime, they encountered another hunting party of three heading into the woods with rifles, a clear advantage to the Robertses' muzzle loader. Taking stock of the situation, the Robertses decided to "let them [the other hunters] do the driving,"[37] and they would wait on the other side of the woods. The plan worked. A doe bolted from the woods directly in front of John, and he shot it. The other hunters emerged from the woods and beheld the triumphant Robertses with their dead deer. Thomas wryly observed that "they were not quite so pleased as we were." It took the rest of the day to haul the carcass back to town, hang it up, and gut it.

Spurred on by success, the Robertses tried again the next day, but the deer were now wary. The men spotted a "large buck with a splendid pair of antlers," but never got within range of a shot. The day after, they did not even see a deer.

Snow was scarce that December. For a fortnight, there was not enough snow to track, and the Robertses took their sleigh out for the first time on the sixteenth, with a scant five inches on the ground. On Christmas morning, Thomas, Walter, and John returned to Lake Calhoun, this time in the sleigh, to take some elderly friends a Christmas present of sugar, coffee, and tea. A sharp, chilling wind blew snow across the expanse of the frozen lake, and sleighing was poor. Thomas reported seeing a great many redpolls, a flock of about a hundred prairie chickens, and some tree sparrows. "One of the latter I shot and skinned," he wrote later in his journal. "Went skating on Johnson's Lake in the afternoon."[38]

Bit by bit, Thomas Roberts was acquiring an eagle eye. But it was not enough just to identify birds. He wanted to understand patterns he was seeing, and he wanted to discuss his ideas with others. He needed the society of other naturalists, and so in the coming year he set about making it happen.

CHAPTER 3

The Young Naturalists' Society

> "Why do you study birds?"
> "Because they are interesting and beautiful and
> because we enjoy it and we think that should be
> answer enough."
>
> — answer from a young birder
> in *The Birds of Minnesota,* 1: 99

O n a Friday evening in March 1875, seven earnest teens gathered in a home on the outskirts of Minneapolis. A bitterly cold winter was losing its grip after months of subzero temperatures, and tufts of prairie grass could be seen protruding from the crusted snow. Most of the boys lived in this neighborhood of two-storied frame houses that lay just west of the business district of First Avenue North, Hennepin Avenue, and Nicollet Avenue. At least two would walk home in the chilly blackness later that night to farms farther out of town.

The boys had recently formed a club, the Young Naturalists' Society, whose purpose was to support the pursuit of natural history. Such clubs were not unusual "back East," where the study of nature was a long-established pastime of educated men. In Minneapolis, an isolated but burgeoning city of thirty-two thousand on the edge of what was termed the "Great Northwest," such groups were uncommon. The Minnesota Academy of Natural Sciences had been established only two years before in St. Paul. Perhaps the idea of an "academy" of their own came from this newly formed gathering of the scientifically inclined.

Following the formality of the like-minded academies, President Thomas Roberts called the society to order, Secretary Clarence Herrick read the minutes to the previous meeting, and Treasurer Frank Clough reported on the society's finances. These procedural duties dispatched, the group settled into the meeting's heart: a discussion on Minnesota's natural world. Their

faces bathed in the rosy gaslight, various members offered reports individually researched during the past two weeks. Frank Clough enlightened the society and fellow classmates on deer. Rob Williams offered a paper on snakes,
and Thomas Roberts reported on "our winter birds," many of which he had
been scrutinizing for the past four months.

Thomas prefaced his essay by cautioning the society that his knowledge on the subject was, as yet, "very slight, only the observation of one or
two winters," so he could say "but little" on his own authority.[1] He himself
had seen only twelve species in the winter, the most common of which he
thought were the White-breasted Nuthatch and the Blue Jay. Drawing on a
list of Minnesota birds published the year before by Philo Hatch, Minnesota
state ornithologist, in the *Bulletin of the Minnesota Academy of Natural Sciences,* Thomas reviewed Minnesota's avian residents. He had seen only one
of the four owls on Hatch's list—a Snowy. He knew two of the three woodpeckers—the Downy and the Hairy, birds "we are all doubtless acquainted
with." He had seen a Bohemian Chatterer and a stunning black and yellow
Evening Grosbeak "in Mr. Howling's curiosity shop, but never alive to my
knowledge," and he had seen crossbills only as specimens in the Minneapolis Athenaeum.[2]

One winter bird Thomas had seen frequently in the past month was the
lovely Pine Grosbeak. Large flocks of the uncommon migrant from the high
Arctic had wandered into the vicinity of Minneapolis that winter. At Lake
Calhoun in late February, where the Pond brothers had built their Indian
Mission School in 1834, he had encountered some feeding on sumac berries.
The flock of about twenty contained mostly birds in the gray and ochre coloration of winter, with one old male feathered a brilliant red. They communicated among themselves in soft calls. Thomas was captivated both by the
birds' tame and peaceful manner and by the artistry of the setting. Nevertheless, he had killed two to take as specimens for his collection.[3]

Speaking at the meeting, Thomas methodically worked his way through
Hatch's list. Since one of the aims of the Young Naturalists' Society (or YNS,
as it was later referred to) was to encourage original observation, Thomas
discussed what he knew about the topic, giving it his best shot.

After additional business, the meeting adjourned, and discussion could
move on to other topics. Perhaps Frank Clough informed the boys about
the new structure being planned to replace the rickety suspension bridge

over the Mississippi River that had been built in 1850. The span was the all-important link between Hennepin Avenue on the west side of the river and Nicollet Island, and the flour mills in St. Anthony on the east bank. His father, as city engineer, was privy to high-level talks about the structure.[4]

No doubt the schoolmates traded stories they had heard about the runaway horse that had gone on a rampage the day before, while they had been at school. Apparently, the runners on the sleigh the horse had been pulling had scraped a bare patch on Nicollet Avenue. The horse spooked and careened toward the central business district, where it collided with a second sleigh. Both vehicles were destroyed, and the horse detached from its conveyance. The frantic animal then dashed north to First Avenue, took out a hitching post, rebounded south, and crashed through the post office window. Bleeding, it recovered enough to head toward the mills and was finally apprehended and put into a temporary hospital at the Cataract Hotel stables. Luckily, no one had been killed. What a shame to have missed the action![5]

The Young Naturalists' Society had been organized in February, the brain-child of Thomas and fellow classmate Clarence Herrick. Their efforts had created a group of boys devoted to the study of natural science. There were seven original members: Thomas and Clarence, and Robert Williams, one year younger—these three would prove to be the driving force of the group—Frank Clough, Frank Ham, Richard Scott, and George Willard. In the nearly four years of its existence, the society would vary between six and seven members, but four remained in the group for its entire existence: Thomas, Clarence, Rob, and Frank Clough.

Thomas met Clarence when both were in their early teens, sharing a desk at Jefferson Public School on Tenth Street and Hennepin Avenue. The two had much in common and established an immediate rapport. Clarence was a natural artist, and his cartoons, drawn on a school slate, amused his bench mate, but often got young Clarence in trouble with the teacher. Tall and lanky with piercing eyes, Clarence roamed the woods and meadows south of Minneapolis with a keen eye to nature. Minnehaha Falls was a favorite site, where he found yellow lady's slippers and maidenhair ferns in the summer. He lived with his parents and brothers on a small subsistence farm south of the city, at what is now Pleasant Avenue and Twenty-Fifth Street. Unlike Thomas, he was occupied with farm chores for part of every day. Clarence's father had been the pastor of the First Freewill Baptist Church in Minneapolis, but he had left that post by the time Clarence was in high school.

Thomas and Clarence had recently exercised their growing independence with a camping trip to Lake Minnetonka the previous summer. It had been Clarence who had climbed the oak tree to assail the eagles' nest and nab the eaglets—a story that had been told and retold in the following months to the great glee of listeners.

Considered by an older Thomas to have been "a genius in many ways," Clarence would later write and illustrate a book on the mammals of Minnesota, a monograph on microscopic pond life, and some 130 other scientific articles. He would go on to study a year in Leipzig and establish an illustrious scientific career, cut tragically short by his early death from tuberculosis at age forty-three.[6]

But at age fifteen, as the friends plotted the formation of a club to study natural history, Clarence was strong and energetic and chiefly "a buggist," as Thomas wrote to Franklin Benner. "Buggist," perhaps, but everything in nature interested Clarence. He matched Thomas's interest in birds and had been the first to spot (and shoot) a Pine Grosbeak that winter.

A third member of the society, whom an older Thomas identified as a propelling member of the group, was Robert Williams. Rob was behind Thomas and Clarence in school and was also bright and keenly interested in nature. He, too, had shot a Pine Grosbeak for his collection that winter. Rob's father, Thomas Hale Williams, owned a bookstore in the central business district of Minneapolis. Sixteen years earlier, he had joined other city businessmen to create the Young Men's Library Association, a member-cooperative library, and its collection of three hundred books was housed in a back room of his store. The organization was now called the Minneapolis Athenaeum, a private subscription library that allowed nonmembers limited access to its collection. Williams was still the librarian.[7]

People of modest means could afford to be subscribers to the Athenaeum. Clarence's family were members from the time the brothers were very young, for their mother read to them from books borrowed from the collection. The Robertses may have also belonged, since Thomas used the Athenaeum to research his reports. He was drawn to the Athenaeum for another reason: it had recently acquired John James Audubon's masterpiece, *The Birds of America*.[8]

Like Clarence, Rob would later distinguish himself in the scientific community. At age twenty, he left Minneapolis for Montana and published observations of the birds of that state. Still later, he became affiliated with the New York Botanical Gardens in the Bronx, where he developed a reputation as an expert on mosses of the world.[9] As a young naturalist, however, he chose to research birds and produced papers on "The Canary Bird," "The House Wren," and "Waxwings," no doubt drawing his inspiration from the birds he saw every day.

A fourth founding member was Frank Clough, whose father had been chief engineer of the Minnesota and St. Louis Railroad and was now city engineer. Frank's selection of topics to report on reveals an interest in geology, covering "Tides," "The Kilaunea Volcano," and "An Argument to Prove the Insolidity of the Earth."

Throughout the life of the society, other young men with an interest in natural history joined the YNS for a while and left when their lives took them out of town. But the three with the deep, compelling love of Minnesota's wildlife continued to meet, week after week, month after month, and share their observations.

In the initial year of the Young Naturalists' Society, there was very little adult guidance of the boys' endeavor. At the end of his first term as secretary, Clarence wrote in his report that they even "lacked reliable books which we need to aid us on many of these subjects," since their interests were large, ranging over the whole of natural history: plants, birds, mammals, insects, rocks and minerals, shells, aquatic invertebrates (termed "pond life"), and anthropology.[10]

Minneapolis High School offered courses in geology, botany, and chemistry, but zoology, an evident passion of both Thomas and Clarence, does not appear on six-week exam reports that the school issued during the course of the school year.[11] They must have been introduced to scientific reasoning at some time, however, since Clarence's report as secretary stresses the point that "it is acknowledged by all that observation comes first and theory afterwards," distinguishing the YNS from those of other young men, "which devote all their time to theorizing and speculation and who lose sight of the true means of making theory into fact."[12]

Both Thomas and Clarence had fathers who nurtured their interest in natural history. John Roberts joined the Minnesota Academy of Natural Sciences a year after the YNS began meeting, and even before this, Thomas regularly chatted with other early members of the academy, including Hatch and William Tiffany. At about the time of the society's formation, Clarence's father scraped together eight dollars from the family's meager funds to buy him a rather crude microscope. It had only a tube sliding in a sleeve for a focus, but the lenses were good, and with it, Clarence could observe the pond life that so interested him. He and his father also discussed evolutionary theory, and together the two explored the religious significance of Darwin's powerful proposals.

Near the end of the first year, despite the members' preference for researched, written presentations, Clarence was allowed to speak off the cuff on the freshwater invertebrate the cyclops. These tiny aquatic crustaceans with a single red eyespot probably inhabited the small lake adjacent to the Herrick farm, the lake he referred to as "Powderhorn." His youthful investigation became the topic for one of three scientific papers that Clarence prepared for publication while still in high school.[13]

The new school year of September 1875 brought changes to the schoolmates and, by extension, to the YNS. Thomas embarked on his junior year at Minneapolis High School but without the companionship of Clarence. Clarence had chosen to leave without graduating and enter the preparatory program at the nascent University of Minnesota.

The university in 1875 was housed in a single building on twenty-five acres on the east bank of the river, at the school's present site. Enlarged that year, the brick building was known as "Old Main" and contained all departments of the school. The first class, two men, graduated in 1873.

The university had been instructed by the state legislature to oversee a survey of Minnesota's geological and natural history. In 1872, the school hired Newton Horace Winchell, a geologist, to direct the survey, which had only recently been organized. Winchell, a man of immense intellectual and physical energy, launched the survey, instigated the formation of the Minnesota Academy of Natural Sciences, and taught geology, botany, and zoology at the university. Three years later, as Herrick entered the school, Winchell proposed to the legislature the establishment of a natural history museum.

A place in Old Main was found for the museum, and specimens from the survey's collection formed the bulk of it.

Clearly, the university had more to offer scientifically oriented young men than the city's high school, which emphasized a classical education heavy on Latin and rhetoric. Within a year, Clarence had attracted the attention of Winchell, who appointed him his assistant. Both Thomas and Rob Williams also would come under Winchell's sphere of influence. Rob followed Clarence's lead and left high school for the university's preparatory program; Thomas would later collect birds for the survey under Winchell's guidance.

Now the young naturalists had their own direct connection to professional scientists. By 1876, the YNS had acquired a small library, financed probably from their ten-cent monthly dues. The library contained bulletins issued by the state survey that Winchell oversaw, those from the Minnesota Academy of Sciences, a report from the state fish commission, and one from the state horticultural society. It also included the first four publications from the Smithsonian United States Museum.

Since their meeting in summer 1874, Thomas had maintained a regular correspondence with Franklin Benner at his home in Astoria, Long Island. Benner, older and more experienced, introduced Thomas to new ideas in the bird world. One of these arrived in the form of a book written by Elliott Coues, who in the 1870s was gaining in reputation as a nationally prominent naturalist. Thomas received the book in May 1875, along with a box of bird skins. He was delighted. "I am ever so much obliged to you. The book will be of great help to me," he wrote to Benner in his next letter.[14]

Thomas soon put the book to practical use after he and his father noticed Black Terns swooping and diving over the surface of Lake Johanna. The coal-black birds, long winged and graceful, were the most abundant terns seen around Minneapolis's many lakes and marshes. That the terns seemed to be nesting on Johanna interested both of them.

Shortly thereafter, his father and William Tiffany made a trip out to Fort Snelling's prairie south of the city, specifically to look for Black Tern nests. The reserve's large expanse of native oak savanna, dotted with small marshes, mature bur oaks, and swathes of prairie grasses was good habitat for these inland terns. (The land would later be developed into the Minneapolis–St. Paul International Airport.) The men returned from the reserve with a good story involving Tiffany wading about in a chilly marsh and the triumphal discovery of nests containing eggs.

Thomas pounced on the description of the nest. He wrote in his journal, "The eggs were in every instance and contrary to Coue's placed in a nest."[15] Coues had written that in his experience (based on an expedition along the northern territorial boundary of the forty-ninth parallel), Black Terns do not build nests. Excited by the possibility that his knowledge of this one bird might contradict the famous Coues, Thomas and his father drove back out to the fort's prairie on June 19, wishing "to see the nest of the Black Tern in its natural position."[16] That night, he recorded in his bird journal a detailed description of the grass-woven nest, its position in relation to the water, the number of eggs in the nests he saw, incubation behavior, and coloration of the egg shells.

Sixty years later, he would include these data in *The Birds of Minnesota*. The eighteen-year-old Thomas, however, announced the results of his field observations much sooner in a paper presented to the Young Naturalists' Society the following June. Titling his report, "A Few Notes concerning the Breeding of Hydrachlidon lariformis in Minnesota," Thomas described the natural history of "the most abundant [tern] in the state."[17] In striking contrast to most of the early reports read at the YNS by him and other members, these "few notes" on Black Terns were all original, empirical observations. Drawing on two breeding seasons of work, Thomas had undertaken meticulous, informed science.

He even observed newly hatched tern chicks: "curious looking little creatures ... with soft fluffy down ... these minute terns are very good swimmers and I am of the opinion that they leave the nest very soon after quitting the egg."[18] He cited Coues's book *Birds of the Northwest* and its difference of opinion, observing that he, Thomas Roberts, had seen only two examples of nestless eggs. But he added cautiously that his observations had been confined to the vicinity of Minneapolis.

At this meeting in June 1876, the YNS decided to switch their meeting place from the Cloughs' house on Hennepin and Tenth Street to the Robertses' residence on First Avenue North and Eighth Street. From then on, the group gathered in Thomas's second-floor bedroom, which he later described as "more of a museum than sleeping quarters." Heated by a small stove, the room housed the large wooden storage cabinets with trays that contained the more than six hundred bird specimens he had collected in his teens.[19]

The serious young men of the Young Naturalists' Society frequently discussed theories and ethics infusing the field of natural history. One hotly debated topic was the wanton killing of animals for recreation, prompted by Franklin Benner, who had been invited to be a corresponding member of the YNS. Benner accepted an invitation to expound on a topic of his choice by writing a letter that expressed his delight in forays into the woods or along the seashore and then launched into a passionate argument against "the destruction of animals [that is] not necessary for their study." He continued: "How much more interesting [live birds] are than to have the bird in your hand, graceful though it is in death, before its life's blood is cold." Florida, he noted, "suffers a great deal in this respect. . . . [There are] thousands of birds of various kinds and lives which come here to enjoy the warmth and sunshine which the frozen North denies them. [Tourists to Florida] are not satisfied to enjoy these things with them but must needs attempt their destruction at every opportunity . . . rudely rousing [the quiet traveler] to a scene of slaughter." Benner closed his letter admitting, "these views may appear pretty strong to the majority of persons but their object is to deprecate the killing of any creature uselessly . . . [that retards] the study of nature."[20]

Indeed, these were uncommon ideas. In 1875, no one questioned "shotgun ornithology." There was no protection for songbirds. The traditional "Christmas Shoot," resulting in piles of dead birds, was still very much supported, and the first book to encourage live bird-watching would not be published for fourteen years.[21] The practice of adorning women's hats with feathers (and sometimes whole birds) had not yet reached its zenith. Thomas himself, during the month in which he pursued his Black Terns, had worked on a hat for a local woman that sported the head and wings of a Forster's Tern. This fashion trend would lead in the coming decades to the slaughter of millions of native birds, bringing some common species, like the Great Blue Heron and the Herring Gull, to the brink of extinction and leading to the formation of the National Audubon Society. In 1875, Benner held radical views.

Other uncommon ideas also found their way into the YNS. Thomas happened upon a copy of George Perkins Marsh's seminal book *Man and Nature* and made a report to the group.[22] Published in 1864, *Man and Nature* was one of the first books to document the destruction of nature by humans. In it, Marsh argued that ancient human civilizations had collapsed because of environmental degradation such as deforestation and soil erosion. Marsh pointed out that these same processes were at work in the United States in the modern age of the nineteenth century.

Another contemporary theory that the YNS returned to several times was that of evolution by natural selection. Charles Darwin had published his theory in 1859; his ideas became known and well received among scientists in the following decade but not so widely understood and accepted in the general populace. The ideas in Darwin's *On the Origin of Species* became a focal point of the YNS in its first year. Minutes from the December 1875 meeting note a "conversation regarding Darwin."[23] Perhaps the impetus to explore Darwin's ideas came from Newton Winchell at the university. Winchell had recently received his master's degree from the University of Michigan, where his brother, Alexander Winchell, was a leading proponent of Darwinian evolution.

The boys revisited the topic a year later when Thomas reported on a recent publication of Alfred Russel Wallace, "Rise and Progress of Modern Views as to the Antiquity and Origin of Man." That the teens in isolated Minneapolis discussed this paper is impressive. It was cutting-edge science. Again, perhaps Winchell had alerted the boys to the paper. Wallace at the time was at the height of his career and had delivered the paper only four months earlier at a Glasgow meeting of the British Association for the Advancement of Science. Clarence Herrick raised the topic of evolution once again two months later when he reported on the evolution of bird lice at one of their weekly meetings.

The young naturalists were beginning to flex their intellectual muscles. Clarence was in his second year at the university. Rob Williams, too, would soon attend the university. And Thomas had entered his final term at the high school, at the top of his class.

In addition to reading papers of original research and actively promoting the knowledge of natural history, the YNS had a third goal: the compilation of verified lists of the flora and fauna of Minnesota. The busy naturalists continually added to their collections of bird skins, pressed plant specimens, insects, and fossils in the four years of the society.

Thomas, of course, was especially keen on this. Hardly a week went by in which he did not shoot and stuff many birds, aiming in his later teens for females, or immatures, or other unusual plumages missing from his collection. He began to record behavioral observations—birdsong, bird food, how they foraged, and where they roosted. He also became very interested in plants, as did his sister, Emma.

Imagine Thomas's bedroom in the Victorian family home, now functioning as both a meeting place and a museum for the society. It gradually became crammed with stuff, not only with stiff, feathered skins but with piles and piles of pressed plants affixed to sturdy paper, and with cigar boxes holding rocks and minerals, fossils and bones, and miscellaneous other finds from the great outdoors.

The very first end-of-term report written by the society's secretary, Clarence, recorded 122 species of birds, 10 of plants, and 13 insect specimens. "Ornithology has taken ... precedence," he noted, "[because] we were all somewhat interested in this subject." Clarence took pains to make clear that only specimens actually held in their possession were included in the lists.[24]

When the YNS was formed, Minnesota had been a state for only sixteen years. Assessment of its plants and animals was low priority; building railroads and establishing industry were more important.[25] Minnesota's biological riches were vast, and the work of describing them, daunting. Under the directorship of Winchell, though, a handful of naturalists launched the task. Philo Hatch published a "Report on the Birds of Minnesota" in 1874. This list gave the boys a starting point—they could confirm the presence of an uncommon bird they had shot, or they could record, as they occasionally did, that it was not on Hatch's list. His list was hardly complete, but this very quality served to whet the young naturalists' appetites for new discoveries.

Thomas's relationship to Hatch had over the years grown into "a fairly intimate acquaintance." Even as a teen, Thomas found the homeopath "an interesting and inspiring personality" but realized that "facts were largely lost sight of in a jubilant effervescing enthusiasm, which, while it was pleasantly contagious, led only to a confusion of ideas."[26] This lack of orderliness clashed with the methodical nature of Thomas's mind. Bird by bird, he began refining Hatch's official list:

OCTOBER 18, 1874 In the list you will see that I have a Red-bellied Nuthatch (*Sitta Canadensis*) which is another bird that Dr. Hatch has not down.[27]

FEBRUARY 13, 1875 The other day I succeeded in identifying a warbler which I shot last fall and had never been able to identify. It proved to be a Blackburnian Warbler (*Dendroica blackburniae*) a male in fall plumage. This is another species that Dr. Hatch has not down in his list. . . . I am of the opinion that many others can be added.[28]

Hatch later received the YNS records, and the club's collecting prowess and careful methodology were recognized by Winchell in his annual report of the survey for the year 1883.

The YNS contributed even more significantly to the state survey's plant list. At the society's beginning, it had only ten plant specimens pressed and identified, but three years later Thomas reported that he thought they might have five hundred. He noted that after three summers of wandering about the prairies and marshes, oak woods, and creek bottoms surrounding Minneapolis, collecting plants they couldn't identify by name, the group had amassed an overwhelming number of specimens. Often there was a backlog of plants that were pressed but unidentified. The collection rapidly became unwieldy. It was eventually turned over to Warren Upham, a young geologist working on the Minnesota survey under Winchell, after the society disbanded and the members scattered.

In June 1877, Thomas became the valedictorian of Minneapolis High School's graduating class of eleven, seven girls and four boys, including Joe Kingman, who would remain a lifelong friend. Graduation ceremonies were held in the large upstairs hall of the elegant Academy of Music, located at the corner of Washington and Hennepin Avenues. The hall's main floor and balcony seated thirteen hundred and were lavish with statuary and frescoes. At the podium before his classmates, family, and neighbors, a callow and earnest Thomas Roberts delivered a valedictory speech that was startling in its originality and clarity of thought and eerily prescient in prescribing the life that he himself would live.

He began by noting that because having money assures a person of influence in the world, people pursue wealth with a vengeance. Most people have no limit on how much money is sufficient. Money does not assure happiness—quite the opposite. To be truly happy and healthy, men need "recreation for the mind," and nothing refreshes a human being more than being attuned to nature's "infinite variety . . . its beautiful and endless forms." In philosophy, there were echoes of Thoreau and Emerson; in language, a discerning listener would have heard Darwin in the great man's closing chapter of *Origin*.

Thomas then noted that almost no one paid any attention to the stunningly intricate natural world. As a people, we were blind to a wondrous world, a blindness that could imperil us, since humans are dependent on nature. Every species plays a role and cannot be obliterated without "a long series of evil" following in the wake of its destruction. For example, Thomas noted, birds keep insect populations in check.

This nascent ecological reasoning could hardly be heard in the hallowed halls of Harvard, much less from a teenager speaking in a young Minneapolis still on the edge of the frontier.

There were several reasons other than survival for paying closer attention to the offerings of nature. It was life enhancing: "it will add new interest to every move in life." Pondering nature's pervasive beauty gave insight into God, for "beauty is God's trademark"—Thomas crossed this out, deciding not to include it in the speech. It would be one of the few times in his long life that he ever referred to a divinity in his written documents.

But the reason that perhaps was most compelling to a boy who was witnessing the initial massive destruction of Minnesota's natural beauty was that appreciation of nature might halt "the ruthless destruction of animal and vegetable life," creatures "far more perfect in . . . detail of structure and finish than the choicest work of man."[29]

Thomas titled the talk "Strangers at Home," and in the coming seven decades of his life, he would not waiver in his belief in the sentiments expressed in that speech. This mature philosophy was also a fruit of the Young Naturalists' Society.

In its fourth and last year, the YNS heard fewer original papers at its meetings and held more discussions of other scientists' contemporary work throughout the country. The members were now in college, and they were busy. Clarence was assisting Winchell as well as working on the family farm. Thomas and Rob were immersed in university coursework. Meetings that had once been held weekly were now once in two weeks. As college students, the boys were poorer too—dues were halved, to five cents a month.

The young naturalists continued to meet into the summer of 1878, through the field season of nesting birds and flowering plants. A young man who had struck up a friendship with Thomas while both were involved in fieldwork for the railroad joined the group. As always, membership was fluid, individuals attending when they were in town and granted a leave of absence when they were not.

Sometime shortly thereafter, however, the society disbanded. It had flourished for three and a half years. Several published papers emerged from the youthful endeavor, and it had left as a legacy a more complete official state list of Minnesota birds and plants.

In March 1879, a founding member, Richard Scott, wrote to Thomas: "I was indeed surprised to hear from you, and much more to learn that our old friend [the YNS] has passed away. From the accounts of the society last summer, one would have supposed it would last forever—but alas! There is an end to all things earthly."[30]

The cradle years as budding naturalists were over. Rob, the scholarly librarian's son, left several months later with fifty-five head of sheep, intending to work a ranch in Montana. Clarence left the university briefly to teach at the Blaisdell School near the Herrick farm (at the present site of the Whittier International School), perhaps to finance study abroad. Thomas would not be leaving home—yet.

〜

CHAPTER 4

College Boy

> Mr. Breckenridge's observations, while studying these
> birds over a period of several days, led him to believe
> these dancing-grounds may in reality be meeting-
> grounds for the cocks and hens.
>
> — *The Birds of Minnesota,* 1: 402

A light breeze tossed the nearly opened lilacs as Thomas Roberts stepped
outside to greet the day. It was May Day 1878, and a chorus of White-
throated Sparrows whistled a clear, melodious song from the trees in the
yard. The bubbling chant of a House Wren mingled with the sparrows' offering. Thomas thought this was the same wren that had nested in a makeshift
birdhouse in their yard last year. A few days before, he had watched as the
bird checked out the place where the birdhouse, a tin can suspended by a
rope, had hung. He had written, "The wren looked in vain for the can, looking at the rope and the place where the can had been from all sides, seeming
to remember that this was the spot where it had reared its family last year."[1]

Thomas was off to the university at the early hour of seven o'clock. It
was more than a three-mile walk from the family home on Eighth Street at
First Avenue North to the school on the east bank of the Mississippi River.
He hiked to campus five days a week, in all kinds of weather, and enjoyed
the trek. It gave him a chance to be outside, looking at birds and observing
the small changes to yards and river bluffs, the falls and the islands, that occurred throughout the year.

Although May 1 was cool with the changeable weather of spring, it had
thus far been a very warm year. During the short days of January, when much
of Thomas's walk to school was made in the dark, temperatures were mild,
with little snow on the ground. Thomas recorded in his journal "quite a large
flock of Purple Finches on the University Campus . . . they were flying about
among the trees and bushes in the ravine through which runs the brook."[2]

Later he noted, "Saw a flock of about forty or fifty Red Polls on the University Campus. They were feeding upon the buds (or undeveloped catkins?) of the white birch . . . very tame and noisy."[3]

Then, in mid-March, when Minneapolis would normally be enduring a succession of wet, heavy snows, pasqueflowers put forth their fuzzy leaves cradling papery lavender blossoms, encouraged by an early rain, which greened up the grass in the neighborhood and opened the lakes. The newspaper reported that Lake Minnetonka was ice-free by March 11.

On a weekend day in late April, Thomas and his father had driven down to Minnehaha Falls and Fort Snelling. They had been dazzled by the wealth of spring flowers and migrating songbirds appearing so early in the year. Early meadow-rue, three-leafed hepatica, and lacy white isopyrum bloomed on the prairie-like knolls along Minnehaha Creek. On a large tract of prairie just north of the fort, thousands of bird's-foot violets in all shades of purple carpeted the ground. On the sandy shore of Lake Amelia (known today as Lake Nokomis), blueberry bushes were lush with flowers.

Thomas recorded these flowers, the spring's first grasshopper, Clay-colored Sparrows, and Black-and-white Warblers in his journal. He was also reasonably certain he heard both Black-throated Green Warblers and Scarlet Tanagers.[4]

It was nice to drive out on excursions with his father, as they were accustomed to do when he was in high school. Now that he was at the university, they had precious little time together.

The walk to school divided itself into several segments. The first few blocks were residential, and Thomas kept an eye out for robins and phoebes, the early nesters in his neighbors' yards. On this morning, he passed crab apples and plum trees, frothy with white blossoms, issuing delicate cascades of discarded petals onto the walks and lawns.

Soon he left behind the neighborhood and turned onto Hennepin Avenue, more urban and less green than First Avenue. The main thoroughfare brought him to Bridge Square, the central business district. In 1878, Minneapolis was a sizable city of forty-five thousand people. As its portion of the nation's wheat market burgeoned, the city's economy bloomed.

Thomas passed Boutell's Furniture, a large store opened in 1877. The following year, a dry goods store, Goodfellow and Eastman, appeared. It would be the forerunner of Minneapolis's premier department store, Dayton's. The Pence Opera House loomed over the corner of Hennepin and Second Street. The yellow brick, three-storied structure dominated the smaller two-storied businesses along the avenue.

But City Hall, at the junction of Hennepin and Nicollet, was its equal. With four stories and a mansard roof, it anchored Bridge Square, the heart of the milling city. City Hall served Minneapolis in several capacities. It housed city offices, the U.S. Postal Service, and the *Minneapolis Tribune*. Accentuating its stature as a power nexus was this novelty: it had a telephone. The first telephone exchange in the city was set up in 1875, linking City Hall with a few prominent businesses, such as the foremost hotel in town, the Nicollet House. Interest in Alexander Graham Bell's invention was growing. Recently, the university's physics professor had connected the school's two buildings by telephone.

Though it was early, Thomas strode past shopkeepers who had opened their doors, clerks and businessmen on their way to work, and early-bird marketers with baskets on their arms. The clip-clop of horse hooves filled the air as wagons clattered down the streets. He crossed Bridge Square, heading for the river. Horse-drawn cars of the street railway slowly eased down Hennepin, back and forth over the bridge. The first public transit in Minneapolis, it consisted of a ten-foot car holding twelve people, gliding on rails, pulled by a single horse. The route originated on Fourth Avenue North, went down Hennepin, navigated the bridge, and terminated on Fourth Street Southeast at the university. Thomas could have taken the street railway to school, but it cost five cents, and the cars were not heated. It was warmer and faster to walk.

The suspension bridge with its castle-like twin tower supports was new. It had opened in 1876, replacing the original suspension bridge, the first bridge to span the mighty Mississippi. This second suspension bridge was already considered inadequate for the growing city. Thomas crossed over to Nicollet Island along its graceful span every day. The island, the largest in the river at Minneapolis, was hardly pristine in 1878. Developers had begun to erect elegant brick and stone houses on its upper section. These residences sold for five thousand dollars, a steep price in the midst of a long-term recession.

St. Anthony Falls itself had been vastly altered since Thomas's childhood. He remembered how the cataract appeared when he visited it as a boy, accompanied by his father. It had been white and frothy, a powerful cascade of water thundering over large limestone boulders that during the millennia had broken off from the ledge that formed the falls. An imprudent attempt to tunnel under the falls in 1869 brought disaster. The limestone ledge had crumbled, and the falls threatened to become merely an extended rapids, of little use in powering the numerous mills dependent on its force. During Thomas's high school years, there were continuous attempts to prevent this from happening. The federal government had even provided a million dollars to construct an apron over the natural falls to stabilize the bedrock. The project had gone on for years, and the work remained unfinished.

As Thomas walked briskly along on the pedestrian walkway of the bridge, though, the cacophonous roar of falling water had lost none of its vigor. On quiet days when the prairie wind eased, he could hear the crash of St. Anthony Falls in his yard a mile away. Even Clarence Herrick heard the falls on calm days while at work on a farm south of the city.

Although the new development would later change things, bird-watching on Nicollet Island was good in 1878. Thomas was fascinated by the beautiful gold and black Evening Grosbeaks that arrived at the island in late fall every year and stayed through the winter. They frequented the sugar maple grove on the north end, drawn to the trees by the elongate, papery seeds, the "keys" that the maples and their relatives the box elders provided. Thomas and his father made many trips to the island specifically to search for grosbeaks. There was magnetism to their coloration, the gentle, confiding way in which they allowed themselves to be approached by a person, and the soft, bell-like whistle of their calls. He did not record any grosbeaks on the island in winter 1878, though. Perhaps it was too warm and they stayed farther north.

Leaving Nicollet Island, Thomas crossed over into East Minneapolis. The graceful steeple of Our Lady of Lourdes Church rose above the business district on Main Street, in stark contrast to the bulky presence of the Winslow House, a pioneer building no longer in use as a hotel. One route to the campus headed southeast on Main Street. The week before along Main, Thomas had noticed a Tree Swallow investigating a knothole in the side of a building under consideration for a nest.

On Main, Thomas could look across the river at Minneapolis's milling district, an industry that had grown by leaps and bounds in the past decade. There the riveting silhouette of the Washburn A mill commanded the attention of pedestrians on the street. Of the eighteen mills in the district, the

Washburn A was the tallest and broadest. It dominated, rising seven and a half stories, a striking limestone structure that promised the city that Minneapolis would soon rule the world in milling supremacy.

What Thomas did not know on May Day 1878 was that the very next evening, when he was safely at home in his parents' house on Eighth Street, particles of airborne grain dust would ignite in the mill's interior, causing the magnificent Washburn A mill to explode. The Robertses, a mile away from the blast, would wonder if they were experiencing an earthquake. Pedestrians on Nicollet, three blocks away, would be knocked flat by the force of expanding air. This force would collapse the walls of the nearby mills, and subsequent fires would roar through the district. In a few hours, a third of the city's mills would be obliterated. Eighteen mill workers would lose their lives.

In recording the historic event in his journal, Thomas described its effect on the city's bird life, almost certainly the only city resident to do so. "During the fire . . . it was curious to see the tame pigeons, which lived about the mills and elevator, flying hither and thither through the thick black smoke. And during the evening, a flock of geese (wild) appeared high [in] the air, passing over the spot. They appeared greatly bewildered and undecided as to what to do. The sight must certainly have been a strange one to them."[5] The smoldering ruins were visible on his daily walks to and from the university for the remainder of spring term. But little in his life changed because of this disaster. His life was not much affected by Minneapolis's flourishing milling industry—yet.

Thomas might have been a little surprised to find himself enrolled in a western university that was only a decade or so old. Many families in Minneapolis with ties to the East Coast sent their sons (and sometimes their daughters) to the older, established schools "back home." Thomas himself entertained the idea of attending Yale. In March 1877, he wrote to Franklin Benner, "I scarcely know what I shall do although it's about time. If I went to college I should prefer a scientific course. Doubt my ability to pass the entering examination at Yale. And not up in all the Geometry required."[6]

In choosing the University of Minnesota, Thomas joined Clarence Herrick and Rob Williams and high school classmate Joe Kingman. The three who had formed the nucleus of the Young Naturalists' Society embarked on a scientific course of study. Clarence and Rob were in a position to assess the school's strengths and weaknesses and speak with some authority on whether the classes were well taught.

Still, the question of his future continued to nag Thomas. In late August, with the start of classes nearly upon him, he again wrote Benner: "You ask me what I intend to do next fall. This question has bothered me much but I have decided not to come East this fall. Shall go to the University with a view to preparing to attempt to enter the Sophomore class of some college next fall. If you have a catalogue of Yale College which you can spare I should be very much obliged if you would send it to me."[7]

To qualify for the University of Minnesota, he took the entrance exam in June, following graduation, tests that covered the spectrum of the high school curriculum from Latin grammar to elementary algebra. His highest score, a ninety-five, was in reading; his lowest, a 55, in English grammar.

Thomas matriculated in September 1877, joining about 350 other young people, men and women. He enrolled in the coursework set out for freshmen, having about four hours of lecture a day. Tuition was free, but there were fees for lab materials, most notably chemistry lab glassware.

Nearing campus on May Day 1878, Thomas crossed over Tuttle Brook, a small creek flowing down to the river. One day, trains would clatter past the northwest boundary of the campus through the narrow valley of the creek, but in 1878, the water was a natural demarcation, separating the university from the bustle of East Minneapolis.

The university campus was situated on a spacious thirty-five acres about a mile downriver from the falls. Native bur oaks shaded the lawn, and the board of regents had hired a Chicago landscape firm to improve its appearance. The main academic building was an elegant structure built of bluish-gray limestone quarried locally from the nearby islands. It had three floors, and from its crowning cupola, one had a dramatic view of the rushing river far below, for the building backed up along the bluff. Its fifty-three rooms were steam heated and equipped with running water and gas lighting. An assembly hall on the third floor seated seven hundred comfortably and a thousand if necessary. In this room the students and faculty gathered at 10:40 A.M. for chapel service and announcements each day.

The first floor of Old Main housed the library, which in 1878 had over twelve thousand volumes. Many had been donated or purchased from private libraries. Included in the holdings were Darwin's *Voyage of the Beagle,* Spencer Fullerton Baird's *Catalogue of North American Birds,* and Alfred Russel Wallace's *The Action of Natural Selection on Man.* Off the library was a reading room, and there a wide array of periodicals could be perused. The university had subscriptions to *Scribner's, Harper's,* the *Atlantic Monthly,* and the *American Agriculturalist,* among others. It received both Twin City daily newspapers, the *Minneapolis Evening Tribune* and the *St. Paul Pioneer Press.* Also on the first floor were two separate student lounges: the gentlemen's cloak room and the ladies' parlor.

In this era before the widespread availability of visual aides, museums were set up to display artifacts to aid students in understanding their subject matter. On Main's second floor in two rooms, the General Museum housed the collected specimens of the state's Geological and Natural History Survey. Room 51 displayed the larger mammals of the "Northwest" and a large set of fossils. Next door was a geological exhibit of the minerals found in Minnesota. The collection numbered in the thousands and increased with each survey field season.

The actual science laboratories were located in the university's Agricultural Building. This building was newer than Main, built in the early 1870s as a result of the Morrill Act of 1862. The act granted tracts of land to the states that they could sell, using the profit to fund universities. But these "land-grant" schools had strings attached: they had to provide instruction in agriculture and "mechanic arts"—civil and mechanical engineering and architecture.

The two-story, brick agriculture building had two wings extending north and south. The former housed the chemistry labs, outfitted with water, gas, and sinks at each station; the latter was a greenhouse used for growing plants for botany and horticulture. It also produced plants to beautify the campus.

Thomas spent about half his time in the ag building. Applied chemistry and molecular physics were both taught there, natural science courses offered by Stephen Peckham, a petroleum chemist by training, who was also the chemist on the geological survey. Peckham encouraged his students to explore their own interests through experimentation and made a small shop available to them for the construction of models and equipment. He was the professor who used his knowledge to link the two university buildings with a telephone line and used a "port luminaire," which showed "magic lantern" slides projected on a screen to illustrate his lectures.

Thomas studied surveying under Mitchell Rhame, a topographer also on the survey. Thomas would use these skills in a few years as a land examiner. He rounded out his academic study reading the Roman historian Livy—in Latin. The distinguished Jabez Brooks, former president of Hamline University, was his professor.

Besides these academic courses, all offered in the morning, Thomas and all other men in the Collegiate Department took part in compulsory military drill. The Morrill Act required it under the belief that well-trained military men are necessary for a democracy. The college students took part in parades and drills, dressed in braided sky-blue uniforms, complete with chasseur-pattern hats, white gloves, and sabers at the sides. In the classroom—for they could not perform drills outside in a Minnesota winter—they studied the manual of arms and learned the duties of commissioned and noncommissioned officers. University president William Watts Folwell reported to the board of regents that a favorite exercise was one employing the bayonet and foil.

Birds were seldom far from Thomas's mind, even as he paraded around the university grounds with his classmates. In his journal, he related a sad tale involving the cannons positioned on the campus that were fired off each morning. "A pair of bluebirds selected one of [the cannons] as a desirable place to move in. Accordingly a nest was constructed. Next morning, this was removed by one of the boys. Another nest was built and removed and so on for several days. Yesterday morning the one whose duty it was to ram the charge into the gun paid no attention to whether there was a nest there but rammed it down with a will. The cannon would not go off and after exploding several primes the charge was withdrawn and the bung of the gun unscrewed which revealed a nest and the *parent bird* mashed to a jelly in the breech of the gun. At noon I saw the other bird going in and out of the cannon as if contemplating rebuilding once again."[8]

Between recitation and laboratory, book work and military drill, to say nothing of walking six miles round-trip every day, there was very little time to wander the tamarack swamps, prairies, and woodlots "doing natural history" as Thomas liked to do. Having survived the first term's finals of his freshman year, he wrote Benner, "My time's pretty much occupied with school, rather more than I like. I am over at the school four hours each day (Monday and Sunday excepted) all of which time is taken up with recitation."[9]

His schedule did not ease as the school year wore on. "I have been very busy at school and with a trip out now and then, my time is completely occupied," he again told Benner.[10] Benner had suggested that he contribute some bird notes to a newly launched magazine, and Thomas had no time to sit down and write anything.

The "trip out now and then" was made possible by the early-out of the school day, sometime around noon. Most of Thomas's excursions were in the vicinity of the university, especially when coursework was demanding. After scrambling around on the limestone cliff below the school one April morning, he wrote, "This morning the river bluff by the University was fairly alive with Yellow-rumped warblers and ruby-crowned wrens, both in full song."[11] But he also reported driving out to Lake Harriet and Sandy Lake with his father, on the lookout for birds to add to his ever-expanding collection.

One particularly favorite haunt was a tamarack swamp "back of town," an easy walk from his home on Eighth Street. The swamp was part of a larger wetland that included what is now Loring Lake, a stream issuing from it, and the low area of the present-day Minneapolis Sculpture Garden. Bassett's Creek, which now flows through downtown in a culvert, meandered into the wetlands from the west.[12] Thomas often took tromps through the wetland on school-day afternoons. He and his brother, Walter, sometimes ran traplines there, catching shrews, deer mice, red-backed voles, and an occasional weasel. In winter, the swamp harbored "numerous tree sparrows," "Lapland Longspurs in abundance," and "a flock of thistle birds."[13] One year, he encountered unusual owls, a Great Gray and a Long-eared Owl, which he watched for a long time, the owl's head swiveling up and down, looking at crows and other birds. "Very comical looking," he commented.[14]

Thomas turned twenty during his first year at the university, and though he was weighed down with studies and consumed by the pursuit of natural history, there was, nonetheless, time in his life for socializing. "Well, I have been doing little else but walk to and from the University and study now and then an evening at the 'Galaxy' or [the Young Naturalists'] Society meetings," he informed Benner in February 1878.[15]

Ah, the Galaxy.

Thomas referred to the Young Naturalists' Society frequently in his journal because of it pertinence to birds. He never mentioned the Galaxy, however. It was a social club to which the Roberts siblings, Thomas and Emma, and their upper-middle-class friends gravitated, and its set was more social than the serious-minded and intellectually inclined naturalists. In the winter of Thomas's freshman year, a friend wrote and staged a play, *The Diamond Necklace*, at the club. Thomas and Emma both had parts. The large cast included friends from public school and the university. Thomas's role as "Officer" was small, but it involved making the arrest of "Princess Lamballe" played by pretty, dark-haired Jennie Cleveland, "for crimes against the state!" Jennie, eighteen and a friend of Emma's, lived down the block from the Robertses. Play practice took up some of the evenings, but the club also met "for much bodily exercise in the way of dancing which latter sometimes claims a very fair share of the evening."[16]

Later in the winter, the Galaxy set partied at the playwright's home, performing charades and dining on oysters, a supper "served in style." Thomas related it all in a letter to Benner,[17] and he saved the play's handbill and a scrap of paper on which were scribbled his and Jennie's lines.

Thomas finished his freshman year with great success, racking up scores in the 90 percent range in all classes but two. In June, the field crew of the Geological and Natural History Survey, led by Professor Winchell, headed to the North Shore of Lake Superior to study the geology and especially the mineralogy of the region. Experts predicted rich deposits of ores—iron, copper, and silver—in northern Minnesota. Several of Thomas's professors accompanied Winchell on the expedition, and at least one fellow student, Benedict Juni, went along, serving as the naturalist. Clarence had collected with the survey in past summers, but this year his job as Winchell's assistant tied him to the museum and Minneapolis.

Thomas would have liked to have gone, but he would have had to shell out his own money. Instead, as he wrote Benner, "I had concluded . . . to try some employment this summer and not 'loaf' away the vacation as I have always done. So I have joined the force of the city engineer and now tramp the city over in the capacity of assistant."[18] It was dry, dusty work, as the crew was out in the summer sun overseeing construction projects each day.

But there was time for a week's camping trip to Dunlap's Island in upper Lake Minnetonka with Walter and Clarence. The fishing was poor, but the young men noted with interest two dead northern pike, choked to death by trying to swallow overlarge sunfish. They also spent time watching the numerous Great Horned Owls on the island, in particular observing them at dusk as they sallied from tree branches, in flycatcher fashion. Thomas finally shot one and discovered it was a juvenile that had been feasting on June bugs.

Thomas and Clarence did some botanizing, too. In Halsted's Bay, they explored a renowned patch of aquatic flowers, the American lotus lily. The flower of this lily is large, ten inches in diameter and pale yellow, and it emits a sweet, vanilla fragrance. The plants grow in large, dense mats in shallow water. A lush growth of these flowers was certainly worth pursuing, but Thomas and Clarence discovered that they were nearly impossible to press for collection. They quickly wilted, blackened, and turned moldy.

Lake Minnetonka was the site of numerous burial mounds of the departed Native American people. The young men searched for a mound that had not been disturbed and eagerly exhumed bone fragments—but no skulls, they were disheartened to find. This blithe disregard for the graves of another culture was common among the Euro-American settlers of the late 1800s. Thomas had a number of bones in his bedroom collection, although he admitted in a letter to Benner that "Father has tried several times to persuade me to bury them."[19]

There was a possible link between the magnificent lotuses and the burial mounds that the men did not know: native people may have planted the lilies in Minnetonka. The natives dined on both the plant's seeds and its thick, starchy roots.

On this trip to Minnetonka, Thomas also took note of a distressing trend: the decline of the heron rookery on Crane Island. He could remember a time three or four years before when the rookery was a noisy, raucous place, filled to brimming with breeding birds. But in the summer of 1878, though it was still squawking, resembling "to a wonderful degree the snarling and yelping of puppies or curdogs," there were noticeably fewer birds. Thomas laid the blame on the steamboats bearing tourists that daily drew close to the shore of the island, blowing their whistles and allowing passengers to fire off guns and pistols. "An inevitable but greatly to be deplored situation," he rued.[20]

The decline of Crane Island's heron rookery was the first in a string of losses for Thomas. As his sophomore year began, in September 1878, he found himself in the lab once again, meticulously weighing and testing compounds in Analytical Chemistry, and fiddling with equipment in Mechanical Physics. He studied logic, taught by President Folwell (known as "Uncle Billy" to some of his students—presumably not to his face), and in spring term, he took zoology with Christopher Webber Hall, who was trained as a geologist. Throughout his college education, Thomas never studied under a zoologist.

Clarence was back at the university with Thomas, but the third member of the trio, Rob Williams, was not. He remained in Minneapolis, though, and he and Thomas shared bird sightings: "Robt. Williams tells me he saw many Lapland Longspurs and Snow buntings on the prairies this morning. These are the first this spring."[21] By midsummer, Rob was gone, leaving Minnesota for life on the frontier of Montana. In the spring term, Clarence, too, left school to take a temporary job teaching at the Blaisdell School near the Herrick farm.

Rob's departure was a blow to the Young Naturalists' Society, but as if in compensation, Frank Benner returned to Minneapolis on June 1, as Thomas's sophomore year was ending. He had come to Minnesota for his health and would remain indefinitely.

Within the week, Thomas and Benner were off on a collecting trip to Herman, Minnesota, a small prairie town in Grant County, in the western reaches of the state. Thomas had heard some time back that white pelicans nested on a big lake nearby and had been itching to get out there. He and Benner took the train to Herman, got settled in a boardinghouse, and began asking around town for the "Pelican camp," but nobody in town knew anything about it. So, while they scouted about for the big white birds, in a fierce wind and passing June showers, they collected the prairie birds they encountered: Marbled Godwits—"a good many . . . they run about on the prairie very much like immense [upland] sandpipers . . . they are not very shy,"[22] Bobolinks, meadowlarks, and Yellow-headed Blackbirds, all abundant.

In the end, the two collectors were stymied in their attempt to find the pelicans. The fortnight took them beyond Herman to Browns Valley and Big Stone Lake, accruing a wealth of prairie birds and taking note of the delicate prairie flowers in bloom. Thomas would later publish an annotated list of the birds taken on this trip in the January 1880 issue of the *Bulletin of the Nuttall Ornithological Club*.

In July 1879, Thomas got his chance to accompany the survey to the North Shore. His task was to collect plants and animals in the area just south of Grand Marais. A party of four took a Canadian steamer from Duluth up the shore to Grand Marais. They expected to be dropped into Lake Superior

with a small boat laden with five weeks' supplies shortly after ten o'clock
in the evening—no steamer being able to actually come ashore in an undeveloped harbor. The party would then row the short distance to the sandy
beach. In his journal, Thomas described the drop:

> There was a considerable sea running but no wind of any account.
> We started off, Prof Weibrecht and I pulling . . . the Captain said
> that he had run within a mile of the coast. As the steamer moved
> off and disappeared in the distance, we began to feel that we were
> actually at sea at night on Superior and in a small, heavily loaded
> boat. Steering by the stars and the dark line of shore we pulled
> away steadily, thinking every little bit that we ought to be close to
> shore, but it was not until half past two o'clock that we really came
> to land. The Captain deceived us badly . . . we must have [been]
> six or eight miles out in the lake. A rather dangerous position,
> all things considered for there is no telling how suddenly storms
> may arise.[23]

At close range of shore, the party saw no place to land. In the gray first light,
they perceived only frothy waves crashing upon a formidable rocky shoreline. None had ever been on this stretch of Superior, and they had no bear-
ings. They made a decision to follow the shoreline to the left—a fortunate
choice, because they were nearly spent—and rowed into Grand Marais's
harbor as the sun was rising. They had endured five hours on open water, a
harrowing experience that Thomas would remember all his life.

Thomas spent the next five weeks collecting plants and birds in the pristine wilderness of Minnesota's Arrowhead, filling his journal with descrip-
tions of the beauty. "The harbor at Grand Marais is a beautiful spot . . . a
promontory projects into the lake which suggests a long, rugged island of
rock connected with the mainland by a sandy beach."[24] Cascade Falls was
"very pretty" with tall evergreens and birches rising high above the bubbling river, and rocks covered with mosses, lichens, and ferns: a "profusion
of verdure" that "seems to set off the more strikingly the little foaming falls."
"There is not the least indication of the presence of man about the falls,"
he added, perhaps thinking of Minnehaha and its heavily trodden banks.[25]

He spent some leisure time gathering agates and thomsonites north of

Caribou Point and collected ferns and bunchberries at Beaver Bay. Birds, however, were not much in evidence, and so, safe from his gun. "I don't think I ever was in a place more deserted of animal life," he wrote, somewhat baffled. "The stillness is so profound that it almost seems a pity to disturb it by talking or shooting."[26]

But it was not a perfectly blissful experience. "Did not sleep much last night from indigestion and was not feeling at all well this morning," he wrote about halfway into the trip. And the next day, "Not feeling well." And again, "Still feeling rather unwell." But was it merely indigestion? Or was it something a good deal more serious, something that would sap his health, consume his energy, waste him away, like his father?[27]

A few days later, he reported hearing "many birds flying over last night. The migration of warblers at least seems to have begun."[28] But that was his last journal entry. The party remained in the field for another two weeks.

In September 1879, Thomas did not return to the university. The college listed him as "on leave."

Thomas's loss of good health was the most personal of the many losses that year. Surely his parents were worried sick over the sudden decline of their eldest. The family had endured John's ill health for many years. What a calamity if Thomas succumbed as well! How unspeakable to imagine such a thing. And unspeakable and unwritten his health was. In his journal, he did not write again about his health that fall. In fact, he would never know definitively what had made him so ill, but assumed it was TB. As summer faded and the trees became gold and yellow, Thomas spent his days out driving with his father, rather than walking to school.

Sometimes he took his shotgun and traipsed out to "Tamarack Swamp," his favorite site, looking for fall-plumage birds to add to the collection. "Shot an orange-crowned warbler, two solitary vireos, two Nashville warblers, a flicker, a clay-colored [sparrow], a [fox] sparrow, a wild pigeon and a female black-throated blue warble," he reported on one particularly fruitful outing.[29]

Yet even the haven of Tamarack Swamp became a source of dismay that fall. One month later, in October, when the needles of the trees in the swamp were a shimmering gold, he wrote, "The far half of tamarack has been cleared off entirely and they are going to cut off the remainder. This spoils one of my best collecting grounds about Minneapolis."[30]

CHAPTER 5

A Gypsy Life

> While surveying in Stearns and adjourning counties
> in 1881, the author saw one or more [Swallow-tailed
> Kites] almost every day.
>
> — *The Birds of Minnesota*, 1: 300

The fall of 1879 was quiet for Thomas Roberts. At twenty-one, he was unfettered by the structure of the school year for the first time. He could freely pursue natural history as he had done in the happy summers of his teens, if his health allowed it.

While at the university, Thomas had lamented the lack of time to write up bird notes for East Coast publications such as *Forest and Stream* and *The Country*, magazines that would gain him national exposure. He now took advantage of his time out of school to complete short articles for publication and pursue correspondence with some of the leading scientific naturalists in America.

George Bird Grinnell, organizer of the first Audubon society and a prominent early conservationist, published young Thomas's bird notes in *Forest and Stream*. E. D. Cope, at the peak of his fame as a paleontologist and a notorious participant in the "Bone Wars" of the decade to come, accepted an article in the *American Naturalist* and promised him complimentary copies. These magazines were geared toward amateur naturalists with a high level of knowledge and skill.

Through letters, Thomas communicated with the Nuttall Ornithology Club of Cambridge, Massachusetts, writing to the editor of its bulletin, J. A. Allen; its founding member William Brewster; and another active member, Henry Henshaw. These young men, just a year or two older than Thomas, would form the nucleus of the American Ornithologists' Union within the decade.

Frank Benner, because of his Long Island origin, had many East Coast contacts. He informed Robert Ridgway of the Smithsonian Institution in Washington, D.C., that Thomas might be able to secure Evening Grosbeak specimens for the museum's collection, and Ridgeway wrote a request. Word then traveled through the ornithological grapevine to William Brewster in Massachusetts, who also asked Thomas for several of the yellow-and-black beauties. Asa Gray of the Harvard Herbarium, Elliott Coues, whose book had been Thomas's earliest reference, and Charles Bendire, another collector for the Smithsonian, all received letters from the bright, ambitious young man of far-off Minneapolis.

Thomas did not crow about his growing recognition as the unofficial expert on Minnesota birds. Still, how satisfying to be noticed.

The following spring, Thomas's health had improved sufficiently for him to take a job. Acting on his father's belief that fresh air was a remedy for TB, Thomas became a land examiner for the St. Paul, Minneapolis and Manitoba Railroad Company, a new enterprise of the fledgling entrepreneur James J. Hill, who was just beginning to build his empire.

The federal government encouraged the construction of transcontinental railways by granting land to the builders. Bold, speculative men like Hill had the drive and connections to undertake such a monumental task and rose to the occasion. The granted lands lay near the railroad rights-of-way. They could be sold by the railroads to finance the laying of track. Hill, though, viewed the lands as a means to populate the unsettled country with prospective passengers on his railroad. He had control of 450,000 acres of granted land, and to offer it for sale to white settlers, he needed to be able to characterize each section's features. Hence, the hiring of land examiners.

Land examiners were not surveyors. The land had already been surveyed, but Thomas's university surveying coursework proved useful in his work. Examiners had to locate the section corners marked by government surveyors, using a compass and pacing. Then within every forty-acre section, they needed to show on a drawn map every lake, marsh, cultivated field, bluff—all physical features of the section—as well as man-made structures like houses, quarries, dams, or mills. They evaluated the slope of the land and its drainage, soil type, and quality (on a scale from one to five). They recorded the native vegetation type and, if a meadow, how much hay, in tons, it could produce. At the end of the day, the field notes were written up and final maps drawn. Sections were evaluated for their best use—farming, logging, hayfield, or other human endeavor.

The work was methodical and thorough, perfectly suited to Thomas's exacting mind and his inclination toward tromping about out of doors. The pay was just adequate, about fifty dollars a month.

Thomas reported to Nathan Butler, who was in charge of all the land examiners hired by the railroad. Butler, in his forties, was a thin man of temperate habits who had found that an outdoor life had restored what he considered to be "a weak constitution." Educated at Colby College in Maine and a surveyor by training, he was a member of Minnesota's Academy of Natural Sciences, where he may first have made the acquaintance of Thomas and his father. Thoughtful and sensitive, Butler would make allowances for Thomas's precarious health, and though Thomas did not like it at the time, he would later credit the older man with saving his life.[1]

Thomas's first exposure to life as a land examiner was daunting. Mid-April 1880, he left Minneapolis on the train, headed for Ada, in northwestern Minnesota, with plans to meet Butler on the way in Fergus Falls. It was a late spring. As the train traveled north of St. Cloud, Thomas looked out on a landscape still in the throes of winter. Ducks, geese, and prairie chickens abounded. Through the windows of the swiftly moving train, he also saw vast numbers of juncos, tree sparrows, and blackbirds.

He met Butler in Fergus Falls and dined with him and some others at the best hotel in town. Together they boarded the northbound train. The others in the party all disembarked at the next station, though, leaving Thomas to continue on to Ada. He was hardly alone, however. The train bound for Ada that wintry spring evening was full of immigrants and land hunters, as well as, Thomas noted, "Two young English bloods with eye-glass and knee-breeches complete."[2]

Arriving in Ada in the dead of night, a sharp prairie wind blowing, he found the one hotel crammed with wayfarers occupying every possible spot, including the floor. He arranged to put up the cot he had brought north from home in the hotel's office, only to find that it had not been taken off the train. Butler's cot, however, had been deposited on the station platform, and Thomas commandeered it for what remained of the night.

Ada, itself, he discovered on a walk about town the next morning, consisted of "a single line of houses on one side of the track, and a station house, elevator and lumber yard on the other."[3] The surrounding prairie was more interesting, harboring godwits, Greater Yellowlegs, meadowlarks, and Horned Larks. He also found many blackbirds, shooting them with a borrowed gun to positively identify them as Rusty, and not Brewer's, Blackbirds.

Butler and the others arrived in the following days, which must have been a relief for Thomas. In the interval between his arrival and Butler's, Ada had experienced a severe spring blizzard that deposited three-foot drifts of snow. The drafty hotel, wracked by howling winds sweeping across the flats of the Red River valley, had provided meager comfort. Thomas had sat by a woodstove in the company of two bridge builders, whom he deemed "intelligent, pleasant persons," but in the barroom downstairs "was a crowd of smoking, swearing, bragging fellows, who are of the lowest type."[4]

Despite the weather, Butler put Thomas to work. Under the constant assault of the wind, he and his boss located the section markers in and about Ada. It was bone-chilling, but the great spectacle of spring migration was ample compensation. Within the week, however, Thomas, the presumed consumptive, was ill with "quite a bad cold." Despite shortness of breath, a bad headache, and poor sleep, he continued to work. His team finished the task at Ada and went farther up the line to Crookston, and from Crookston to Euclid, "an embryo town," on a train coated with solid ice and snow.

The country north of Ada remained in the grip of midwinter. Thick snow blanketed the ground, and more fell in the nights they were there. Thomas got sicker and longed to remain in bed, "but did not like to give up, so went." More wind, more chill. The examiners, out beyond Crookston, expected to remain in the field for hours after sunset until the eleven o'clock train came through, but were thrilled when a special freight train came by and picked them up shortly after dark.

Back in Ada, Thomas worsened. Feverish and fitful, he spent the next day in bed, at Butler's suggestion. He dosed himself with aconite, commonly known as wolfsbane, a medicinal herb used to treat fevers and one considered a bit risky since it was easy to overdose. Too weak to walk steadily, he remained in bed until Butler decided the following day that the party could not work productively in the wintry conditions.

The men arrived back in Minneapolis on the evening of April 29, 1880. Even in the city, it was still cold enough for ice to form. At home under his mother's care, it took Thomas three weeks to recover sufficient health to resume his journal.

The educated Butler had learned that young men with some college background made the best land examiners, particularly if they had civil engineering coursework and were considering it for a career. They were eager to learn, less entrenched in their ways, and more likely to heed his instructions. Thomas fell into this employee profile and would work closely with several others like him in the coming summers.

He met the first of these compatriots in June 1880, as he set off with the team to examine land north of Minneapolis in Ramsey County, along the east bank of the Mississippi. In the party were Butler, Thomas, John Cobb, whom Thomas had known at the university, and a cook. The group set off with a newly purchased covered wagon pulled by two horses, a nine-by-twelve-foot tent, a cookstove, and all provisions needed for a four-month stay in unsettled country. The cook acted as driver and was the only team member to ride. The others traversed the rough road to Long Lake in northern Ramsey County on foot.

That first fortnight, his small party moved frequently and quickly made their way toward Anoka. Much of the area was marshy. The June weather was warm and humid, and the men were plagued by biting insects. "The flies and gnats were very bad," Thomas wrote on June 30. And the next day, "The mosquitoes were very bad last night despite our best efforts to keep them from the tent. The poor horses suffered terribly and their ceaseless stamping and moving about the trees to which they were tied kept me awake almost as much as the mosquitoes in the tent."[5]

When they were not swatting mosquitoes, the examiners were tramping across the wet marshes and sandy soil, looking for section corners. They noted the vegetation: tamarack, oak, marshland. Thomas's expert familiarity with flowers allowed him to precisely identify them. "On some peculiar sand hills . . . I found the Hudsonia tomentosa (false heather) growing abundantly. I have only found it before [in Duluth] on Minnesota Point."[6]

One memorable day, Thomas encountered a hognose snake, a harmless reptile that puts on an impressive, cobra-like show of hisses and strikes. It is entirely possible he had never seen this great bluffer of the Minnesota prairie.

He killed it, tucked it into a baking powder box, and sent it off to his father that same day, conveyed via train by Butler, who had ridden into Minneapolis. Frank Benner examined the snake on a visit to the Robertses. By mail, John Roberts informed his son, "Mr. Butler called on Friday the 2nd about dusk and left me the letter and the box with the snake. . . . We put the snake into alcohol in a jar that was in your room. A 'Puffing Adder,' Benner says."[7]

The deerflies by day and the mosquitoes by night were so relentless that Butler was inclined to let his men take the train into the city for the Fourth of July. They did not leave, however, and were treated, instead, to a celebratory dinner: "Peas, blueberries, butter, bread, custard (pudding), ham, potatoes, tea, peaches, tomatoes, pie." Thomas ate with relish and then "spent the rest of the day sewing on a curtain around the bottom of the tent to keep out the mosquitoes."[8] The nation's birthday was a day off. The crew slept in and lounged about camp, talking, reading, and writing letters.

By mid-July, the biting insects had waned, but sultry days and frequent violent thunderstorms swept over the countryside. Butler often assigned Thomas the less rigorous task of setting up and breaking camp. He was also in charge of copying the field notes and reproducing the maps, a task he performed in pencil with a precise, meticulous hand. "My duty in the party has undergone a change," Thomas confided to his journal on July 27. "I am undecided whether I shall like it or not and never feel as well after sitting still and writing several hours."[9]

In August, two additional men joined the examiners, who were now camped outside Big Lake, a town consisting of a store, a meetinghouse, a blacksmith, a grain elevator, and a rail station. The first to arrive was Henry Nachtrieb, a robust native of Ohio, who had come to the University of Minnesota the year before. Nachtrieb, like Roberts, would soon prove to be as interested in the plants and animals they encountered in their work as the work itself. The second, also a university student, was Edson Gaylord, whom Thomas had known in high school. The three would become lifelong friends.

Examining the railroad land proved a slower process than Butler and his superiors had anticipated. Thomas's party had gotten a late start in the season, the area was much more marshy and harder to evaluate than they had originally thought, and frequently rain or extreme heat shortened the workday.

Thomas was again assigned to the field. He and Gaylord took on the tamaracks, cattails, and brushlands. "In company with Gaylord went entirely around Section 29 but although we walked 7 or 8 miles through swamps and brush, accomplished nothing of any account since we could find no [section] corners," he penned in his journal after a particularly discouraging day.[10]

The life of a land examiner was paradoxical. Although the men traversed rough, uncultivated country and had little in the way of creature comforts—clumsy canvas tents, blankets as bedrolls, and simple, filling food prepared over a cookstove—they were never far from a rail line and could catch trains and reach Minneapolis in a matter of hours.

"The Boss," Butler, was constantly on the move. A second team of examiners worked another portion of the line. He kept a close eye on both camps, observing how well the men carried out the work, the detail and clarity of their notes, and the various ancillary skills needed for this nomadic life. Butler's on-again, off-again presence in camp meant that often the examiners were laboring under somewhat vague or out-of-date instructions. But Butler was a fair and likable supervisor, and Thomas's journal presented a picture of a tranquil, domestic camp life. "We pitched camp and were soon comfortably fixed. Put our horses in Mr. Babcock's stable [a nearby farm]. About supper time, Mr. Butler came walking into camp. We had not expected him but were pleased to see him."[11]

In the first week of September 1880, the crew knocked off work to spend a few days in Minneapolis. Thomas had not been home since June. A steady stream of letters had passed between the family home on Eighth Street and the camp in the hinterlands, and also between Thomas and Frank Benner. Unlike those in the Young Naturalists' Society, Benner moved in Thomas's social circle as well as sharing his scientific interests. Benner constantly fed Thomas tidbits of gossip of concerts, parties, and rumors. In one letter, Frank pitched an appeal: "The world moves on very quietly here. The only thing on the programme at present is a surprise party to be given to your sister before she goes. Harry Neiler is getting it up. Don't you want to come home for a day or two and go to it"?[12]

But it was a newsy letter from his sister, Emma, that carried the announcement of perhaps keenest interest to Thomas: after weeks away in Chicago, Jennie Cleveland was coming home to Minneapolis. Although busy with ice-cream socials, archery, and band concerts, Emma anticipated the arrival: "She is coming at last on this afternoon's train."[13]

Five weeks later, Thomas received a reprieve from camp life. It coincided with the Great Exposition, Minneapolis's answer to archrival St. Paul and its Minnesota State Fair. He went with his father to see the exposition's displays and a highly publicized horse race between two women equestrians. He returned a second time with Jennie, Emma, and Benner. The highlighted event that day was a women's running race, which Thomas found "a rather vulgar low display not at all elevating in tendency."[14] The foursome returned home for tea with the elder Robertses.

The land examiners returned to the field after a five-day break. They were back in the vicinity of Anoka, on a spreading glacial outwash, the Anoka sand plain. Thomas wrote of this landscape: "We are now in a section of country that has long been settled but which is yet as desolate, worthless a region as we had to examine. . . . There are great numbers of abandoned farms here that have been deserted in years gone by and are growing up in weeds and scattering brush. . . . The land is nothing but clear sand and will yield only middling crops after being most thoroughly worked. It is said that there are not as many settlers here now as there were in 1860."[15]

But the sand grew wild cranberries, which they picked and cooked. There was time to record bird life, too. Thomas observed a Pileated Woodpecker, the second he had ever seen, and a screech owl near camp. Migrating ducks, geese, and Sandhill Cranes frequented the many wetlands. The weather was beautiful that fall. The insects that had so plagued them were long gone, the heat, as well, and the examiners enjoyed bright, sunny days and cool nights. Thomas relished what he termed a "gypsy life" and wrote in his letters of living "very comfortably indeed—having all the conveniences possible and not a few luxuries."[16]

Then, in mid-October and with little warning, the weather changed. A storm moved in, bringing high winds and dark skies. The examiners feared their tent would blow down and were glad they had pitched it on the lee side of a hill. On October 16, 1880, the men awoke to heavy snow that almost broke the ridgepoles of the tents. The wet snow blanketed trees and shrubs, and it continued throughout the day. In the evening, the temperature dropped. The following morning, the weather was still wild. Large flocks of Snow Geese passed in Vs overhead. They were flying high and headed south.

It was a couple of days before Cobb and Gaylord could make their way to the nearest town, St. Francis. When they did, they learned that the storm had laid siege to a widespread area, blocking the railroads as far south as Iowa.[17] It was the start to "The Long Winter" of 1880–81, legendary in the accounts of farmers and other homesteaders riding out one snowy assault after another. Several hundred miles west, holed up as a girl on the Dakota prairie, Laura Ingalls Wilder would immortalize the season in a book of the same name.

The land examiners living in their canvas tents on the sand plain, though, naturally thought that an October snowfall would soon melt. Butler had not been in camp when the first storm struck, but the examiners had their instructions to carry on the work. However, after a week in camp, hindered by successive snows at night, they hoped to see Butler return with directions to break camp and "come in." Instead, they received word to continue. "We were some put out but concluded to make the best of it and stick to it," Thomas wrote that night.[18] The team purchased potatoes, sorghum (a sweetener), and mutton and prepared to move camp.

Although pleasant days followed the initial blizzard, the threat of snow was ever present. The early snow had left the roads rough and muddy. The men lacked heavy winter clothes. They hoped for a shipment of blankets from St. Paul, as the nights were getting cold, but were disappointed. Ponds developed sheets of ice. Still Butler did not come.

Three weeks after the onset of snow, Nachtrieb and Gaylord left camp to begin winter term at the university. This left Thomas and Cobb in camp with the cook. Thomas assured his concerned parents in letters home that living conditions were comfortable. In one tent was the cookstove, and there they ate, copied field notes, wrote letters, and passed the time. In the other, where they slept, it was less crowded, especially with the departure of the university students. "Cobb and I sleep together (spoon fashion) and have five pairs of blankets—besides our overcoats," Thomas wrote Benner in mid-November. "Last night was the coldest we have had. The whole inside of the tent was white with frost—tent poles, blankets, the canvas, etc. so that a rap on the tent brought down a perfect shower of frost."[19]

Worried over his son's health, which had been so tenuous at the start of the summer, John Roberts wrote and urged Thomas to come home.[20] Indeed, with frequent snow squalls and subfreezing temperatures, it seemed unlikely that any more work would be done that year. On a trip into Princeton, the examiners noted that the town folk had traded wheels for runners to travel about.

Finally, on a bright, cold November 18, 1880, a full month after the first storm, The Boss strode into camp. The next day, the team dismantled the tents, packed the wagon, and headed for town. They caught the nearest train bound for Minneapolis at Elk River and arrived in the evening. The remainder of the Long Winter would be endured in the civilized life of Minneapolis.

The 1881 land-examining field season started in early May for Thomas, at the height of the spring bird migration. He had missed this euphoric (for bird-watchers) season the year before, recovering from the bad cold he had caught in Ada. In 1881, however, he became immersed in the grand event.

The team of examiners headed north out of Minneapolis and then west of Monticello and the Mississippi, crossing the river by ferry to reach the campsite. The party consisted of men whom Thomas had worked with the previous year—Edson Gaylord and Nathan Butler—and several older men whom Thomas also knew. There was also a short, burly French cook who specialized in blue language. He lasted about a week under Butler, but while he reigned over the cookstove, Thomas regarded him as "the most profane man I ever met," adding, "as a cook he was far from a success."[21] All the men in camp were relieved to see him go.

Every evening, Thomas filled his journal with lists of the newly arrived birds that he saw while out in the field: yellow-red poll warblers (Palm Warblers), Rose-breasted Grosbeaks, and whip-poor-wills one day; Ovenbirds, Black-and-white Warblers, and Black-billed Cuckoos the next; Black-throated Green Warblers, Nashville Warblers, Golden-winged Warblers, Least Flycatchers, and Veeries the day after—and all this unaided by binoculars. The May days were clear and very warm with a south wind.

The land was flush with spring flowers, as well. Thomas's work in the Young Naturalists' Society had honed his identification skills, and in his journal, he recorded marsh blue violets, large-flowered bellworts, Juneberries, wild plums, wild strawberries, and dandelions.

Soon there were nests: "Found a whippoorwill's nest in thick brush along the edge of a wheat field. The two eggs were fresh . . . also found a pigeon's nest containing a single fresh egg. The male was sitting."[22] Where there were nests, there were eggs and opportunities to enhance his egg collection. Thomas was nimble in the treetops, having gained his experience as a boy, and it was a skill he would use well into middle age. "Found a Red-tailed Hawk's nest in the top of a tall white oak tree. Leaving my boots and part of my clothing on the ground, I managed a pretty hard climb for me to reach the nest. It contained two eggs which I blew in the tree. One of them was nearly fresh while the other contained a small embryo. Wrapping each in a handkerchief and putting them in my shooting coat pockets I reached the ground without breaking them."[23]

The next stop for the team was in Stearns County, with the railroad station at St. Joseph. Within hours of arrival, Thomas ascertained that "all the residents in this place seem to be Germans of the genuine type."[24]

Stearns County was fairly settled with farms by 1881, but the examiners did encounter both brushy areas, which were difficult to navigate, and open prairies, which were much preferred. The examiners arrived during a rainy spell and found the roads muddy and "terribly bad." The horses sometimes became mired in mud, requiring the crew to unload the wagon to ease the burden on the beasts. On occasion, the wagon needed to be dislodged with a rope. The going was slow.

The birding, however, was fine. Part of the county had been burned, and Mourning Warblers were abundant, as were Chestnut-sided Warblers, nesting in brush that had sprung up after the fire. Outside of Avon, he shot a Golden-winged Warbler with an aberrant song. Northwest of Cold Spring, he spotted several Swallow-tailed Kites.

In mid-June, Thomas took the empty wagon to St. Joseph for supplies. Passing through Cold Spring, "a prettily situated village lying in a wooded valley" he came across a celebration in midweek. "[These] Germans are Catholic and are great church goers during the week as well as Sundays. Today was one of their holidays . . . and they were all out in force. At every church in the country and in the towns there were numerous little bowers of evergreens . . . decorated after the manner of a chancel in a church. With ornamented carpet and stools in front, apparently to kneel upon. All the men and women were in their holiday attire and parading the streets and churchyards and according to the customs of these people crowding the beer saloons."[25]

The examiners continued moving westward, to Paynesville and then to the glacial ridges north of Willmar. At the next big town, Benson, Thomas was assigned the task of describing Benson itself, all the buildings and lots. He wrote to his father, "I began taking an account of the property in the entire town. There are 42 blocks with from 12 to 24 lots in each. . . . I was pacing off buildings and lots all day Saturday and shall be again tomorrow. It excited the people so seeing me pacing, dodging into alleys and looking up at every building that I didn't know but I should be arrested upon some charge or other."[26]

The cook who had replaced the notable swearer did not work out either, and at Benson, Butler used a ruse to trick the cook into leaving peaceably. Thomas disapproved of the deception ("a method I did not like," he wrote his father). But the replacement proved an excellent choice:

> He is an old land examiner himself and able to find his way about the country with plat and compass as well as anybody which enables him to move camp alone while the examiners are all at work. The other cook could not tell whether he would the next minute come in sight of Big Stone Lake or Lake Superior and accordingly [could] go nowhere alone. I have become pretty well acquainted with the new man and so far think him an improvement in every way over all the other cooks I have seen. He is a German, talks broken English and has some peculiar notions. He is as clean and orderly about his cooking as any woman could be. The first thing he did was to pull everything out of the wagon, clean it until it fairly shone, repack and rearrange everything. He has a notion how everything ought to be and it must be that way or no way. The boys will hardly recognize the culinary department when they get back.[27]

Thomas ended his lengthy letter home with a reassurance to his parents: "Am in good health—much better than when I was in camp last year. I like working in the field better than staying in camp." And a request: "I suppose Jennie Cleveland is home by this time. Remember me to her."[28]

After a short break in Minneapolis, Butler moved his land examiners up the line to the Crookston area in northwestern Minnesota. They were now in the broad expanse of the Red River valley. What a difference from when Thomas had first come to this valley in the wintry April of 1880! Upon his second arrival, it was the height of summer. The northern prairie was very warm, and

Thomas noted, "reed birds are very abundant here."[29] The terrain was still flat as a pancake, of course, and good drinking water was hard to find.

Arriving in Crookston, the examiners crossed paths with Warren Upham and Horace Winchell, who were that summer surveying the shoreline of Glacial Lake Agassiz for the Minnesota Geological and Natural History Survey. Thomas knew both men personally; Horace, a teenager that summer, was the oldest son of Newton Winchell, head of the survey. The surveyors visited the land examiners' camp outside of town after supper that evening and regaled the examiners with stories of their time in the field.[30]

The work in the valley was enlivened by something new: transportation problems of the equine variety. One horse, Jerry, refused to pull the wagon. On another occasion, the team pulling the covered wagon ran away "full speed across the prairie." In a letter to his father, Thomas confided that though he had been present at the event, he took no responsibility. "It came about through following out Mr. B.'s orders—to let the cook [Eggert] move alone and see how he would manage. . . . He is no horseman. . . . [Who would] hitch a pair of restless horses to a wagon without putting the bridles on?"[31]

There was also a pony, which had been acquired to pull a buckboard, a four-wheeled open conveyance. Thomas termed it "a perfect circus outfit." The pony ("the ugliest-dispositioned animal I ever saw") never truly acquiesced to the wagon. "[It] would buck on all occasions and at last the front of the buckboard (a most appropriate name) was in a sadly demoralized condition as also was the harness," Thomas wrote to his father.[32] The men called the pony "Boomerang." Thomas refused to have anything to do with her.

The men endured the temperamental animals for a month. Then, in early September, the Boss appeared one morning, driving a country wagon hitched to a pair of mules. Two days later, Butler departed with the horses, leaving the crew the mules, "a trade with which we were much pleased."[33]

Within weeks, Thomas was back in Minneapolis for good. Edson Gaylord and Henry Nachtrieb were once more students at the university, and Nachtrieb had rented a room over Gray's Drugstore near the university for living quarters. The three friends, along with John Cobb, arranged a photo with their boss, Butler, all five dressed in their examiner outfits to commemorate the happy summer of hard work, camaraderie, and recalcitrant horses.

CHAPTER 6

The Medical Student

The flight of the Marsh Hawk is easy and graceful . . .
at times it soars in the air at considerable height.

— *The Birds of Minnesota*, 1: 342

Three days after Christmas in 1881, Thomas Roberts, slim and fair at age twenty-three, boarded the twelve o'clock train of the Chicago, Milwaukee and St. Paul Railroad to Philadelphia. Under the solstice sun hanging low in a bright blue sky, a small delegation consisting of his father and brother, Frank Benner, John Cobb, and high school chum Harry Robinson gathered on the platform of the elegant Italianate depot on Washington Avenue to see him off. When the eastbound train stopped in St. Paul, another group, which included Nathan Butler and Harry Neiler, gave him a second send-off.

John Roberts wrote in his journal that night that Thomas was headed to Philadelphia merely to "visit friends for some time."[1] Yet the trip was more portentous than his father would admit. The past three weeks, at the wane of the old year, exuded an air of finality about them. Thomas spent time with Warren Upham of the Geological Survey, compiling the list of plants that he and the other Young Naturalists had identified during the time of the society's existence. He had dental work done. He shopped with his mother for dress shirts and readied his woolen clothes for travel by brushing and cleaning them. He called on the Clevelands, with hopes of seeing Jennie, but the family was out. He carefully packed away all his bird skins. Life was about to change for Thomas Sadler Roberts, and those closest to him sensed that fact.

When Thomas was seventeen and still in high school, he had written Benner, "I have not yet settled on exactly what I will do or be in the future although I suppose it is about time I had. What makes you think I would do for a doctor?"[2] In casting about for a career, he apparently never seriously considered pursuing his love of birds in a professional way, even though Clarence Herrick was already immersed in natural history at the University of Minnesota. Perhaps he did not view it as a gentlemanly vocation. All around him were examples of men—William Tiffany, William Dunwoody, Philo Hatch, his own father—who made money in business or the professions while pursuing nature on the side. Philadelphia, Thomas's ancestral city, had spawned dozens of "secondary" naturalists, like Thomas Say and Thomas Nuttall. Many, in fact, had been Quakers, like the Robertses: John Bartram, considered the first American naturalist, and his son, William; Say (with a phoebe named after him); and John Townsend (with a warbler named after *him*); and a number of women who were illustrators of plants and shells. Thomas left no record of his inner deliberation, but in the fall of 1881, he came out of the field season with plans to investigate a career in medicine.

In the mid-1800s, most physicians trained as apprentices to an established doctor. It was not necessary to attend a formal medical school with a set curriculum, nor did states license practicing physicians. By the 1880s, however, that system was fading. Long-established medical schools, incorporating the recent explosion of scientific knowledge, offered solid coursework as background in training doctors. Most of these schools, though, still retained remnants of the apprenticeship. Medical students paid their fees directly to the lecturers whose classes they attended—one fee to the anatomy professor, another to the surgery lecturer, and so forth. This did nothing to weed out incompetents, since there were no entrance standards, and lecturers maximized their income by letting all comers into their courses.

The University of Pennsylvania Medical School was among the early few that had enacted a series of reforms to enhance competency of its graduates. By 1882, it had abolished individual lecture fees. Students paid tuition directly to the school, and thus, professors were part of a unified faculty. The school also set requirements for entrance—either passage of an exam or the completion of a two-year college course of study. The University of Pennsylvania was the oldest medical school in the nation, established in 1765, and it was leading medical education into the modern era.

By contrast, medical education in Minnesota could be obtained from several small schools. Minnesota College Hospital, founded in 1881, was renting the old Winslow House in East Minneapolis. There was also the St. Paul Medical College and the Minnesota College of Homeopathic Medicine. These three would merge to form the University of Minnesota medical school in 1888. The Minneapolis College of Physicians and Surgeons, later affiliated with Hamline University, would become part of the University of Minnesota in later years, but the unified medical school would not be housed on campus until 1892. By then, Thomas had completed a residency and been practicing general medicine in Minneapolis for six years.

Shortly before leaving for Philadelphia, Thomas sought advice on how best to pursue training from Dr. Hance, a Minneapolis physician with a practice on Nicollet Avenue and a social friend of his parents. "He gave me a rather diffuse account of medical schools, the methods pursued and requisites necessary to the study of medicine," Thomas summarized in his journal. "He seemed a little opposed to the service of entering a physician's office as a student and thought it better to enter college direct . . . the tenor of his advice, however, was that I should first attend to my health even though my studies were neglected. An energetic, well man of only moderate attainments succeeds better than the brilliant intellect supported by a weak body."[3]

Hance must have been referring to Thomas's previous bout with apparent tuberculosis, which had subsided. His health was now good. Hance's advice to aim for "moderate attainments" did not resonate with young Thomas, who was competitive and accustomed to being at the head of his class. Having once considered Yale for a college degree, he now prepared to investigate the University of Pennsylvania for a medical education.

Philadelphia! A vigorous, venerable city in 1882, with two hundred years of history and a population of nearly a million. The city buildings were taller, the neighborhoods older, the rivers broader, and the slums more decrepit than anything Minneapolis knew. Coal mines to the west of the city provided a nearly limitless fuel supply to Philadelphia's large and growing clothing, iron, textiles, and locomotive industries. Railroads were prominent in the City of Brotherly Love, the single most important enterprise in town. The city was also a thriving seaport, second only to New York, and home to an extensive network of horse car lines—264 miles of track, longer than any other American urban area.

In 1876, Philadelphia had hosted the Centennial Exposition to commemorate the hundredth anniversary of the signing of the Declaration of Independence. Thomas had visited this first "World's Fair" with his family and become reacquainted with the haunts of his early childhood. He had gone out to the ancestral farm in Germantown and spent time with cousins he had left behind in his move to Minnesota.

In the six years since that trip, Philadelphia had continued to press into its industrial future. Alexander Graham Bell had introduced his telephone at the exposition. Now the contraption had spread into daily life. Some city businesses had electrified, including the nation's first department store, Wanamaker's, anchoring the downtown business district. One block over, Chestnut Street's entire length was lit by electric lights.

Thomas had aunts, an uncle, cousins, and family friends on his father's side waiting for him when he arrived in town. Accompanied by a cousin, he went directly to Germantown in the northern portion of the city, and there he stayed with his aunt Cornelia Roberts, widow of his father's brother.

Although his father had characterized the trip as a social visit undertaken in the dreary days of a Minnesota winter, Thomas's actions made clear that he was on a fact-finding mission. Within twelve hours of arrival in town, he had called on two medical contacts, Drs. Benjamin and Arthur Wilson, father and son, and discussed with them the university's medical school, a call Thomas found "very pleasant and profitable."

The Wilsons arranged to show Thomas the facilities at the school. Several days later, he trekked to West Philadelphia, across the Schuylkill River, and located Medical Hall. This spacious new building had been erected in 1874 on land that had previously been meadow. Five stories of brick and stone, with countless gables and chimneys, it was the counterpart of the university's College Hall, where undergraduates took classes. Across the road was the equally impressive Hospital of the University of Pennsylvania, affiliated with the medical school. Its proximity allowed students ample clinical experience as well as academic training, a rare situation in 1882. The school's faculty was a dazzling constellation of stars in the medical world. It included Joseph Leidy, teaching anatomy (but also a renowned parasitologist, who had established that trichinosis in pork was parasite caused), and the brilliant surgeon David Hayes Agnew, an attendant to President James A. Garfield after he was shot by an assassin in 1881.

Accompanied by Arthur Wilson, Thomas sat in on lectures. He listened to a discourse on the kidneys and their diseases, followed by a demonstration on "morbid anatomy" that included specimens in dissection pans passed about the class. At Agnew's lecture, Thomas was amazed by the uninterest of the class: "Some were lying at full length on the benches, some asleep, others were reading books or newspapers, some talking among themselves and others supremely indifferent without being employed at anything."[4]

He enjoyed a clinic on skin diseases at University Hospital, but "the dissecting room was a strange and startling place to me it being my first visit to any place of this kind."[5] This from the young man who had skinned hundreds of bloodied birds!

All in all, he must have liked what he saw. Soon after, he went downtown to Lippincott's and bought a copy of *Gray's Anatomy*, his first definitive act as a medical student.

Courses began at the school in early October and ended in mid-April. Thomas's arrival in Philadelphia in January meant that he could not begin the academic sequence immediately. On his visit he did enroll, however, in the school for the 1882–83 session.

These first months in Philadelphia gave him an opportunity to put down a few roots of his own in his father's town. He spent time with his male Harper cousins, sons of his father's sister, Susie, and he became better acquainted with Thomas Shipley, his father's close friend and accountant, who would write the checks for Thomas's living expenses for the next five years. He rode the street cars and browsed the collection of the Philadelphia Academy of Natural Sciences, the institution that had nurtured Meriwether Lewis before his western expedition.

Not least, he lived daily in the presence of a Quaker culture that had been the Robertses' birthright for two hundred years. Philadelphia had been founded by William Penn as a haven for Quakers, but by 1882 the Friends were a notable minority. The family had left its ties to the Friends behind when they moved to Minnesota, though John had retained his Quaker sensibilities and Thomas would later attribute the family's tranquil atmosphere to their Quaker heritage. Now young Roberts moved in a social circle of people who lived simply, dressed plainly, and sometimes spoke in "thees" and "thous." Perhaps their presence afforded the son more insight into his beloved father.

Even so, Thomas was viewed as an outsider in the City of Brotherly Love. Natives considered him a "raw Westerner" living on the far side of the Mississippi River. Indeed, how many of his fellow medical students had ever dealt with a runaway pony hitched to a buckboard or slept outdoors in a canvas tent for months on end? It would take him several years to break through the social reserve of Philadelphians, and as an old man, he would credit this toehold to his interest in natural history and his Welsh-Quaker heritage.[6]

The trees along the Schuylkill River were waxing yellow when Thomas arrived at the University of Pennsylvania campus to begin his first year. The summery East Coast humidity still hung in the air, though, and it dampened his hair, his skin, and his three-piece suit. Plants thrived in this hothouse atmosphere. The banks of the Schuylkill supported a richer, more verdant growth than the mighty Mississippi, skirting the edge of the prairie, ever would.

To the east, the smokestacks and steeples of Philadelphia rose in gritty determination. Before him, West Philadelphia was more pastoral—the young campus with its pink stone buildings, grassy expanse, and two relatively new and substantial hospitals, one skirted by farm fields running down to the river. This was the leading edge of suburban development, with new streets, new residences, slender boulevard trees, and wooden sidewalks.

Few prospective doctors enter medical school undaunted. The training required to become a physician was rigorous and exhausting. Thomas had never encountered any subject too difficult to master, but that was back in Minnesota. How would he fare in an established, highly competitive eastern university?

He made his way up the steps to Medical Hall, past the rosy marble pillars topped with a frill of stone-carved oak leaves, through the solid double doors, and into the building. Before him yawned a splendid, ornate staircase that rose upward three flights, stairs that would carry him into the lecture hall and the laboratory—into a new life.

That life, as a first-year student, would be a grind of basic science courses accompanied by hours of laboratory work. Thomas began each week Monday morning at nine o'clock in Dr. Wormley's lecture hall, pondering the world of General Chemistry. Wormley, a noted naturalist, was highly regarded for his book on the chemistry of poisons, the first ever written. The chemistry course was bolstered by four hours of lab work on two successive mornings.

There was also General Pathology, taught by James Tyson, whose particular skill was in microscopy, used in the new sciences of histology and pathology. He had published a book on Bright's disease and diabetes the year before. Joseph Leidy taught Anatomy, a two-year undertaking, and this year Thomas would wield scalpel and forceps three evenings a week, Monday, Wednesday, and Friday, until ten o'clock, dissecting his cadaver in the dim of the gaslit laboratory.

Hygiene, Physiology, and Pharmacy labs and the quaintly titled course Materia Medica (today referred to as pharmacology, the science of drugs) rounded out his schedule. Saturday mornings until 1:00 P.M. were given over to clinical demonstrations at Philadelphia City Hospital (also known as Blockley) or University Hospital, both near campus.

Thomas took rooms close to school, in a new neighborhood on a hill north of campus. The boardinghouse at 3205 Baring Street was an Italianate, stuccoed duplex, with tall, narrow windows and heavy oaken front doors. It was run by Mary Pancoast, a Quaker who had physicians in her family, and Thomas found the house a convivial place, referring to it as a "household" and "the family." The turnover at Miss Pancoast's was low—Thomas boarded at 3205 for half his years in Philadelphia—and the tenants often spent the evening together playing whist.

It was here that Thomas met Carroll Williams, a young lawyer newly established at the bar, who would become a close friend. Thomas and Carroll shared a suite of rooms that included a sitting room, where they could host young women without scandal. On one fall evening, Thomas described the social scene: "We spent the latter part of the evening until quite late playing whist. Between 11.30 and 12 we entertained the ladies in our sitting room previous to retiring. Showed them Emma's floral portfolio which was much admired."[7] (Emma had recently become interested in watercolors of wildflowers.)

Carroll was a Quaker, born on the family farm in Bucks County, Pennsylvania, north of Philadelphia. Exactly Thomas's age, he was a graduate of Swarthmore College, where his uncle was president, and of the University of Pennsylvania law school. He was working in a downtown law firm when the two met in 1882. The young men, both first-born from old Quaker families, with sisters the same age and younger brothers, had much in common. As young bachelors in the cosmopolitan city, the two roamed Philadelphia in their free time, attending private parties, the theater, and concerts. They often went to church on Sundays, at either the Episcopal or Unitarian church, and then sometimes went on to Sunday dinner at Aunt Cornelia's in Germantown.

The Williamses' Bucks County farm was near enough for a weekend visit, and occasionally the men took a late afternoon train on Saturday out to the country. One lovely October weekend, the eastern hardwoods glowing with fall color, Thomas went home with Carroll.[8] He met the family, gathered chestnuts on the estate, and spent an evening boiling the nuts and listening to Carroll's sister Agnes read aloud. On a January visit, Carroll took Thomas and Agnes, wedged together in the backseat, on a memorable sleigh ride with two very fast horses that passed all others on the road. Thomas was impressed by the remarkable pace of thirteen miles in one hour and ten minutes.

The second year, Thomas's coursework increased to almost fifty hours of lecture, laboratory, and clinical rounds a week. Anatomy continued to soak up the most time, with three hours of lecture and five evenings of dissection per week. And yet, this intense contact was not what it had been. Thomas recorded in his journal, "In his lecture today Dr. D. Hayes Agnew said that in his younger days, he was accustomed to spend from 10 to 16 hours daily in the dissecting room for six years. He thinks that dissecting is not carried on as extensively as a few years back."[9]

Anatomy lectures were held in an amphitheater with tiered seating, the bearded and dignified Leidy holding forth from the circular pit at the bottom. A photo from the time shows the young males—women were not admitted to University of Pennsylvania's medical school until 1913—thoughtfully regarding the professor and his array of models and specimens lined up on a long, rectangular table. All students are dressed in wool jackets over high-buttoned waistcoats, behind which peep high-collared white shirts and neckties.

On his first exposure to medical school, Thomas had described students at lecture as asleep or inattentive. Now sitting in the same place, he was neither. "At college all day and dissecting all evening" he often wrote in his journal.[10]

Although no longer trained as apprentices, medical students at the university did align themselves with experienced physicians, termed preceptors, with whom they had contact when they were not in school. Thomas came to Philadelphia without a preceptor, but by his second year, he had settled on Amos Abbott, who had a general practice in Minneapolis. Abbott, not yet forty, was an energetic, high-profile doctor in town. He had been instrumental in establishing the Minnesota College Hospital and taught anatomy and gynecology there. He was also chief of staff at St. Barnabas Hospital and conducted a thriving practice out of his residence in the fashionable neighborhood at Tenth Street and Harmon Place. Thomas had spent time with him at his office and had done urinalysis for him the summer between his first and second years of medical school.

Thomas corresponded with Abbott from time to time throughout medical school, and Abbott dispensed commonsense advice in a hurriedly written, nearly illegible scrawl, hinting about the time constraints of a busy GP. Abbott was pleased that his protégé was receiving good training in the new fields of microscopy and pathology. He weighed in on the desirable optics of microscopes and urged Thomas to "get a firm stand and a low firm adjustment. Try the instrument before you take it."[11] Thomas purchased one for eighty dollars, soon after Abbott's letter arrived.[12] He also bought another tool of the trade that year, his first stethoscope, presumably for use in clinic.

It was in the fall of his second year of school, when he was twenty-five, that Thomas suffered his first abdominal pain. The onset was sudden and severe, confining him to his room and keeping him from sleep. He applied a mustard plaster and took tincture of opium (laudanum) for the pain. He thought the pain might have been due to overexertion at the gym several days before. He had recently joined the athletic association, aiming to build up his chest muscles.

When the pain intensified, he became "a little frightened" and sent for the doctor, who agreed that he had "probably strained the attachments of the caecum and ascending colon, and ordered rest, light diet, and a fly blister."[13] A fly blister was another plaster, made from an ointment derived from a certain species of Spanish fly and used for internal inflammation.

Within a day, Thomas was pain-free and somewhat surprised to find himself "none the worse" for having spent an entire week in bed. He felt so good, in fact, that in rapid succession he attended a wedding, ate Thanksgiving Day dinner with friends, strolled the galleries at the Academy of Fine Arts on a date, and went to the Chestnut Street Opera House with Carroll to see *The Merchant of Venice*.

Despite the exhausting grind of medical school, there was always time in a young man's life for fun. Thomas frequently went out to Aunt Cornelia Roberts's in Germantown to spend what little weekend was allotted to him. He caught an afternoon train on Saturday, when the hospital clinics were over, and spent the evening with family and friends playing cards or talking. Sometimes he would take tea at Shipley's before heading back to West Philadelphia.

Shipley had a daughter, Alice, whom Thomas occasionally escorted to concerts. There were other women of interest, too—young ladies in a boarding school a short distance from 3205 Baring, and Carroll's cousin Beatrice Magill, whose father was president of Swarthmore College. Carroll's sister, Agnes, lived in another boardinghouse, and Thomas and Carroll sometimes spent evenings with her, playing cards. But young Roberts was discreet: there was hardly a whisper of romance on the pages of his journal, perhaps for the simple fact that his demanding schedule did not allow time for much wooing.

The other pursuit not followed in these busy years was that of birds. The relative absence of feathered creatures foreshadowed how all-consuming a medical life would be for Thomas. His journals contain almost no references to avian presence, either on campus or on his walks to school above the Schuylkill. In his later years, he was known to be intensely interested only in Minnesota birds, shunning even those on the Wisconsin side of the St. Croix River, and perhaps that predilection played a role in his neglect.[14] But birds did not vanish entirely. In the fall of his second year, he received a letter from C. Hart Merriam of Locust Grove, New York, informing him that he had been invited to become an active member of the fledgling American Ornithologists' Union formed in September 1883, an invitation that Thomas readily accepted.[15]

A photo of Thomas taken in Philadelphia shortly before Christmas 1883 shows the young man who was so diligently balancing an exhausting schedule, a duty to family, and some semblance of a social life, gazing off to one side. In the photo he is elegantly dressed in a topcoat of sturdy wool. A subtly patterned ascot is clinched with a stick pin, the head of which is a miniature gold owl clutching a branch. His eyes are level, his expression is serious, and he is sporting an admirable mustache, which makes his youthful features more mature. The mustache was new. He would keep it for the rest of his life.

That Christmas, Thomas remained on the East Coast and passed the holiday with his mother's sister in Baltimore. Emma met him there, and the siblings spent time catching up and enjoying Baltimore's sights.

Henry Nachtrieb, Thomas's fellow land examiner, was an assistant in the Biology Department at Johns Hopkins, undertaking graduate work after obtaining his degree from the University of Minnesota. They arranged to meet in the days after Christmas, and Thomas got a tour of Johns Hopkins's new physiology lab and also the medical school, which he deemed "far inferior" to the University of Pennsylvania's. The new hospital, however, still under construction, was quite impressive. He and Henry also took in some culture: they spent an evening at the theater and toured the art gallery at the Peabody Institute.

The end of each school term was capped by oral examination in mid-April. Thomas and his classmates prepared for these with intensive study, both individually and in study groups of two or three. These studious endeavors were punctuated by breaks. The second spring, when he was twenty-six, Thomas went on a tennis jag, rolling a court with a fellow medical student, investing in a new racquet, and letting off steam in frequent matches.

When Thomas finally stood for his exams, his preparedness showed. He was examined by Professor Allen in physiology on April 14. ("What is the function of saliva?" was one question), and he scored 100 percent. The next appearance was before Professor Wormley in medical chemistry ("What do you understand by lactic acid fermentation?"). Score: 97 percent. Finally, there was the formidable Professor Leidy in anatomy, testing the culmination of two years of exhaustive study ("What is the larynx?" "How many cervical ganglia?") Score: 100 percent.

Leidy was most likely the professor who had called him into his office after a prior exam, when Thomas's written answers had been nearly identical to the textbook. The professor, skeptical, had decided to follow up with an oral exam and was astonished when the student before him could quote the textbook verbatim, exhibiting a nearly photographic memory. Thomas would get mileage out of this story for the rest of his life.[16]

Year three of medical school for Thomas opened on October 1, 1884. Third-year students had increased clinical time, and he spent the early afternoon of every day and most of Wednesday and Saturday in the clinic or on the wards of University Hospital. He also spent time in the operating room now and took lectures and practice in the methods of bandaging.

William Osler joined the medical school faculty that year as chair of clinical medicine. Osler, later to be known as the father of modern medicine, was only thirty-five, in the early years of his remarkable career. He had already developed a focus on clinical education for medical students, and his coming significantly improved the students' clinical experience.[17] Osler was famous for his buoyant personality as well as his practical jokes, and he soon took a particular interest in Thomas's education.

The time-consuming dissection labs were over for third-year students, but there were lectures to attend in morbid anatomy, obstetrics, ophthalmology, therapeutics, and surgery, in addition to hospital time. The class of 119 third-year students was divided into smaller sections now, so each student could get individual instruction.

In addition, each student had to prepare a thesis. In a pre-typewriter world, the school catalog stipulated that the work "must be in the candidate's own handwriting, written on thesis paper, the alternative pages being blank; [and] bound."[18] Thomas had been elected to the Stillé Medical Society in his second year, a mark of distinction. Its members met once a week to read papers on the theory and practice of medicine. Thomas's choice of thesis topic, "Case Illustrating the Value of Massage to the General Surgeon," may have emerged after presenting a paper at one of these meetings.

The third year was also a time to consider residency programs. A residency was not required of physicians practicing in Minnesota. In fact, the state had only recently required its doctors to register their diplomas with a board of examiners, and it would be two years before doctors were required to take three full courses of lectures of six months each (University of Pennsylvania's standards) and apply for a license to practice.[19] Thomas decided, however, to apply for a residency, and he opted for one in Philadelphia. In the past, a residency position was gotten by appointment—a social or political connection of some sort, which a Minnesotan would be lacking, of course. This system sometimes resulted in terrible, incompetent care and poor reputations for teaching hospitals. But qualifying exams changed that. Thomas applied for programs that required an exam, turning down an offer to apply at Philadelphia's Presbyterian Hospital, which did not have one.

Thomas took the exam for resident physician at Children's Hospital and was voted in that same day for a term beginning June 1, 1885. The next week, he was also awarded a post at Philadelphia General Hospital, thanks to his high score. There may have been overlap in the terms of the two appointments, something he apparently worked out in late summer.

Three days later, on May 1, 1885, the University of Pennsylvania medical school held its commencement exercises at the American Academy of Music downtown, and Thomas Roberts became Doctor Roberts. His total accumulated percentage in coursework over the three years was 97.3 percent, making him fifth in his graduating class. (Prior to graduation, he himself had figured this out, listing on the back of an envelope all his final scores in every class and the final percentages and names of the top twenty-five of his classmates.)

Thomas had sent invitations to the graduation to two of his mentors back home—Professor Winchell and Dr. Abbott. Neither one could make the thousand-mile trip, but each sent his congratulations, and Abbott also promised the new MD a teaching position in Abbott's new medical school when he finished his residency.[20]

A residency in Children's Hospital was a plum, well-deserved by the high-achieving young doctor. The institution was the first pediatrics hospital in the nation, founded in 1855. A new building had been erected in 1867 on Twenty-Second Avenue between Walnut and Locust Streets downtown. Pediatrics was a young field, only about twenty years old. By taking this residency, Thomas was acquiring expertise that would distinguish him from other general practitioners and would enable him eventually to teach pediatrics at the University of Minnesota. The hospital's prime concerns were the vitamin deficiency diseases, scurvy and rickets; diarrhea; and the infectious childhood diseases.

A residency at Philadelphia General Hospital was a plum of a different kind. The program consisted of work in several different and generally un-related institutions, each challenging in its own way. There was the general hospital itself, a large, one-thousand bed facility, built and funded by the city; the insane asylum, which housed patients with diverse psychiatric disease; and the almshouse for Philadelphia's poor. Associated with the almshouse was a farm, the "poor farm"; nearby, orphan children were housed in the farmhouse; and across the road was a one-acre "potter's field," the final resting place of many of the unfortunate inhabitants.

The whole community was referred to as Blockley, the name of the former owner of the farm on which it had been built. It was situated on the west bank of the Schuylkill River, immediately adjacent to University Hospital.

"Blockley Hospital" sounds less institutional than "Philadelphia General," but in the 1880s, the name conjured up images of raving lunatics, ragged indigents, and wretched patients submitting to incompetent care on massive wards. Medical staff regretted the association of the hospital with the almshouse, since it tainted it unfairly. After establishing the requirement of a resident's qualifying exam, care at Blockley was good. Nevertheless, there was a stigma attached to seeking treatment there, and it was considered in the popular mind to be the last resort for those who could not afford other hospitals.

Ironically, students and professors alike highly regarded a residency at Blockley. It offered opportunity to extensively study the chronic diseases of alcoholism and mental illness. There was a steady stream of unclaimed bodies on which to perform autopsies—a desirable skill for general practitioners, who were likely to become coroners in smaller communities—and the extent of instruction by teaching MDs in the amphitheater and at the bedside was unmatched by other programs. Blockley had fourteen resident physicians in 1885–86, many at the top of their class. It is not surprising that Thomas, always committed to mastery of any field, would be attracted to such a program. It was almost guaranteed that the new doctor had never seen life as it was lived within the walls of Blockley.

Thomas started Blockley's residency program in the fall of 1885, after employment in the summer months at Children's. By then, he may have worked through the most unnerving of the existential doubts that torment a newly minted MD: What if I see symptoms I don't recognize? What if I do irreparable harm? What if I kill someone?

Blockley was built of gray stone, four massive buildings arranged to form a square, three stories high with dormer roofs. In the central courtyard were the shops needed to maintain such a giant institution: the bakery, the carpenter, the wheelwright, among others. The floors of the various buildings were dedicated to specific specialties: a maternity ward, the "Drunk House" consisting of ten beds (usually occupied) where alcoholics were placed when in the throes of delirium tremens, separate men's and women's wards. The hospital was apart from the almshouse. The insane department had its own wing. The year Thomas started, it had been reduced to two floors, because of damage from a fire the year before.

Blockley was unwieldy by today's standards, but the governing board, known as the Guardians of the Poor, had made recent changes that greatly improved medical care. The competitive residents' exam was one; the hiring of trained nurses and the start-up of a school of nursing (also housed in the complex) was another. The use of trained nurses had a marked influence on the decline of maternal and infant mortality.[21] In 1883, a maternity pavilion had been added. In 1885, epileptic patients were transferred from the insane department to the care of a neurologist.

The fourteen residents (including one woman) lived in the residents' quarters, located on the third floor of the almshouse for women. Most of them, including Thomas's study partners at the University of Pennsylvania, who were also in the program, had attended a Philadelphia medical school.

The resident doctors lived in pairs (save for the woman, who had her own room at the far end of the hall) in spacious rooms, each with a high ceiling and one large window. They were lit by gas and heated by a woodstove, which cast a cheerful glow during the dark, cold days of winter.

The meals, taken in the staff dining hall, were institutional. Heavy on tough cuts of meat like beefsteak and mutton, they sometimes inspired complaints about rancid butter and sour milk. Residents frequently missed meals while out on ambulance runs or tied up on the wards, and were given to scrounging for cold fare in the kitchen's icebox.

New residents were issued a uniform of blue cloth with brass buttons and gold piping and stars, supposedly a replica of a uniform of a U.S. naval surgeon. These they wore while on duty, whether rounding, in clinic, or in the operating room. There were no surgical scrubs. Surgeons and all assistants wore street clothing.[22]

Residents were rousted from their beds at 7:30 A.M. by a runner's voice announcing "Half past seven, Doctors; half past seven; half past!" Breakfast was served at eight, and then rounds on the wards kept them busy until noon. The afternoons were spent writing up case histories—charts—for the attending doctors before evening rounds.

Depending on the schedule, this routine might have been frequently interrupted by ambulance calls. Residents accompanied the horse-drawn wagon that responded to emergency summons to fetch a sick or injured soul. Ambulance rides brought the young residents into the darkest, most destitute slums of Philadelphia, exposing them to a degree of poverty most had never seen.

In America in 1885, Sunday was generally observed as a day of rest. This was true even for heavily worked medical students—but not, alas, for residents, whose only indication that it was Sunday was the distant church bells ringing through the windows of the wards. "There are easier stations in life than that occupied by a resident physician at Blockley," observed one man.[23]

And yet, youthful exuberance will out. The dormitory rooms opened onto a large hallway, and this was transformed into a playing field for sports. The resident physician-in-chief, Thomas MacLaughlin, played the fiddle, and residents were known to hold "stag balls," gallivanting about with each other. This same instrument provided similar dances in the insane department quarters, affording the inmates some form of recreation.

The Guardians of the Poor, Blockley's directors, maintained a second-floor clinic on Seventh Street in the city in a dilapidated house. It received and examined patients for entrance into the hospital. Blockley residents staffed this each morning, passing judgment with each exam on who was allowed a bed and a meal at Blockley.

Generally speaking, most young doctors embark on their careers with a high level of idealism. The profession is a healing one; the opportunity to ease suffering and ward off death is a daily reality. Yet rarely do doctors remain idealistic—physicians are usually nobody's fools, and it is in places like the upstairs clinic on Seventh Street that the tempering begins.

Applicants to Blockley were often chronic alcoholics. If admitted to the "Drunk Ward" and nursed through the worst of delirium tremens, they were most likely to be seen again, and again, with the same malady, until they died, usually from bronchopneumonia or liver disease.[24]

Other petitioners might wheedle, charm, lie, or attempt to bribe their way into free room and board—or a chance at medicinal whiskey. For all the masses of impoverished, ill, and broken humanity seeking shelter at Blockley, there were enough wheedlers to hone the edge of shrewd skepticism in the greenest of young MDs. This was also a useful medical skill that Thomas would later employ in his practice.

Other aspects of Blockley were more conventional. Thomas rotated through obstetrics, where the ward was a busy place, with most patients being young, unmarried women, "ignorant, without any self-control," according to one resident.[25] It was presided over by a midwife with vast experience who trained in the inexperienced residents in their first deliveries. "Her manner towards us was a quaint combination of motherly interest, good-natured amusement and professional respect," a resident observed.[26] Few precautions were taken to maintain sterile conditions, and one entire ward was devoted to women with postpartum infection.

Thomas also worked in neurology, another specialty with much to offer at Blockley. By 1885, the number of patients had outstripped the hospital's capacity, and those with nervous disorders were housed in long, single-storied wooden pavilions, poorly lit and uninsulated. Yet, the best neurologists in Philadelphia served these wards of the hospital, and residents were exposed to a large number of common and not-so-common maladies.

Residents assisted in surgery. Only two years before Thomas's residency at Blockley, another resident had noted that nothing was sterilized, and if an instrument fell to the floor, it was frequently wiped with a towel and put to use again.[27] This seems hard to believe, since the English surgeon Joseph Lister had developed sterile practices, such as washing hands and instruments in carbolic acid solution, in the 1870s and had published his findings; and Robert Koch in Germany was using heat to sterilize surgical instruments by 1881.[28]

The operating room was a great lecture amphitheater, where residents and medical students could sit and observe the surgeons at work. Thomas had sat in this room in his medical school days and now found himself back again as a resident. The most instructive surgical operations were undertaken on Saturday morning around noon, when residents and students could observe and natural lighting was most intense.

Thomas also became proficient at autopsies. These were undertaken in the postmortem lab, or dead house, called euphemistically the "green room." There, residents might excise tumors or other pathologic tissue of academic interest, to be preserved for teaching or research. In Thomas's day, the dead room was ornamented by the embalmed severed head of a former patient of the insane department, adorned with a pair of femurs crossed behind it. An attendant of the green room, "Cadaver Charlie," was responsible for the gruesome artwork.[29] Such a callous disregard for human remains is shocking today. In the 1880s, it was an indication that the sometimes grisly work at Blockley was offset by a gallows humor that the young residents wouldn't find funny under other circumstances.

In later years, Thomas recalled one autopsy particularly well. Dr. Osler had adopted a habit of requesting that young Dr. Roberts accompany him on his rounds at Blockley, even though Thomas was not his appointed intern. A certain patient, very ill, interested Osler, and the physician instructed Thomas to be sure to get permission to do an autopsy when this man died, as it seemed certain he would do.

Soon after seeing the sick man, Osler dropped in at the hospital in the late afternoon accompanied by a visiting physician, both in evening clothes, dressed for a dinner engagement. Thomas encountered the two and informed Osler that the patient had died and that he had obtained permission to do the autopsy, but it had to be done immediately.

Osler said, "Oh my, oh my. Too bad, too bad." He paused, considered, and spoke to his companion. Then, brightening and taking both his friend and Thomas by the elbow, he steered them down the hall, saying, "Well, let's go down to the dead room anyway and have a look around."

The dead room was empty (save for the corpse), so Osler took off his evening coat and donned a gown and soon was immersed in the task. Three hours later, an intricate autopsy was complete. The brain had been removed, and both middle ear cavities revealed, and it was no longer possible for Osler and his friend to be even fashionably late to the dinner party.[30]

Thomas lived at Blockley for almost one year. The stark reality of Philadelphia's dark underbelly must have made that year seem like a "time out of joint"—abnormal, dislocated—to the young man from Minneapolis with a passion for birds. But we will never know that, for the journal that he had kept for a decade fell silent in the third year of medical school and remained so through his residency.

Yet, as in all things, by taking a residency at Blockley, young Dr. Roberts pursued excellence, gained broad experience in the field, practiced meticulous work, and, in the grueling process, made lifelong friends.

At the end of his term, there were opportunities for Thomas to remain in Philadelphia with his extended family and the cultivated life he appreciated. But life was waiting for him in the Mill City. It was time to go home.

CHAPTER 7

A Family Man

> Love-making is accompanied by the more arduous
> occupation of nest-building.
>
> — *The Birds of Minnesota,* 2: 210

Thomas Roberts studied the creamy, high-quality stationery as he read the letters from his high school friends Joe Kingman and Harry Robinson. The missives had been mailed from Minneapolis on the same day, June 10, 1885. Once more in Philadelphia's steamy, summer warmth after a visit home, Thomas took in the exuberant, almost chortling joy of his friends. The news of his engagement to dark-haired Jennie Cleveland had made its way through their social set back home rather quickly.

"My dear Tom," Joe's letter began. "The pleasantest duty I have had to perform in a long time [is] to congratulate the luckiest fellow in Philadelphia and the most fortunate young lady in Minneapolis." "Delighted I am and pleased without end," enthused Harry's letter. "I should so like to take you by the hand and say so." "But don't think you've surprised us, Tom. We've been waiting for it," Joe's letter added. "As we stood on the corner of Nicollet Ave. the day before you left, I told you that you had done the *old crowd* honor. . . . [Now] our faith in you is increased the more," chimed Harry's letter.[1]

Thomas had arrived in the Mill City in May 1885, triumphant as a newly minted MD following the graduation ceremonies at the University of Pennsylvania medical school. Too soon he would embark on the first of his rigorous residencies, at Children's Hospital in Philadelphia, but in the break between the end of medical school and the start of residency, he traveled home to see his parents, catch up with friends, and seal a long-running romance with a marriage proposal.

Jennie and Thomas had known each other for a long time. She was born Jane Lyon Cleveland in Conneault, Ohio, on the far eastern border of the state. Known to friends as "Jennie," she had moved to Minnesota with her parents as a child. The Cleveland family home at 710 First Avenue North had been just around the corner from the Robertses'. Jennie and Emma Roberts, the same age, had been close friends since grade school. It was not uncommon for Jennie to spend the night in the Robertses' home.

Her father had owned Northwestern Stove Works, a wholesale manufacturer of cast-iron stoves with an attached foundry in south Minneapolis on the main road to Fort Snelling. An older brother took over the business when the father died, and another brother also worked in the family business.

There is no telling when the attraction between the two began. Maybe it was during rehearsals of *The Diamond Necklace,* the play Thomas and Jennie took part in at the Galaxy, when they were both in their teens. Perhaps it was sometime later, when he took her on a double date to the fair while on furlough from his summer land examiner job. He made a point to call on her before leaving for Philadelphia and medical school, and in letters home written when he was a land examiner, he asked his parents to remember him to her, but her name does not appear once in the journal he kept while a medical student.

Discreet and decorous though they apparently were, their engagement did not surprise their Minneapolis friends. She had waited for him during the long years he was in Philadelphia, he had chosen her when his schooling was done and he was free to marry, and the family and friends that had known both so long were happy.

Thomas and Jennie were nothing if not responsible. They were not especially young—he was twenty-seven and she soon to turn twenty-five. Engaged on the cusp of Thomas's grueling residency year, they waited to marry until after he had returned to Minneapolis and established himself in a medical practice—a long, two-year engagement.

After his residency, Thomas returned to Minneapolis in fall 1886. His preceptor in the city, the energetic Amos Abbott, had previously promised the young physician a teaching position in the school he had just launched, but in July 1886, as Thomas was winding up his stint at Blockley and set to return, Abbott withdrew the offer. Apparently, John Roberts had declined a request to invest in Abbott's endeavor, and the position, that of teaching physiology, went to someone who had.

Abbott softened the blow, however: "I think we can find a place for you in the dispensary and possibly something better," he wrote that July. He added that he was giving up his general practice "as fast as I can" and that he might be able to pass along to Thomas "some good families."[2]

With this vague promise of professional aid, Dr. Roberts, age twenty-eight and still sporting the luxuriant blond walrus mustache, moved back into his parents' home at 27 North Eighth Street. Once more he settled into his boyhood bedroom filled with bird skins, collected nests, and blown eggs, after four and a half years away. Emma and Walter were also still at home, and the tight-knit Roberts clan must have felt a certain satisfaction at being together under one roof once more.

Thomas rented office space downtown at 22 South Fourth Street and hung out his shingle. A new addition to the medical community, however, even a hometown boy, was not necessarily welcomed warmly. In the 1880s, there was a limited demand for doctors, and one popular book advising physicians cautioned that rivalry with other doctors was to be expected. The caveat went on to liken the situation to that of the European cuckoo, a nest parasite whose nestlings are raised by other birds; the interlopers eventually grow big enough and become sufficiently strong to hurl the rightful occupants out of the nest![3]

This particular newcomer, though, made a favorable impression on his medical colleagues very quickly. One year later he was invited to become a charter member of an elite new society, the Minnesota Academy of Medicine. The academy, comprised of physicians and surgeons of Minneapolis and St. Paul, set an initial limit on charter members, and at the first meeting on October 7, 1887, organized a committee to solicit other appropriate members "up to forty." Thomas's name was already on the roster, but he did not attend that first meeting or, apparently, the next the week after.

The young doctor's schedule was booked in other matters that month, for one week later, on a Tuesday, October 18, he and Jennie were finally married. He was twenty-nine, she, twenty-seven. The quiet ceremony was presided over by the Reverend T. B. Wells, of St. Mark's Episcopal Church, and the Reverend James Tuttle of the Universalist Church of the Redeemer, the Clevelands' congregation. George H. Christian, a prominent miller with the Washburn-Crosby mill and a member of St. Mark's, signed the certificate as a witness to the vows. None of the local papers carried a wedding announcement, and no photograph was taken commemorating the rite.

Married life did not bring about a change of address for Thomas, at least not immediately. The young couple may have taken a short honeymoon;

like about other details of the romance, they left no record. But they apparently moved into the Robertses' family home after the wedding, and the elder Robertses, and eventually Emma, left for an extended stay in the southern United States.

By late 1887, John Roberts's health had seriously deteriorated, and a long vacation in a warm place to avoid the worst of Minnesota's winter seemed warranted. The trip south was combined with a visit to Maryland to see Lizzie's family, particularly her father, Thomas Sadler, Thomas's last surviving grandparent, who at ninety-one was ailing.

After New Year's, John and Lizzie and Lizzie's sister Kate went on to Aiken, South Carolina, on the state's border with Georgia, which had become a "tuberculosis resort." There they met other Minneapolitans, the R. P. Russells—he was a pharmacist in the city—and spent the winter months. Emma joined them in March and provided companionship to the Russells' adult son, who also suffered from TB. He would not survive the year.

Meanwhile, in the Mill City, the newlyweds adjusted to life together in the snowy days of a Minnesota winter. That January 1888, a particularly fierce and unexpected blizzard killed hundreds of children living on the prairie, "out west" of Minneapolis, but had little effect in town. What did grab the city's attention was the fire that followed immediately after the blizzard. The large and prestigious Church of the Redeemer in downtown Minneapolis burned to the ground, leaving behind a charred shell encased entirely in ice.

A year after he set up shop, Thomas's practice was taking off, and he spent a good deal of time traveling by horse and buggy, or sleigh, to his patients' homes and keeping regular office hours at his downtown office.[4] When not pondering medical cases, Thomas had something new to think about: Jennie was pregnant and due in October. Now, in addition to adapting to a sleeping partner, a domestic companion, and another's constant presence in the home, the young couple was introduced to the mysteries of morning sickness, appetite changes, and an expanding girth.

There was precious little time to devote to birds, although Thomas kept an eye on the winter residents flocking in the hedgerows or feeding on mountain ash berries, as he rounded on his patients. As winter waned, though, and the early avian migrants began appearing, he could not resist scribbling the first signs of spring in a small notebook that had been lying about the house. "April 8—*robins* (first), 42 degrees, rained all day; other

birds—red crossbills on 8th St.," read one entry.[5] In an April notable for
its cold temperature and frozen puddles, Thomas recorded "white-bellied
swallows flying over the house" (April 13), "a pair of bluebirds preparing
to build in a bird box in an ash tree on 10th Avenue South" (also April 13),
and "the pie plant is coming up in the garden" (April 17). (Thomas used the
old-fashioned term to refer to rhubarb.) But other things in his life were so
pressing that he could not even continue the observations to the end of the
month—the record ends abruptly on April 21.

The elder Robertses and Emma arrived back in Minneapolis in mid-May.
Thomas and Walter were at the depot to greet them. Minnesota's weather
provided a dose of reality to the erstwhile "Southerners"—there was ice on
the hillsides when they arrived, and it snowed in the city the next day.

Thomas and Jennie moved to her mother's place to await the readiness of
their newly rented home.[6] Two weeks later, they moved into a brown brick duplex at 810 Sixth Avenue South, just around the corner from Jennie's mother.
Thomas left his office downtown and established an exam room in his home,
a common custom in that time period. The young couple, still in the first year
of marriage, settled into a routine that they would keep for many years.

Thomas dropped by to see his parents nearly every day. It was a short,
ten-minute walk from the duplex on Sixth Avenue to 27 North Eighth, and
he often visited both morning and evening. This may have been the devo-
tion of a dutiful son, but it also was the diligence of an attending physician,
as Thomas resumed medical care of his father. A winter in the South had
done nothing to relieve John's tuberculosis, and he frequently recorded
feeling unwell in his journal. Fresh air was still considered healthful for the
consumptive, and because Thomas was busy with other patients, it was the
pregnant Jennie, apparently in the bloom of good health, who now called
many summer mornings for her frail father-in-law and took him out riding.

Thomas and Jennie were frequent guests at the elder Robertses' dinner table, and they also reciprocated. Sunday suppers were especially good
times to entertain the parents or Emma—the constant press of ill patients
not bearing quite so heavily on the day of rest.

Thomas apparently took possession of the Robertses' horse and buggy,
which he needed to reach patients who lived beyond a short walk from his
house. Although he may not have read the doctors' "bible," *The Physician*

Himself, the use of a horse and carriage was de rigueur for an up-and-coming doctor: the manual made clear that "a [horse and buggy] shows your practice is growing, and anyone can ride into a full practice much quicker than he can walk into one."[7] Furthermore, by riding, rather than walking, the physician arrives at a patient's house ready to examine him—not breathless and sweaty—and one is less likely to be detained in conversation if one is in a buggy—one needs only to wave a friendly "hello" and not have to stop and talk.

That first summer of married life, Thomas also began taking his father with him in the carriage as he made house calls, much in the same way the two had gone out looking for birds together when Thomas was a boy. It was another way for John to take in fresh air, as well as giving father and son time together. It had also, incidentally, the stamp of approval from *The Physician Himself,* which advocated that a doctor take along another person when on rounds—someone to tie up the horse and tend it, so the doctor did not waste valuable time, and so the horse would not wander off while the doctor was in with his patient.

Despite all indications that Thomas's general practice was thriving, John recorded giving him an occasional fifty dollars—a goodly sum in 1888—and he also bought four tons of coal for the newlyweds for the coming winter when he placed his own order for the house on Eighth Street.

General practitioners in 1888 were often unable to live on what they made on patients' fees. Not everyone paid or could afford to pay the doctor, and especially during times of epidemics, physicians were too busy to chase down people who had not made good on their bill. Studies estimated that only a quarter of graduates from nineteenth-century medical schools earned enough to not have to take a second job.[8]

Negligence in collecting fees was frowned upon by *The Physician Himself.* That worthy manual told practitioners to charge special "night-visit fees" to ensure the doctor's sleep would be interrupted only when absolutely necessary. It also pointed out that a speaking tube from the office front door to the bedroom was a convenient device to have.

Early on October 11, 1888, a clear fall morning with the city trees shedding leaves in earnest, Anna Cleveland made her way up Eighth Street to tell the elder Robertses that her sister Jennie had given birth to a baby boy in the predawn hours. Mother and child were doing well. Thomas, who had attended the birth, dropped in a short time later, and Emma hurried down to meet the new nephew and rejoice with her sister-in-law. Thomas and Jennie called the baby Thomas Cleveland Roberts—the newest of a long succession of Thomas Roberts dating back at least to the late 1600s in Wales.

There were a lot of women nearby to help with a newborn. Mrs. Cleveland and Anna were close by, and Lizzie Roberts and Emma were a short walk away, but the young couple also hired a nurse to aid in child care. All the help was particularly opportune when three weeks later guests from Philadelphia—Carroll Williams and a traveling companion—appeared on their doorstep for a week's visit as they journeyed to California.

A mere fifteen months later, as John Roberts was still referring to this grandchild as "Baby" in his journal, Jennie was in labor again. This time, Thomas himself arrived at the close of a cold January day to tell his parents that Jennie had given birth to a daughter around ten o'clock that morning. The baby was healthy, and Jennie was fine. The blond little girl was named Catharine Lyon, after her mother and maternal grandmother.

In the briefest span of time, Thomas had transformed from a young, single physician to a settled family man, father of two. He did not record—he probably did not have time to put pen to paper—any frustration at having his time completely occupied by professional and familial responsibilities. With relatives and hired help, Jennie must have had no problem managing the household, because even as little Thomas was a newborn, Thomas expanded his participation in the fledgling Minnesota Academy of Medicine. In January 1889, he accepted an appointment to the Microscopical Committee, charged with staining and preparing slides of specimens to be presented at the academy's monthly meetings; and in April 1890, shortly after the birth of Catharine, he was elected to the academy's governing board.[9]

Meetings of the academy were held once a month in the evening and included socializing over supper. They were held alternately in downtown St. Paul and Minneapolis and did not break up until 10:00 P.M. Active participation, while valuable in professional networking and in continuing education, required a substantial time commitment. This, in addition to middle-of-the-night visits to sick patients and rounding on house calls (almost no one hospitalized patients in the late 1880s, unless they were indigent), left Jennie and the nurse alone with two babies much of the time.

With a burgeoning medical practice, additional professional obligations, a wife and babies, and ailing parents, Thomas found it nearly impossible to tromp in the woods in search of birds. Still, John Roberts recorded one precious Sunday in May 1888, when Thomas and Frank Benner took off to the country across the Mississippi to take in the blooming spring wildflowers and the neotropical bird migration. It must have been a great year to observe the brightly colored warblers. Bird-watchers relish the springs in which the trees are slow to leaf out and the birds are easily spotted; May 1888 was such a year. Thomas and Benner returned from their jaunt reporting that the trees were still bare and "everything backward."[10]

It was in this time that Thomas added a needed bit of technology to his home and office at 810 Sixth Avenue South: a telephone. Almost no private residence had one in 1889. Calls to the doctor would have had to be made from a nearby business. John and Lizzie did not have a phone, but Dr. Abbott did. *The Physician Himself* observed that "a telephone is both a luxury and a necessity."[11]

The appearance of a telephone at the Dr. Roberts residence reflected the rapid strides into modernity that Minneapolis was undergoing. Following the explosion of the Washburn A Mill in 1878, the company had rebuilt with new technology, and in 1880 the Pillsbury Company had followed suit. Flour production tripled in the following decade to six million barrels per year, catapulting the city to the flour capital of the United States.[12] Sawmills, feeding on the rapid deforestation of Minnesota's pine forests, also burgeoned.

The boom in industry brought a corresponding expansion in building and an influx of people. Minneapolis's population nearly tripled, from 45,000 to 129,000 in the five-year span from 1880 to 1885.[13] Former residential neighborhoods sprouted large brick commercial buildings, as the little "New England–like" town grew into an urban area. "Houses which have long been landmarks in the older parts of the city are, by the dozens, on wheels and trundling off to remote sections of the city," reported the *Minneapolis Tribune* in 1882.[14]

But the rapid expansion of building and population had a swift environmental toll. Excavation of former residential sites that would soon support five-story structures often uncovered cesspools or the remains of outhouses. The medical director of the Minneapolis Board of Health described one such scene on Washington Avenue between First and Second Avenues South: "The centre of the excavation was the site of a privy vault and cess pool, and for the entire distance each way, it was found that the entire mass was saturated with stinking filth. . . . Water taken from a well nearly 200 feet distant was putrid."[15]

The medical community was well aware that typhoid and cholera were spread by poor sanitation. In a city of over 130,000, the existing sewer system and garbage collection were woefully inadequate, and too many residents depended on shallow wells for drinking water. "It seems strange that such conditions should have been so long tolerated," the Board of Health observed, "but the people at large are slow to act on the dictations of a few sanitarians . . . especially when private rights and conveniences stand in the way. . . . Proper disposal of sewerage [sic] in communities require[s] combined action, and it is difficult to get municipal corporations to act on scientific principles, especially when it is thought a little false economy will better serve political interests."[16]

The laying of sewers, however, had unanticipated and undesirable environmental effects in this city of wetlands, too. A notable one was the drying up of the creek that flowed out of Loring Lake and into a broad valley between what is now downtown and the Bryn Mawr neighborhood. In 1883, the land surrounding Loring Lake was made Minneapolis's first city park. Known initially as Central Park, it was a draw for city dwellers, who strolled or drove conveyances around the park's paths. The elder Robertses frequently availed themselves of the proximity of the new park, only a few blocks from their house. The lake originally had very marshy margins. It was fed by many springs, and the overflow spilled out into a small creek that flowed over the land occupied today by the intersection of Harmon Place and Hennepin Avenue and then traveled northwest to empty into Bassett's Creek (now running in a buried culvert). A sewer line laid down along Fifteenth Street on the southern fringe of the lake dried up the flow of the stream. Absent running water, the lake froze entirely in winter, resulting in winterkill of the fish.[17]

Thomas had lost his beloved "Tamarack Swamp" to development in 1879. The swamp was actually part of the same wetland system as Loring Lake and its creek. The hydrogeology of the entire valley west of downtown Minneapolis, what an early author called the "Hollow of the Hills,"[18] was disrupted very early in the rapid expansion of the city, and Thomas's favorite boyhood haunts, those he could reach on foot from his house, disappeared. A second assault on the Loring Lake/"Lost Brook" marsh came in 1886 when dirt from Lowry Hill was used to fill in more of the marsh to create a forty-six-acre park that became known as the Parade Grounds.

It must have been shocking for those who cherished nature to witness the rapid pace of its destruction in this decade. By 1892, the farmland south of Franklin Avenue was all platted, although frame houses clustered close to downtown, and few homes were actually built near the chain of lakes. Thomas had patients living on farms or lake homes on Calhoun, and he sometimes stayed overnight "at the lake" when someone in the family was sick.

Lakes Harriet and Calhoun in the late 1880s had large pavilions on their shores, where fifteen years before the Robertses had carried shotguns, hunting for deer. Calhoun had a boat clubhouse and was a draw for sailboats and other recreational craft. A large bathhouse provided a changing place for swimmers.

Closer to the booming business district, Nicollet Island, once a winter home to stunning Evening Grosbeaks, also succumbed to development. A number of small businesses clustered at its southern tip, including a sash and door factory, a box factory, and a rye flour mill. The northern end sprouted large, fashionable houses; residences fronted Hennepin Avenue where it crossed the island.

North of downtown, in present-day "Shoreham," railroads built a massive service station with an engine house, round table, car shop, machine shop, blacksmith, and boiler. The bountiful Sandy Lake vanished; its shoreline, at about Central Avenue and Twenty-Eighth Avenue Northeast, was platted. John Roberts described a visit out there in June 1888: "That part of town is now built up where I formerly went to shoot plover, ducks, etc."[19]

Perhaps thinking of the plenteous day of hunting in July 1874, John again drove to the prairie remnant around the lake in August 1890, "to look for Bartram's sandpipers [upland sandpipers] but did not see one."[20] Earlier, John had reported a similar trip in which he had come home empty-handed: "I got a horse and buggy at the livery stable and ... went across the [Mississippi] River and drove about 10 miles looking for Pigeons where I have shot a great [many] in former times but did not see one. The country is altered

a great deal and fenced in."[21] Thomas would later observe that the last Passenger Pigeon in Minnesota was recorded in 1895.

John returned to the area, this time with Thomas. It was a special outing,
one snatched from the doctor's hectic workweek. John, apparently feeling
unusually well, rented a carriage from the local livery at 6:00 A.M., picked
Thomas up, and in the early hours of a fresh May morning, again crossed the
river and drove to the woods, this time in search of Field Sparrows. Thomas
had been surprised to encounter this species, with the chestnut cap and
sweet, plaintive whistle, four years before in northern Ramsey County. Field
Sparrows were considered a southern species but apparently were extending
their range northward.[22] Thomas shot three that morning in 1890, further
documentation that they were indeed moving north. The outing, covering
familiar ground and of short duration (the men were home in time for noon
dinner), was, in retrospect, a poignant one. It would be the last time Thomas
and John would drive out to collect birds.

Even land far away from the city center was not safe from the frenzy of
development that gripped Minneapolis in the boom decade. On a windy
day in early September 1888, John and Lizzie drove out to Medicine Lake,
west of the city. "[We] ate our lunch on the east side and spent a couple of
hours there, and then drove around the lower side of the lake. The ground
around the lake has been bought and is laid out in town lots—8 or 9 miles
from the city."[23]

And expansion occurred in the neighborhood. A new hotel opened on
Hennepin Avenue, above Eighth Street, only a block from the Robertses'
once-suburban home, with its barn, woodshed, fruit trees, and garden. Late
in the decade, the Robertses received an unsolicited offer to buy their house
and adjacent lot. John was actually inclined to sell, but the would-be developer never followed through with details. Nonetheless, what once had been
a purely residential neighborhood was now an island in the business district.

John Roberts would not live to sell out to a developer, nor would he see the
birth of his third grandchild, a boy named for him, John Carroll Roberts, in
March 1892. As he approached seventy, his body, long wracked by tuberculosis, finally succumbed.

Although earlier in the decade Robert Koch had discovered that bacteria caused TB, no cure was forthcoming. As his doctor, Thomas prescribed

for John at various times quinine, wild cherry bark and whiskey, castor oil, and rhubarb (for constipation). Nothing halted the inexorable spiral downward—the nausea, the expectorating of bright red arterial blood, and the coughing, coughing, coughing. On September 12, 1890, a feminine hand left a final entry in John's journal: "This day was the saddest one in my whole life. My dear, kind husband left me for his heavenly home. We were married Jan. 1, 1857. E. J. Roberts."[24]

The birth of the blond, robust John Carroll—Thomas and Jennie called him "Carroll" in honor of Carroll Williams of Philadelphia—made the living quarters at 810 Sixth Avenue South more cramped. Several months after his birth, they moved their brood of three—Tommy, not yet four; Catharine, two; and baby Carroll—to a new duplex at 1015 Harmon Place. Emma and the widowed Lizzie moved next door. As at the former place, Thomas conducted his clinic from his home. Office hours were in the afternoon from two to five o'clock.

Clarence Herrick came to this office from his home in Denison, Ohio, in 1894, suffering the symptoms of TB, to be examined by his trusted friend. Thomas recommended the treatment that had proven efficacious in his own experience, fresh air, and Clarence and his family moved west to New Mexico, but Thomas would sadly endure his friend's untimely death in 1904 at the age of forty-two.[25]

In old age, Thomas recalled one illustrious visitor to Harmon Place: his former medical school professor William Osler. As Thomas recounted it, the bedside telephone rang early one morning, before Thomas was up. Osler was on the other end, asking for breakfast, and by the time Thomas was dressed, the exuberant man was pounding at the door. He was in Minneapolis to visit a former resident from Johns Hopkins, who was dying.

Thomas and Jennie seated him at the breakfast table, where he met and befriended all three small children. After the meal, the parents attended to matters of the day, and the children took Osler in hand. When Thomas went looking for his guest, he could not be found. Searching, he discovered Osler in the attic, sitting on the floor, attending a party, drinking imaginary tea from a little cup, and eating imaginary wafers, with children and an assortment of stuffed animals gathered round. He was, Thomas noted, exhibiting the buoyant enthusiasm for which he was famous.[26]

The Robertses moved their family one more time, four years later, when the children were school-age, to a plum-colored frame duplex at 1603 Fourth Avenue South, just skirting downtown.[27] They modernized the place, installing, first, indoor plumbing and, later, electricity, replacing the gas lighting. Again, Thomas carved a medical office out of the spacious residence. The office/family home received many people, both patients and personal friends, and in that house the children grew up. Thomas and Jennie grieved the death of their mothers there, Elizabeth Roberts in 1904 and Lydia Cleveland in 1913. Frank Chapman of the American Museum of Natural History in New York came to 1603 to escape the rigors of his work and recuperate from illness, and many illustrious speakers on birds, in town for a lecture, were overnight houseguests.

In the "middle years" at 1603, Thomas and Jennie would see Walter Roberts move out of state, and Emma become the art director of the Minneapolis public schools. Daughter Catharine received and then married, in 1914, "best beau" Joseph Seybold in the comfortable family home. Thomas conducted his medical practice out of this address until closing it in 1915.

In later years, people would remark on the sociability of Dr. and Mrs. Roberts. One magazine article from the 1930s noted that "Dr. Roberts cut quite a figure as the town's fashionable medic."[28] Thomas did not take in many concerts or plays in the early years—one wonders if he would have been able to sit through a performance without being interrupted—but in his forties, he learned to waltz and two-step and discovered he enjoyed a turn around the dance floor. He and Jennie joined the Cotillion Club, which held balls—on weeknights—during the winter. They were frequent guests at dinner parties, and sometimes Jennie went unaccompanied, as doctors' wives learn to do, if an emergency called Thomas away. They ran with a well-to-do crowd that included many friends from childhood.

Thomas was a member of the Minnekahda Club, which maintained a clubhouse and stables, a caddie house, and a boathouse; the Minneapolis Club; and the Six O'Clock Club, a civic organization of the time. It is not known if he had the time to put in an appearance at any of these—much less to play a round of golf!

For a time, he and Jennie considered investing in a summer home on an island off the shore of Isle Royale, in the middle of Lake Superior. A handful of people from the Cities were going together in the buy-in, and the Robertses knew who their neighbors would be. The deal did not go through.

Although they employed at various times maids and a cook, and always a driver, the Robertses were not in the top echelon of Minneapolis society. In a revealing series of letters written in winter 1913, when they were in their fifties, Jennie told Thomas, who was recuperating from exhaustion in Bermuda, that their elder son was working in the office of Washburn-Crosby, coming in early and staying late, "an all round utility man."[29] The younger son turned twenty-one during that time, and Jennie took pains to explain to Thomas why she purchased a gold-filled watch and not a silver one, letting him know the exact cost. In the same letter, she mentioned that daughter Catharine, "Sis," was sewing her spring and summer clothes, because she had been asked to be in a friend's wedding and was fretting about the cost of the gown.[30] What a change from Thomas's youth, when Emma had a seamstress in residence for a week to sew dresses for her! Jennie also told him that she had been asked to accompany a friend on a trip to Panama, and she blanched at the price tag: six hundred dollars![31]

The correspondence that remains conveys the sense that the Robertses were surrounded by a warm, convivial group of friends of long standing, who knew each other well and chased around together—out to the Long Meadow Gun Club on the Minnesota River for a Sunday dinner, or perhaps to someone's farm for a party, dinner at the Minneapolis Club, an evening spent playing cards or dancing, whiling away the frosty winter nights and humid summer evenings, making the most of life in Minneapolis.

CHAPTER 8

The Busy Physician

> The Golden-eye, or Whistler, is one of the few
> Ducks that is able to get a living and exist in apparent
> comfort through the long Minnesota winter.
>
> — *The Birds of Minnesota*, 1: 267

D r. Roberts stepped briskly from his buggy to the massive oak door of his patient's imposing residence, black bag in hand. He was dressed in a single-breasted, knee-length, dark wool coat over a starched white shirt with a high collar and a checkered tie anchored by a stickpin. A bowler sat atop his head. The mustachioed doctor paused at the front entrance before ringing the bell, checking his gold pocket watch, always mindful of the minutes ticking away and anxious to be on schedule for the start of office hours at two o'clock. The door creaked open, and as the hired girl stood aside to admit him, he had a final glimpse of his horse and driver before entering the hall and making his way to the sickroom.

Described as a "hard-driven, hard-working" physician,[1] Roberts kept up a pressing pace, rising early and retiring late, meeting the demands of patient house calls, office hours, hospital rounds, and administrative duties all in the course of a twenty-four-hour day. The practice that had begun slowly in 1886 became ever more complex in the twenty-five years that followed.

True to the advice of *The Physician Himself*, Roberts had hired a driver after the death of his father in 1890. That loss had deprived him of a companion when he "rounded" on patients, someone who could tend to the horse as the tightly scheduled doctor looked in on the sick. The driver, John Nordquist, was a Swedish immigrant a few years younger than Roberts, and his life would be intimately entwined with the Roberts family for thirty-five years. While a bachelor, he rented living quarters from the family, an arrangement that gave him the opportunity to meet, woo, and wed the Robertses' second maid, Mary Hansen.

The Nordquists set up housekeeping in the same neighborhood as the doctor's family, so John would be available for medical emergencies. One never knew when the doctor might need to dash off to some distant locale in the wee hours. The driver would tend the doctor's horse into the twentieth century and later master the automobile and continue driving his employer around, even after Roberts left his medical practice. Roberts himself, competent though he was in nearly everything, never learned how to drive well. Perhaps his absent-minded collision with a streetcar early in the learning process soured him on the venture. Over the years, he owned a number of cars, among them a Maxwell, an electric Cadillac that charged in the garage, a Buick, and a Nash.[2] Nordquist, though, oversaw their care.

Together, Roberts and Nordquist maintained a flexible schedule of morning house calls around town until about one thirty. Then later, after lunch and office hours, there might be more calls until dinnertime and, alas, even after-dinner calls until as late as midnight.

At some point during those morning rounds in the years 1894 to 1900, when he was in his late thirties, Roberts also stopped at St. Barnabas Hospital, fifteen blocks away, where he was chief of staff. There, he attended to administrative duties and sometimes rounded on a patient who had been hospitalized.

Afternoons were spent at 1603 Fourth Avenue South. His small home office was notable for being kept at a warm temperature, often as high as eighty-five degrees. Patients came and went, not always during set office hours. A particularly ill patient, maybe someone who had reached him by telephone, might need to be seen after five o'clock, and a house call might be warranted.

Roberts seldom got home for dinner before seven o'clock and often ate as late as nine. Jennie and the children saw little of him. Certainly, he could not devote the time to his children that his beloved father had to him. But having his medical office in his home, a situation adhered to by other, but not all, doctors in Minneapolis, meant that the family lived his medical life with him. They were accustomed to the creak of the office door as patients entered and exited, the ring of the telephone, and the presence of the office bookkeeper, Mabel Densmore. Mabel would later play a large role in Roberts's bird work, but in the 1890s, the bright, dark-haired young woman from Red Wing, Minnesota, billed patients, received payments, served as lab technician, and generally kept the office in order.

Despite the frantic schedule, Roberts spent time chatting with his patients, particularly if birds were a topic of discussion, sharing with them his interest in wrens nesting in drainpipes and hummingbirds visiting the daylilies. He was quick, though, to detect a false interest in things avian.

The doctor maintained the habit of making a final visit to a recuperated patient. He entered this in his account book as "p.c.," or "parting call," and charged nothing for the visit. Jennie tartly observed that "p.c." more accurately stood for "pleasant chat"! Otherwise, Roberts's charges were standard at two dollars for an office visit and three dollars for a house call, which he increased to five dollars in later years.

Although his patients appreciated his sympathetic attentiveness, Jennie fretted over his lack of time to relax and catch his breath. The stress on family life must have been severe, because her solution to his lack of leisure at the dinner table now seems drastic. Even though both of them were involved in community efforts to curb lung disease—particularly TB—she encouraged him to take up smoking in his forties, in the hope that he would linger at the table after a meal. And he did it![3]

Like most general practitioners, Dr. Roberts maintained an active obstetrics practice, delivering about fourteen babies a year. Babies born to married couples were almost always delivered at home, so when a messenger or the telephone interrupted the quiet of the night, the physician, and presumably Nordquist, would dress and drive through the gaslit streets of Minneapolis to answer the summons. The erratic nature of birth made for some bone-weary days, but delivering babies, that sacred moment of first breath and blessed wail, offset the somber grind of disease, decay, suffering, and death that filled most of a family doctor's days.

At the start of his practice, Roberts had built his patient base from several sources. Abbott probably passed some of his patients on to him as he had promised; his father's friendships with owners of Minneapolis's early flour mills, particularly William H. Dunwoody, who came to hold a high position in the Washburn-Crosby Company, also provided him with contacts; and Roberts's own high school days in Minneapolis yielded future patients. Social friends who were also patients, and there were many, called him "Dr. Tom." Over the years, these friends became intensely loyal to their dedicated physician, as loyal as he remained to them.

One high school classmate-turned-patient was Clara Hampton, two years his junior, who had been an academic standout in the halls of the close-knit high school. Clara had married a Norwegian immigrant lawyer while Roberts was away at medical school, and become Clara Ueland. She would later rise to fame in the drive to give Minnesota women the right to vote, but in the 1890s, she was mother to a string of children, several of whom Dr. Tom delivered at the Ueland farm on the south shore of Lake Calhoun. After a trio of blondies, the fourth baby girl was different, and Roberts hailed her as having "very dark plumage." This daughter—Brenda—later recorded the story of her birth.[4]

Another high school classmate refiguring in Roberts's life was Joe Kingman, the writer of the gleeful letter congratulating Roberts on his engagement. A partner in the Minneapolis law firm of Woods, Kingman, and Wallace, he became the Robertses' lawyer—and Roberts became their family doctor, delivering the Kingmans' fourth child.

Assorted Boveys, friends from his early years, became patients. Caroline Bovey remained a close friend of both Emma and Jennie. Dr. Tom delivered the children of her brothers, Charles and William, and decades later, long after Roberts had retired from medical practice, Charles Bovey's family kept a room waiting for him out at Lake Minnetonka, should he feel inclined to visit the lake.[5]

A connection to Minneapolis's signature business, the Washburn-Crosby flour mill, later to become General Mills, ran like a gold thread through Roberts's patient population. Charles and William Bovey were both associated with Washburn-Crosby. The Crosby sons of founder John Crosby and their wives were also patients. Roberts delivered nine Crosby babies in the first decade and a half of the 1900s. Washburn babies were also escorted into the world by Roberts, including one at the lavish Fair Oaks mansion in south Minneapolis. Perhaps the most significant patient connection, one that Roberts could hardly have predicted in the years when he used his stethoscope more than his field glasses, was that of the Bell family: James Stroud Bell, president of the Washburn-Crosby Company, and his son, James Ford Bell. Jim Bell, though younger by nineteen years, became a personal friend of Roberts. Besides sharing a Philadelphia birthplace, the two had much in common: a love of nature, particularly birds, and an interest in wildlife photography, which was in its infancy when they met.

DeLaittres, Boveys, Christians, McKnights, Heffelfingers, Washburns, Crosbys, Bells—there was a great deal of intermarriage among the wealthiest families in town. Roberts delivered babies who were siblings, babies who were first cousins, and babies who were neighbors, as sisters and sisters-in-law passed along the name of their modern and competent baby doctor, one who was knowledgeable in good prenatal care and whose soothing bedside manner and broad experience had brought them safely through the perilous passage of childbirth.

Summer babies of these wealthy elite were frequently born at their seasonal homes on Lake Minnetonka, on a rocky, wooded peninsula dividing Wayzata Bay and Brown's Bay that Roberts simply noted as "Ferndale." Ferndale was a collection of large, rambling cottages, similar to those found at Bar Harbor, Maine, during that time period. The compounds typically included a main house, guest cottages, a carriage house, and a boathouse, providing a retreat for the owners to engage in sailing or boating on the lake, in tennis and croquet on the land. "Going to the lake" was the common response to summer heat, but those expectant mothers who fled the sultry environs of the city and chose to deliver their babies out at the lake took a gamble. Their physician might not make it in time. When labor started, they could use the telephone to summon the doctor, but in the early years of his practice, Dr. Tom was entirely dependent on the Great Northern Line to get out to Ferndale. Thanks to a friendship between James J. Hill and Frank Peavey, Ferndale had its own stop on the line, but even so, there were one or two babies who arrived before the doctor.

But not all of Roberts's obstetric work was devoted to Minneapolis's upper crust. He was also the physician to his driver's wife and delivered their two daughters, and was on staff not only at St. Barnabas but also at Swedish Hospital and City Hospital (later to become Hennepin General and then Hennepin County Medical Center), both in the immediate vicinity of St. Barnabas. He very likely did not keep records of the deliveries of poor, unmarried women—women who might give their babies up for adoption, women who stayed at these hospitals in the last days of their pregnancies before giving birth, women who had come in to Minneapolis from small towns or farms for the protection of anonymity from what was then a scandalous situation.

Roberts had a remarkable delivery record. Out of 262 births, he did not record losing a single mother or baby to postpartum infection. In the days of his practice, before antibiotics or sulfa drugs, puerperal fever caused by strep or staph infection was a common occurrence. It was rampant at Blockley Hospital when he did his residency there. But Roberts set up his practice just as antiseptic measures were gaining acceptance in the United States, and he was well informed about them. He had lectured to St. Barnabas's nursing students in 1895 on those very practices. These would have included acts as simple as hand washing and sterilization of tools, such as forceps and scissors. He did not record doing such measures—perhaps it was a routine taken for granted. He did record the repair of perineal tears, using chloroform as an anesthetic and catgut—still used today—to make the stitches.

He often took a nurse with him to assist on deliveries, particularly in the second half of his career. These young women, dressed in long, white aprons over pinstriped gowns with leg-of-mutton sleeves and in starched, winged caps, were often trained at St. Barnabas's nursing program. His relationship with his nurses was warm and often enduring. He was invited to their weddings, and he sent flowers to celebrate the events.

Maintaining a practice with a large core of well-to-do patients who paid their bills made Roberts financially solvent in an age when physicians were generally not well compensated. As late as 1913, the American Medical Association estimated that only 10 percent of the nation's doctors earned a comfortable income.[6] Moreover, Roberts did not solely serve the wealthy. Indeed, riffling through the physician's accumulated correspondence over the length of a year, one would find the vast preponderance written by people of humble means, ones who sometimes paid bills in increments. He had a long-standing association with the Home for Aged Women and Children, a charitable enterprise, and remained closely associated with St. Barnabas Hospital, whose focus was on ministering to the poor.

Imagine Dr. Roberts moving purposefully down the light, airy hallway of the new St. Barnabas's first floor. The high ceilings contributed to the capacious feel of both patient rooms and passageways, and staff and directors alike were proud of the hospital's perfect ventilation system. Long-skirted nurses passed him in the hall and greeted him in subdued voices. Loud talking in the hospital was considered disruptive and not conducive to healing. In fact, perfect silence was observed when physicians attended patients on the wards. St. Barnabas also banned the following: profane language, vulgar or indecent conversation, betting and gambling, smoking, spitting on the floor, drinking, and immoral literature. But patients were free to subscribe to a daily newspaper, which was delivered to their rooms, and were welcomed at Sunday services in the hospital's chapel. Morning prayer was held daily at 7:00 A.M. with the nurses in attendance.[7]

Roberts was the chief of staff of St. Barnabas, the first hospital in Minneapolis, from 1893 to 1900.[8] Initiated by an Episcopal congregation, it had continued its affiliation with the church in the intervening twenty-five years. In its early years, volunteers provided the money and goods to run the institution. In 1897, members from the city's Episcopalian congregations still gave gifts of fresh eggs and milk, hand-hemmed linens, hospital gowns, and homemade jellies, courtesy of women's circles. Because so many of the poor were malnourished, there was a lot of emphasis on good diet for convalescing patients, and the hospital maintained a garden on its grounds.

The brick and stone building, new in 1894, with its elegant, semicircular portico serving as a front entrance, made it possible to launch a much-needed nursing program. Members of the medical staff lectured the young nurses-in-training during the school's first year. Roberts's two lectures were both concerned with obstetrics: the first, "Natural Labor," discussed preliminary preparations for labor, the position of the fetus, and what to do in an emergency. His second covered "The Puerperal State"—cleanliness, articles required, the immediate care of the infant, and infant feeding.[9]

St. Barnabas was recognized for its excellent surgical facilities. The new building was considered "a model in the perfection and completeness" of its operating room. In his chief of staff report, Roberts noted that 573 operations had been performed in 1897–98, as many as three or four a day in the winter. The operating room was in such demand, in fact, that the staff felt compelled to petition the hospital board of trustees that surgeons working at St. Barnabas be permitted to reserve the room every day until eleven o'clock.[10] Surgeons on staff at other hospitals could use St. Barnabas's state-of-the-art facility after that time—a common practice in Minneapolis at the turn of the century.

In his last annual report in 1900, Roberts wrote that St. Barnabas was so busy that it had to turn patients away. Although St. Barnabas, like most hospitals, was instituted to care for the poor and those far from the loving care of relatives, the progression of medical technology in the 1890s had transformed it into a "modern" institution of healing. But this was increasingly costly and required the hospital to court paying patients. Under Roberts's supervision, St. Barnabas had been able to do this. The bustling operating room proved also to be a good training ground for St. Barnabas nurses, especially acquainting them with the modern antiseptic obstetric methods. Roberts vouched for the high quality of the nursing students, and overall he praised the "harmonious staff" of the hospital.[11]

In 1900, Roberts stepped down as chief of staff. He was forty-two years old, and he had been in practice for thirteen years. His medical work was rich and complex, and his reputation in obstetrics was blooming. But he was terrifically overworked, and in the year preceding his decision to leave the post, he repeatedly fretted over his frantic schedule in letters: "When really busy I have absolutely no time for anything else night or day. It's a great trial and disappointment, but there is no attenuation."[12] Something had to give. The nonpaying administrative job was the logical choice. Roberts "resigned on account of not being able to devote sufficient time to the work," but he remained on the medical staff.[13]

Sometime in the late 1890s, he met Dr. Leslie Dart, who in 1901 served as senior intern for St. Barnabas. Dart was a homegrown Minnesota boy with an unusual avocation: he loved watching birds. Even before Dart's affiliation with St. Barnabas, Roberts invited him along on bird outings, and the two developed a multifaceted friendship. Later, Dart would function as an assistant and a quasi-medical partner in the remaining years of Roberts's practice.

In the age when telephones were a luxury that only doctors and some businesses required, Roberts received a variety of handwritten and, occasionally, typewritten notes from patients alerting him to their need for medical attention:

> Dear Dr. Roberts: Will you kindly call at 1408 Stephens Ave? I am suffering from La Grippe and would like to have you call this evening. Yours respectfully, —— I wish to be able to attend school tomorrow.

> Dr. Thos. Roberts: [I] give you the plain facts: Agnes is daily growing weaker and those plain blue capsules are, apparently, doing her no good. . . . she has taken five boxes already of them.

I want to thank you for the kindness and interest you manifested for me during my illness and also for the generous way in which you have discounted the remuneration for your attention to me.

Dear Sir! I received your medicine and have been taking the same according to your instructions, have half of it used and I find it is keeping my bowels in very nice shape.

I have great faith that you will relieve my trouble.[14]

Many times, the notes began apologetically, acknowledging his harried schedule: "My dear Dr. Roberts, I feel so guilty in asking a favor of anyone who has so little free time as you." And usually they continued on to describe a grave situation, as this one did: "But we are in pretty serious trouble ... my grandfather is rapidly losing his mind, and while he has sane intervals, it is almost impossible for us to care for him."[15]

Infrequently, the notes are frankly flirtatious: "My dear Doctor Roberts— after waiting in vain for a pink or blue box to come in response to the valentine I sent out, I have come to the conclusion that in order to save my feelings, you have decided not to send the yellow and red ones.... [This is] a crushing blow." But apparently not too crushing, for the letter writer adds as a postscript: "I won't be the one to forget that invitation for the next waltz." And one can only imagine the good doctor's reaction to others such as this one: "My dear Dr. Roberts—If you have any respect for my feelings, do send me something for my nerves ... give me something strong this time, I assure you I need it."[16]

There were queries about treatment for syphilis and sexual dysfunction, menstrual cramps and bowel upset, "inflammatory rheumatism," and infectious hepatitis. He treated pinkeye, scarlet fever, depression, and urinary tract infections. Clara Ueland was concerned that young Brenda ran a fever after her smallpox vaccination.[17] The American Medical Association, conducting a survey, solicited his opinion on whether to treat diphtheria with antitoxin. Roberts's phenomenal memory (recall the test incident in medical school) aided his ability to accurately and incisively assess symptoms. One legend that circulated in his later years was that by the time of his retirement in 1915, the Mayo brothers of Rochester—who were personal friends— regarded him as one of the top five diagnosticians in the country.[18]

Typhoid fever was a recurrent problem for all physicians in Minneapolis. This bacterial disease, caused by *Salmonella typhi*, infected people via contaminated water or food. Wells located too near outhouses or cesspools were the most common source, and the disease appeared with regularity in epidemics. In 1897 the disease was epidemic, and St. Barnabas treated many of the sick. The hospital admitted sufferers of typhoid fever because spread of the disease could be controlled through simple rules of hygiene. Those infected with communicable diseases that could not be controlled, like the terrifying smallpox, were not admitted at most hospitals.

But smallpox sometimes presented as typhoid fever. This was the case in June 1900, when a man, apparently in the early stages of typhoid fever, was admitted to St. Barnabas. Within hours staff realized the misdiagnosis. He was immediately removed to Quarantine Hospital in the city, and the two nurses who had cared for him were quickly isolated. One fell ill with a particularly severe, disfiguring, though not fatal, case. Trenchant action had prevented the entire hospital from being shut down, but the incident had happened under Chief of Staff Roberts's watch. Even though he had not been at the hospital at the time—he had been in northern Minnesota collecting bird specimens—he and the hospital received a sharp reprimand from the quarantine officer of the city of Minneapolis.[19]

The infectious disease that perhaps cut closest to Roberts's bone was the one that so shaped his childhood: tuberculosis. In the age of antibiotics, it is hard for modern readers to imagine the devastation that tuberculosis wreaked in the nineteenth and early twentieth centuries. It was called "The Great White Plague," and it killed one in every seven people on the planet.[20] The toll was higher for those in productive adulthood: one in three. Tuberculosis infiltrated every part of society in the years of Roberts's medical practice—rich and poor, young and old, the milling elite living on Park Avenue and those eking out a miserable existence on Bohemian Flats. Physicians knew what caused it—a bacterium—but were helpless to cure it. So Roberts watched as his witty and intelligent patient Caroline Crosby, whose keen observations on birds and plants filled her letters to him, grew increasingly worse from the disease. About the same time, Clarence Herrick, who had become a brilliant and prolific professor at Denison University in Ohio, also came under his care. Miss Crosby recovered; Herrick did not, TB indifferent to accomplishment or genius.

By the 1890s, it was widely accepted, at least among physicians, that as an infectious disease, tuberculosis could be limited in scope. They knew that tuberculosis bacilli inhabited saliva, could cling to dust particles, and if inhaled, could cause infection. This suggested ideas on how to curtail transmission of the disease.

In 1902, Roberts authored a paper, "The Prophylaxis of Tuberculosis," presented it to the annual meeting of the Minnesota State Sanitary Association, and illustrated it with slides. The venue underscored the fact that this paper was not an academic treatise or even a clinical piece with doctors as an audience, but a paper designed to effect societal change in the attitudes toward TB.[21] Calling TB "this arch fiend," Roberts noted that "we are all so used to it and complacent about it" that it had been hard to convince the general populace that they themselves could do much to make tuberculosis a much less prevalent disease. The paper was methodical and comprehensive. In it, Roberts ticked off measures that individuals, society, and government could undertake to bring rampant infection under control: Dairy herds should be monitored and kept clean from disease—it was not known if bovine tuberculosis was transmittable to people, but it might be, and if not, he reasoned, no one wants to drink milk from sick cows, anyway. Human saliva contained millions of bacilli. No one should kiss a consumptive on the mouth—a practice to which many small children were subjected. (Was he thinking of his own young children and his sick father?) Eating utensils and dishes needed to be carefully washed. In factories that crafted handmade cigars and cigarettes, workers should not moisten the wrappers with their saliva—a known route of transfer of the tubercular agent.

Roberts devoted a large portion of the paper to the conundrum of sputum. Noting that seven billion bacteria were given off by the adult consumptive in one day and that "Americans are a spitting race," Roberts said that controlling and properly destroying the expectorate of consumptives was crucial. "Handkerchiefs of specially prepared paper" were available to be used once and burned. Public cuspidors should be at least three feet high (ensuring better aim), and they should be easy to disinfect. Trains and streetcars should prohibit spitting on the floor and display signage to that effect. (Philadelphia already did this, he noted.) Women needed to adopt the fashion of wearing shorter skirts that cleared the dirty sidewalks (the current fads of bicycling and golf helped in this regard). Trailing dresses were "a foolish fashion" when sidewalks were filthy with spittle—more deplorable, he thought, than the fashion of wearing the feathers of native birds on hats, and that practice had already been outlawed in some states.

Tuberculosis was a menace, and the poor could not afford some of the measures that needed to be taken. Government programs should pay for necessary disinfection. But above all, widespread public education was necessary, so that every person became convinced that adopting these measures was in his own best interest.

The next year, the Anti-Tuberculosis Committee of the Associated Charities of Minneapolis was formed. Roberts was one of a number of physicians serving on this committee. Chaired by George C. Christian and with charitable donations spanning the spectrum of the city's wealth, it aimed to promote education on the control of TB. Members delivered public lectures, hired nurses to make home visits, placed articles in the newspapers, gave talks to the Trade and Loan Assembly, and hosted a touring National Tuberculosis Exhibit in the Hennepin County courthouse that drew twenty-eight thousand visitors. Most of the actions that Roberts had called for in his paper were taken. A pamphlet published in 1907 bore the familiar red "Christmas Seal" logo and was titled "The War on the White Plague in Minneapolis." It proclaimed that this mammoth undertaking, involving so many, delivered the "gospel of hope" to the tens of thousands of residents consumed by the disease.

The years of grueling medical work were beginning to tell on Roberts. An undated photo taken sometime in his forties shows a man who has seen his full share of human joy and suffering. His face is still thin, his hair still full, though darker, his mustache still bristling, but his eyes, nonetheless, are weary. His gaze is steady, but he looks tired. He does not smile at the camera.

After leaving the post of chief of staff at St. Barnabas, Roberts enjoyed a short interlude devoting his professional energies solely to his private practice. Then in 1901, he was appointed professor of pediatrics at the University of Minnesota, an unpaid post.[22]

Though he had not earned a degree there, Roberts returned to the university as a native son. The campus had grown in the two decades he had been away, and it was a time of great expansion for the medical school. The school had not even existed when Roberts was a student at the university. It had begun modestly in 1888 and quickly grown. In 1901, at his return, it was a collection of buildings near Old Main, including a 1896 structure, Wesbrook Hall.[23] The newest additions at that time were a dispensary built at Seven Corners on the West Bank to serve as a walk-in clinic for the poor (a bridge accommodating streetcars made the location accessible to the campus) and a new anatomy building with a morgue, cold storage vaults for cadavers, and refrigeration equipment.[24]

In 1906, Professor Roberts assumed a new title, that of clinical professor of the diseases of children. This post, too, was unpaid—large numbers of practicing physicians came into the medical school for a few hours each week to give clinical instruction.

In 1905 the school received a bequest that would fully fund a university hospital, something the school had badly needed for clinical classes.[25] The administration formed committees to locate a site for the new hospital and also for the medical school, which to this point had been expanding willy-nilly without plan. Though it seemed unlikely that the busy Dr. Roberts would take on additional responsibility, perhaps duty called, because he did. He sat on both committees and participated in the first concern of the hospital committee, that of raising money to buy land for the hospital.

The next year, the committee recommended that the hospital be located on four blocks of land between Washington Avenue and the Mississippi River, and several years later, it recommended that the entire medical school be moved to a twenty-six-acre plot of land south of Washington between Union Street and the river. The hospital was dedicated September 1911. W. J. Mayo, a member of the board of regents, gave the dedicatory address. Referring to the fact that hospital operations would be funded by the legislature, he declared that "enlightened socialism is the keynote of modern civilization."[26]

In 1912, the atmosphere in the medical school grew increasingly ugly, as the school locked horns with a new university president. The relationship between the administration and the medical and surgical faculty became tense; rumors flew that the president wanted to reduce the number of faculty on staff at the medical school, though it was unclear why. It was not a cost-saving move, since most were not paid. The tension culminated in what a chronicler of the medical school's history later called "the convulsion of 1913."[27] The entire core faculty of the school resigned, paving the way for a complete restructuring. Though he was not part of the core, Roberts resigned also, as did his associate, Leslie Dart.

Less than one month later, Roberts was headed on a steamer for Bermuda, on a four-week vacation, apart from Jennie and in the company of a Minneapolis businessman and his wife and daughter. Since he rarely took vacations and seldom traveled away from Minnesota, this was indeed an odd situation Roberts found himself in, but apparently one brought about in desperation: he was exhausted. The grind of general practice, the high drama at the university, and perhaps his increasing frustration over his inability to devote more time to birds finally took their toll. He would turn fifty-five on the trip.

Jennie stayed behind with the children, now young adults out in the work world and all living at home. They would have been fine on their own, but Jennie was, as she put it, "in charge," fielding patient calls that came for Dr. Roberts in his absence and referring them to Dr. Dart. A week after his departure, she expressed her hope that he was "beginning to get rested," noted the "not . . . very cheerful tone" of his first letter home, and added, "I did not expect you to recover in so short of time from years of overwork, but knowing your recuperative powers to be good, I have great hope that a month will do wonders for you."[28]

Unaccustomed to idleness, Roberts spent a restorative four weeks at an island resort. He played bridge. He took tea on the porch with a panoramic view of the Atlantic. He wrote postcards to the kids and Jennie. He told young Tom that the overall look of Bermuda was oddly like Isle Royale—the water, the wind, the islands. Did the passionate birdman revel in Bermuda's exotic avifauna? He did not mention it.

Nearly a month later, in her last letter sent before he was scheduled to come home, Jennie breathed her relief at the change in mood that was evident from his postings: "Your good letter . . . came yesterday. It did me a world of good, darling boy, for I was very, very anxious about you before you went away. I feel more than justified for having sent you away."[29]

Carroll's twenty-first birthday was the next day. Roberts would miss the celebration. Carroll had invited a girl to his birthday dinner and was "whistling a cheerful tune." Roberts would miss the dinner, too. Young Tom was sleeping in on Sunday morning, and "Sis's" "best beau" (soon to be her fiancé) had taken her out Saturday afternoon to lunch at a ritzy Minneapolis restaurant. Jennie closed the letter, "We will all be so glad to see dear Daddy, especially his loving wife."

The physical exhaustion had been a warning sign. His good health and remarkable stamina had their limits. Yet, there is momentum in a general medical practice. Taking on a new obstetrics patient meant an eight-month commitment, at least. Each new baby was a new little patient, whose care continued through childhood. It was difficult to say no to pregnant women whose friends had sung praises of their wonderful baby doctor. Many patients refused to transfer their medical care to young Dr. Dart or to any other physician.

Roberts's natural inclination toward "doing his duty" and bearing the yoke of responsibility under the most adverse of circumstances, and the fervent loyalty he inspired in those around him, now fused to work against his best interests.

When the summons came in the black wee hours of the morning, Dr. Roberts reluctantly rose from his warm bed to see what was amiss. The rap on the door disturbed the quiet house. His wife and his three offspring all slumbered. A messenger on the doorstep or the shrill ring of the telephone might mean anything: a high fever, an accident, a deathbed. That night, like many nights, it was a woman in labor, about to give birth. Contractions were regular, hard, and only minutes apart. The baby was early. Dr. Roberts calculated her due date as April 15, but babies were often early. The woman and her husband had been through this before and knew what to expect. This would be their third child.

The messenger waited while Dr. Roberts dressed and called his nurse, Miss Tennyson. Early in his practice, he seldom used an obstetrics nurse, but trained nurses were more available in 1914 and greatly helped in keeping a hygienic, semi-sterile environment, crucial for births in the home.

The April night was chilly. There would be frost before morning. The balmy nights of Bermuda seemed a lifetime ago, although he had been back little more than a month. The gaslights only partially lit the city streets as Roberts traveled eastward toward the river, toward a new part of town with modest frame houses.

Lights blazed in the house when he arrived. Upstairs, he found his patient, an older woman, in bed, dressed in a nightgown, her hair in plaits. She grimaced with each contraction. Dr. Roberts took off his winter coat and hat, rolled up his white shirtsleeves, and carefully washed his hands. The first task was to check the patient's cervix, to gauge the stage of labor, which he did, modestly, of course, with a clean sheet draped over the patient's knees. She was almost complete. He was pleased. The baby appeared at 2:30 A.M., an eight-pound baby girl, healthy and well formed, thank God. He clamped the umbilical cord, clipped it, and handed the baby over to the nurse. The placenta was delivered, inspected, and disposed of; the bleeding ebbed. The new mother had suffered a small tear, which Roberts promptly sewed up, after she got several whiffs of chloroform.

Meanwhile, Miss Tennyson had taken the baby, given her a bath, and wrapped her warmly in a blanket. She now handed her over to her mother. The bedroom had a serenity to it in the wake of the pain and tension of the delivery.

As the bone-weary Dr. Roberts left the house, the eastern horizon was pink with the coming day. It was April 5, 1913, a Sunday, the day of rest, and soon the city church bells would be pealing. Chickadees were whistling their two-noted spring song. Flocks of juncos, heading north to their breeding grounds, trilled from the trees.

This was his second delivery in April. He would be called out to another one on Monday morning and to two more later in the month.

CHAPTER 9

The Empty Day

> [The Kingbird] is probably one of the best known
> birds in the state. It is everywhere from early May
> until September, in forests, in orchards, on prairies,
> and in the outskirts of towns and cities.
>
> — *The Birds of Minnesota*, 2: 6

In 1889, Thomas Roberts received a letter from a man in Jackson County, in southwestern Minnesota, whom he had not met. The man, Thomas Miller, was a market hunter, one who made a living shooting large numbers of waterfowl—one hundred ducks, easily, in a single morning—and sending them to the East Coast to hang in butcher shops or grace the linen-clad tables of fancy restaurants. Miller lived on the edge of a vast shallow lake that teemed, he wrote, with birds: white pelicans and Trumpeter Swans, Whooping and Sandhill Cranes, and thousands of ducks. The wetlands were a stopover for untold numbers of migrating birds, particularly shorebirds, including the Eskimo Curlew. There was a large Black-crowned Night-Heron colony, for which the lake was named, and incredible numbers of Franklin's Gulls. "If you can spare the time you ought to visit," Miller wrote. "You would see a sight well worth going a long way to see."[1]

But it was not easy for the young physician to get away in 1889. He was thirty-one years old, he had been in practice two years, he was a new father, and his wife was pregnant again. His duty lay in building his practice, especially with another baby on the way.

Miller had not contacted Roberts out of the blue. Roberts had written him earlier, sending him a copy of a report issued by the Geological and Natural History Survey and asking if he would document birds in the Heron Lake region. Did Miller feel well versed enough to do that? Miller replied that he knew waterbirds intimately but had only recently begun identifying land birds. But his letter indicated that he was a very close observer and that the bird life was abundant in the area.

In the following months, Roberts became a father again, his own father succumbed to tuberculosis, and he settled John's financial affairs, securing the welfare of his mother and sister. Another baby appeared, the third in four years; the family moved, and the medical practice burgeoned. There was just not time for birds.

In 1892, Philo Hatch, Roberts's former mentor, authored *Notes on the Birds of Minnesota*, a clothbound, substantial-looking book that belied the term "notes."[2] At first glance, it seemed that Hatch had usurped Roberts's dream of writing the definitive book on Minnesota birds.

Hatch had been asked many years before, when he had been considered the foremost authority, to write a report on Minnesota's birds for the state's Natural History Survey. Roberts had been a boy then. He had always liked Hatch (his ebullient personality was infectious), but even as a boy Roberts had recognized that Hatch's record keeping left much to be desired. Hatch had delayed the report to the survey many times. He had an active medical practice, and the survey had not pressed for his report, being more interested in the prospects of iron ore mining in northern Minnesota. Hatch had published a couple of briefly annotated lists before 1892, but his final contribution was submitted after he had retired to California, poor in health and resources. By this time he had lost most of his notes and compiled his bird list from memory.

When the report appeared, Roberts realized that many of Hatch's observations were "largely fictitious" and "the result of confusion of data." So did the head of the Natural History Survey, Henry Nachtrieb. Nachtrieb, Roberts's old friend from his land examiner days, had returned to Minnesota and taken a teaching position at the university. When he became the departmental head of Animal Biology, he assumed the role of head of the Natural History Survey as well.

Nachtrieb wrote the introduction to Hatch's erroneous report and tried to distance himself from it. He declared to the university's board of regents, to whom the report was addressed, that he had "not assumed any editorial responsibilities and privileges, but simply those as a transmitter."[3] He added in his introduction that a *report* on the state's birds was under way and would soon be published.

To Roberts, Nachtrieb wrote that "Our good Dr. Hvoslef [a meticulous ornithologist from Lanesboro, Minnesota] is very much cut up by Hatch's treatment of his [Hvoslef's] careful observations. I tried my best to write him a soothing letter." Nachtrieb added sagely and with perhaps a twinkle in his eye that the publication of the bad report would prove to be a great incentive to the legislature to publish Roberts's forthcoming and more accurate report.[4]

With the unreliable Hatch report available to ornithologists, an accurate account of Minnesota's birds suddenly took on more urgency. Roberts made plans to visit Heron Lake, and in 1893, they came to fruition. Traveling alone, he took the train to the tiny town on the northwest shore, rented a room at a hotel, engaged a team and buggy, and went in search of Miller.

By 1893, many letters had passed back and forth between the physician and Miller, and the hunter-farmer had demonstrated that he had a keen eye and a philosophical turn of mind. Still, the letters had been untidy scrawls, full of creative spelling and lacking punctuation. Upon their first meeting, Roberts found him "a red-haired, red-shaggy-bearded, horny handed Scotchman of rather uncouth and forbidding exterior but with a straightforward sincere manner and correct comprehensive speech."[5]

Heron Lake itself proved a lovely place. A large, shallow lake constricted in the middle, forming two large basins ringed by reeds and other emergent plants, Heron Lake received its name from the myriad Black-crowned Night-Herons nesting in its luxuriant vegetation. The Dakota had called it "Hokabena," their name for the herons' nesting place. In May, the bird activity was dazzling, but Roberts would not return to the lake for another five years.

Roberts's young family and his medical practice had weathered his absence during his trip to Heron Lake, so in 1894, he planned another trip, this time to northern Minnesota. His companion on this trip was the Reverend Herbert W. Gleason, an interesting fellow. Lanky and bearded, he towered over the five-foot-eight Roberts. Like Roberts, he was in his thirties and an ardent outdoorsman. Raised in Massachusetts, he was an ordained Congregational minister who had served a church in Minneapolis, but by 1894, he had left the ministry to be the editor of a small church-related newspaper.

Thomas Sadler Roberts, about eighteen months, 1859.
Courtesy of Nancy C. Roberts.

Minneapolis in 1867, as the newly arrived Roberts family saw it.
The photograph looks south down Second Street from Nicollet Avenue.
Courtesy of the Hennepin County Library, Minneapolis Collection, BR0137.

The family of John and
Elizabeth Roberts,
circa 1867. From left:
John, Thomas, Emma,
Elizabeth, and Walter Roberts.
Courtesy of Nancy C. Roberts.

Old Main, University of Minnesota, circa 1878. Courtesy of the University of Minnesota Archives, University of Minnesota–Twin Cities.

The land examiners, 1881. Seated, from left: Thomas Roberts, Edson Gaylord. Standing, from left: John Cobb, Nathan Butler (crew boss), Henry Nachtrieb. Courtesy of the University of Minnesota Archives, University of Minnesota–Twin Cities.

Thomas Sadler Roberts, as a medical student in 1883.
Courtesy of Nancy C. Roberts.

Jane Cleveland Roberts with children Carroll (on lap), Thomas ("Tom"), and Catharine, 1892. Courtesy of Nancy C. Roberts.

*Dr. Roberts's medical office at his residence at 1603 Fourth Avenue, Minneapolis.
His secretary, Mabel Densmore, is with Tom and Catharine Roberts, circa 1898.
Photograph by T. S. Roberts. Courtesy of the Bell Museum of Natural History,
University of Minnesota.*

*Old Tiger and buggy
at 624 South Ninth
Street, Minneapolis,
circa 1899. Tiger
conveyed Dr. Roberts
on his medical calls to
patients. Photograph
by T. S. Roberts.
Courtesy of
Nancy C. Roberts.*

Thomas Sadler Roberts (right) and assistant Leslie O. Dart at Long Meadow, 1900. Courtesy of the Bell Museum of Natural History, University of Minnesota.

Thomas Sadler Roberts photographs a flycatcher's nest at Heron Lake, 1899. Tom Miller holds the ladder, 1899. Courtesy of the Bell Museum of Natural History, University of Minnesota.

Thomas Sadler Roberts photographs a Chipping Sparrow's nest at Long Meadow, 1900. Courtesy of the Bell Museum of Natural History, University of Minnesota.

Mabel Densmore, birding, circa 1900. Photograph by T. S. Roberts. Courtesy of the University of Minnesota Archives, University of Minnesota–Twin Cities.

Camp at Moose River, Marshall County, 1900. Left to right:
Thomas S. Roberts, Leslie O. Dart, Thomas G. Lee, E. L. Brown (guide).
Courtesy of the Bell Museum of Natural History, University of Minnesota.

The Roberts family picnics at the present site of Douglas Lodge, Itasca State Park,
1902. Courtesy of the Bell Museum of Natural History, University of Minnesota.

Bird study room, Zoology Building, University of Minnesota (undated).
Courtesy of the Bell Museum of Natural History, University of Minnesota.

Thomas Sadler Roberts, circa 1916.
Courtesy of Nancy C. Roberts.

Bird class, 1923, studying ducks at Lake Vadnais, Vadnais Heights, Minnesota. Courtesy of the Bell Museum of Natural History, University of Minnesota.

Bird blind at Lake Calhoun. John Nordquist (driver) assists in taking a photograph of a Killdeer, 1921. Photograph by T. S. Roberts. Courtesy of the Bell Museum of Natural History, University of Minnesota.

The University of Minnesota, circa 1916. Elliot Hospital is on far right; Zoology Building is the prominent building at right center. Roberts frequently took classes to bird along the east bank of the river south of campus. Courtesy of the University of Minnesota Archives, University of Minnesota–Twin Cities.

Bird class, 1919. Olga Lakela, future professor at Duluth State Teachers' College, is on Roberts's left. Courtesy of the Bell Museum of Natural History, University of Minnesota.

Thomas S. and Jennie Roberts at Itasca State Park, circa 1917. Courtesy of the University of Minnesota Archives, University of Minnesota–Twin Cities.

Breckenridge wedding, July 26, 1933. Left to right: Elizabeth Shogren, Dorothy Shogren Breckenridge, Walter Breckenridge, Thomas Roberts. Courtesy of Barbara Breckenridge Franklin.

Construction of the Museum of Natural History, 1939 (Folwell Hall in background). Courtesy of the University of Minnesota Archives, University of Minnesota–Twin Cities.

James Ford Bell at Ristigouche River, New Brunswick, Canada, 1939. Courtesy of Lucy Bell Hartwell.

Francis Lee Jaques, painting background for wolf diorama. Courtesy of the Bell Museum of Natural History, University of Minnesota.

Florence Page Jaques. Courtesy of the University of Minnesota Press.

Schoolchildren tour the museum, circa 1941. George Rysgaard, tour guide. Courtesy of the Bell Museum of Natural History, University of Minnesota.

Thomas S. and Agnes Williams Roberts, 1940. Courtesy of the University of Minnesota Archives, University of Minnesota–Twin Cities.

Siblings Emma Roberts and Thomas S. Roberts, circa 1942. Courtesy of Nancy C. Roberts.

Gleason would later become a nationally renowned nature photographer, recognized for his work on the writings of Thoreau, his depiction of landscapes in the national parks, and his highly popular slide presentations. His speaking engagements would draw a thousand people. But on this trip, it might be said that both he and Roberts were in embryonic form—established professionals who also had a deep, urgent affinity for the natural world, which had yet to blossom.

The men boarded a train in Minneapolis that took them to Two Harbors and from there across the Iron Range to the mining town of Tower on the shores of Lake Vermilion. Roberts described the Arrowhead region in 1894 as "wild, desolate and forbidding in appearance—rocky ridges covered with stunted pines, often burned over larger areas."[6] After three days at the Vermilion, Tower's best hotel, the collectors headed out by steamboat to the head of the big lake. Roberts was rather dubious about the seaworthiness of the *Jeannett,* observing that it seemed "built to blow up, burn, or be wrecked on the rocks."[7] Nevertheless, the *Jeannett* brought them safely to the far western shore, where they set up their tent on a bare rocky point and went out with their guns to collect. They did not fire a shot. The fishing, on the other hand, was fine. Gleason even went out trolling in a birch-bark canoe. And of course, it being June, the "mosquitoes [were] very thick," "in swarms," "in a cloud."[8]

The boreal forest of northeastern Minnesota was the breeding grounds of many of the jewel-bright warblers that migrated through Minneapolis each spring and fall. On Lake Vermilion, Roberts had the chance to nail down the territorial songs of these northern birds: "Mr. Gleason shot three Blackburnian Warblers (2 males and 1 female) and thus identified the song which we were at a loss to place as the birds keep high up among the tops of the tall pines. . . . [It] is a fine screeping effort of little musical merit . . . once heard is easily recognized again." Again, "Heard a number of Black-throated Green Warblers . . . the song is . . . four or five notes . . . all pitched differently . . . fine and wiry and have a peculiar way of sliding one into the other up and down." And again, "Saw an olive-sided flycatcher at an old burn. It was uttering its loud ringing call of 2 notes [of] different pitch from the topmost branch of some dead tree."[9]

In the afternoon of the next day, the rickety *Jeannett* arrived and transported the men to Jack Pine Island, about seven miles from Tower. They liked the island's attractive appearance and arranged with the steamboat's captain to stay two days but were disconcerted to discover "the island is solid rock with . . . very little soil so that was difficult to drive [tent] pins. Had to use rocks in part to stay the tent." Upon closer inspection, Roberts found "the island is full of birds, especially warblers, and there must be hundreds of interesting nests on it," adding, "it would appear profitable working ground for a couple of weeks instead of one day."[10] The bright yellow, rusty-capped Palm Warbler was especially abundant, moving restlessly in the thick lower branches of the trees, not easily seen. Reflecting that night in his journal, Roberts wrote, "I remember now hearing this song in nearly all open pine woods. . . . The bird is undoubtedly quite common in all suitable habitats."[11]

There were warblers galore—redstarts, chestnut sideds, Ovenbirds, waterthrushes. Mourning Warblers tended a nest near the tent, and Red-breasted Nuthatches moved through the conifers "in little roving bands." Roberts shot a Pileated Woodpecker, and Gleason a black-backed three-toed woodpecker (known today as an Arctic Three-toed woodpecker). The rhythm of the day was to rise early and collect birds in the morning and then put up the skins after noon dinner, a pattern that would mark all Roberts's future trips.

Eight days after they arrived in Tower, the collectors left again by train, Roberts getting off at Two Harbors for a few days collecting along Lake Superior, the Reverend Gleason bound for Minneapolis, called suddenly home by business. The sociable Roberts missed his company. "I was sorry to be left alone," he wrote in his journal.[12] They would not collect together again but maintained a warm, cordial correspondence for the rest of their lives.

In 1898, the year he turned forty, Roberts returned to Heron Lake, this time with camera equipment in tow. The camera was a new tool for him, and this was the first time he had tried it afield. He had bought a Long Focus Premo camera that could be used to take shots of objects at some distance. Some members of the American Ornithologists' Union, like Frank Chapman and William Dutcher, had begun to employ a camera in bird study, but it was a very new field. Roberts was the one of the first in Minnesota to turn a lens on the feathered world, and he often consulted with Chapman about various details—paper thickness, magnification of the lens, magic lantern features.

By 1898, Roberts had forged a close friendship with Frank Chapman of the American Museum of Natural History in New York City. The beginnings of the friendship are not known. Most likely, they met at an American Ornithologists' Union meeting in a year when the physician had been able to tear himself away from his patients for a week on the East Coast. Chapman was younger than Roberts by six years, but the two had much in common. Both came from wealthy families and were comfortable in the world of opera and cotillions; neither had any formal training in ornithology.[13] Chapman had an exuberant personality that radiated across half a continent. Roberts appreciated men with a zest for living that matched his own. And the two had similar interests, including the new field of wildlife photography.

Until recently, exposed plates—no film was used in this early camera—had had to be developed while still wet, so an outdoor photographer needed to haul a "dark-tent" with him, in addition to everything else. But in the late 1880s, George Eastman had invented a dry plate that did not need immediate developing, and this accelerated the interest in outdoor work.

Roberts's new camera was heavy, built of solid mahogany with a black leather case. It required an awkward tripod to hold it steady. The thick glass plates that served as "film" were carted out in a sturdy wooden box. The whole assemblage was unwieldy; thus, it was a very determined photographer who attempted to transport such a contraption on a train, in a wagon, over hill and dale, and in a boat across a lake. It was also a carefully balanced photographer who waded through the muck of a marsh to get his shots, because to stumble and fall would spell disaster to the expensive equipment.

Heron Lake was extremely shallow that spring, requiring the party of Roberts and several others to alternately row and pole their skiffs across the broad expanse of water for over an hour. They then "left [the boats] and waded the remaining distance—perhaps an eighth of a mile and through water and mud, knee and sometimes thigh-deep and a part of the way through quill reeds much higher than our heads. The sun was very bright and it was intensely hot." The cumbersome camera and tripod, of course, came, too. But, Roberts wrote, "the sight at the Heronry repaid us all the trouble. . . . There seemed to be many hundreds of herons and at an approach, they rose in a cloud with a great squawking and remained flying about during our stay."[14]

With the local game warden, Roberts examined nests, counted eggs, and observed the gangly nestlings—"comical looking gray and white streaked creatures . . . when annoyed, they would rise up and strike quite viciously."[15] Roberts exposed all the glass plates he had brought out to the heron colony, and that ended the expedition for the day. The next day, though, he went out to photograph Forster's Terns, nesting coots and grebes, and red-headed ducks. Overall, he was satisfied with the results of his new camera and reported to one of his colleagues that "it opened a new and most fascinating field."[16] He became aware that the camera enhanced his appreciation for nature's beauty and artistry, and he liked the fact that he could "shoot" a bird without bloodshed and destruction. It was not that he had lost interest in collecting but that a camera allowed him to show to others the living bird, and even by 1898 some birds were becoming less common.[17]

Roberts pursued bird photography for the rest of the summer of 1898. After his return from Heron Lake in late May, he spent a few days along the Mississippi River below Lake Pepin, collecting, studying, and photographing birds and bird nests in June. On this jaunt, he took Leslie Dart along, whom he had already identified as a "first class Bird Man." In 1898, Dart, a man of thirty, sporting a dark, bushy mustache, was about to begin his studies at the University of Minnesota Medical School. How he developed his interest or skill in birds is not known, but he would accompany Roberts on several collecting trips in the decade to come. That first summer, he chased enthusiastically after Prothonotary Warblers on the Mississippi, as Roberts aimed to document the northernmost edge of the species' range.

The trip was undertaken in a little boat, which they paddled through the Mississippi's winding channels. They collected at Barn Bluff in Red Wing, the one that Thoreau had climbed in 1861, and then made their way downriver. Prothonotary Warblers, small beauties of bright yellow with gray wings, nest in tree cavities in flooded bottomlands. The men skirted the riverbanks, knocking on all trees with holes, likely candidates for warbler nests. They disturbed a variety of cavity nesters, including the warblers, Downy Woodpeckers, and mice.

When they came upon a chickadee nest, the noon lighting was perfect for photography, and they decided to seize the opportunity. The cavity proved just a bit too high for the camera's tripod, but Roberts was ready for this: he pulled out a saw, sawed off the trunk below the cavity, then propped it up against a forked stick positioned in the riverbed. The birds took the de-elevation of their nest quite calmly, and Roberts got great shots of baby birds and attending parents.

Later that summer, he turned his camera on the ground-nesting Killdeer, this time in company with Bert Gleason. The bird was nesting in a cornfield near town, and the photography was not rigorous fieldwork but a pleasant diversion on a summer afternoon. The men devised a system to foil a wary mother bird. Gleason observed through binoculars and communicated with Roberts, hidden on his belly in the grass, via a line attached to Roberts's wrist. Roberts took the photo when Gleason yanked on the line. A woman—perhaps Jennie?—was an onlooker to the antics and witheringly commented on the maturity of the enthusiastic photographers: "About four years of age, I should think, instead of forty."[18]

When at home in Minneapolis, Roberts set Dart to work experimenting with the making of lantern slides, assisted by the versatile office help, Mabel Densmore. The role of Roberts in this enterprise was, as he put it, "simply superintending and criticizing."[19] Photos produced by the new camera were fine for publication in magazines, but Roberts was interested in giving talks to audiences.

Densmore had just begun working for the doctor that year. Orphaned as a teenager, she was only twenty-three but proved to be smart, capable, and meticulous. She soon picked up the birding bug. When she quit the job two years later, she returned to her hometown of Red Wing and began sending reports to Roberts on the nesting habits of birds around town.

The lantern slides that Roberts had Dart and Densmore producing were the forerunners of the classic slide show. Powered by a small generator, a "magic lantern" shone a photographic image on a screen or bare wall. In the days before silent films, the shows were very popular and were used by professionals to illustrate lectures. Roberts's photos were black and white, but the images were frequently hand colored by his sister, Emma, who was now a professional artist. He also sent a young woman to be trained in New York to do the exacting work.

Roberts assembled the slides of that first summer with the camera—the chickadees, warblers, Killdeers, bitterns, Downy Woodpeckers—and showed them at the American Ornithologists' Union meeting that fall in Washington, D.C. They were widely admired, and requests for duplicates came through the mail for months after. But the images soon found a much larger audience: in January 1899, Chapman launched *Bird-Lore* magazine, aimed at members of the fledgling Audubon chapters that were springing to life on the East Coast, and he prevailed upon his friend to submit the photos and a story for the first issue. Roberts complied with a how-to article on "The Camera as an Aid in the Study of Birds," published on page five of the inaugural issue. The Killdeer story made it into April's issue. *Bird-Lore,* with the slogan "A bird in the bush is worth two in the hand," rode the wave of the popularization of bird-watching; decades of bird lovers pored over its illustrations and stories. In time, its name was changed to *Audubon Magazine,* the publication of National Audubon. With uncharacteristic modesty, Chapman wrote to Roberts, "I trust . . . you will find Bird-Lore a worthy medium for the publication of your beautiful photographs."[20]

The next spring, 1899, Roberts returned to Heron Lake, this time accompanied by Dart, to photograph Franklin's Gulls, which built semifloating nests amid the rushes and reeds. Thomas Miller had at one time estimated the gull colony at two thousand birds.

Franklin's Gulls are unusually beautiful. Besides the gull-like white-and-gray plumage, they have rosy pink underparts that flash as they fly. Roberts was drawn, in part, by this aesthetic appeal, lauding their "exquisite beauty." He relished their "thrilling performance" of plunging headlong toward earth in a deep dive, which he thought was not a nuptial display since he witnessed it in October, and he marveled at "these glorious birds."[21] Aesthetics would mark future studies as well.

Heron Lake's water level was high that spring, and as he took pictures, Roberts was both intrigued and dismayed to discover that newly hatched gull chicks frequently wandered off the nest and ended in the drink, floating off into the wider lake and probable death. The "old birds" attempted to rescue their wayward chicks by grabbing them by the neck with their beaks and flinging them three or four feet back toward the nest, often successfully. However, the chicks were often exhausted and bloodied.

Roberts was patient enough to obtain a photo of one such "chick toss"; in it, the youngster can be seen flying through the air, the parent gull hovering above. This graphic slide was enthusiastically received at the November 1899 American Ornithologists' Union meeting in Philadelphia. One witness to the talk observed: "Dr. Roberts' views [slides] of the Franklin's Gull story were simply astonishing and his story captivating. One view was loudly applauded . . . [it was of] a beautiful gull, exquisitely colored, standing, the bird at least a foot long. Soaring just over the nest another graceful gull in the *act* of throwing a refractory young one that had left the nest and was floating away in the winds, back into the nest. The young bird was *in the air* half-way between the old bird's bill and the nest center. Loud applause greeted this wonderful view."[22]

In the fall of 1899, Roberts got the word out that he was interested in membership in the Long Meadow Gun Club. The gun club was a gentlemen's retreat on the shores of Long Meadow Lake, on the floodplain of the Minnesota River, upstream from Fort Snelling. The club had been in existence since 1884 and was housed in a rambling, two-storied frame lodge, spanned by a broad screen porch overlooking the lake. The yawning expanse of the Minnesota, with its quiet backwater sloughs and fens, attracted huge numbers of migrating waterfowl spring and fall. It was a duck hunter's paradise.

Inside the clubhouse were rooms where hunters could sleep overnight. The eight-mile drive out from Minneapolis took over an hour by horse and buggy, and hunters sometimes spent the night. Dark wooden lockers provided hunters a place to store their guns and gear. Women were allowed at the club but had to dress appropriately—in outdoor clothing, not dressed for a tea—and could under no circumstances carry a gun. Mixed parties, including children, often drove out in the spring and summer for Sunday dinner.

Membership in the exclusive club was limited. Roberts had to buy a share from someone willing to sell, but this proved no obstacle. By April 1900, in time for the breeding season, he received notification that he could go out to Long Meadow anytime.

Roberts was well acquainted with the floodplain of the Minnesota, which he had called "Minnesota Bottoms" as a boy. He and his father had taken many long drives out to the fort and the river below it, looking for birds. He knew many of the gun club members in 1900—they were in his social set in Minneapolis. Some were patients, others were longtime friends. Some he first met in public school. Over the years, he would visit the gun club at least once each fall for a day of duck hunting. All members recorded the number of ducks taken on a day's outing. Roberts was one of the very few who exactly enumerated the species shot. On October 10, 1900, for example, in the company of a fellow physician, he bagged two wigeons, two teal, and nine Ring-necked Ducks, which he called "blue bills."

His take for a day of hunting was always modest in comparison to many others. Where some would shoot 20 or 30 birds in a day, he would shoot 8 or 10. In 1904, he tallied 34 ducks over the entire season. Some members had taken as many as 150. Possibly, this was a result of his impossible schedule. Most years, he made it out to Long Meadow for only one or two days in October. But friends noted that he was not a voracious duck hunter. "He'd dream around in a boat and shoot an occasional duck, but he really went down there to study the yellow-winged [sic] blackbirds, their nesting and their habits," a friend observed.[23] Indeed, the first thing he did after securing membership was to launch a study of the brilliantly plumed Yellow-headed Blackbirds in May 1900.

For those acquainted only with Red-winged Blackbirds, their yellow-headed cousins strike observers as both gaudy and bizarre. Males brandish bright buttercup yellow heads and bibs. Females are only slightly less colorful. The males' song, charitably termed by Roberts as an "unbird-like effort," was later described by him like this: "[They strain] every nerve in an attempt that results . . . in a seemingly painful choking spell, which terminates in a long-drawn, rasping squeal that is nothing short of harrowing." He added, "It has always seemed as though some day a Yellowhead would be found that could sing the song they are all trying so hard to render, but thus far not a single note of the dreadful discord has been improved upon, and it always ends in the same disappointing failure."[24]

Nevertheless, the breeding colony at Long Meadow was compelling, if cacophonous, and occupied Roberts for two seasons. He spent long hours amid the dense reed beds locating many hundreds of nests and observing behavior. Some days he lugged the camera and tripod along to photograph nestlings. The raucous noise of singing males must have rung in his ears.

The second year of the study, 1901, he sent Mabel Densmore to the gun club to live for four weeks during the study. She served as a field assistant to Roberts and collected data on her own when he was not there.

The field season of 1900 was not solely devoted to the blackbirds at Long Meadow. After preliminary work on the yellowhead's natural history in spring, Roberts and Dart, later joined by Thomas Lee, an embryologist at the university and accomplished birder, traveled by train to Warren, Minnesota, in the northwestern corner of the state. Their goal was to collect birds in the remote area, focusing on Thief and Mud Lakes in eastern Marshall County. In his journal, Roberts described the region as "a vast sea-like expanse of meadow and marsh with islands of poplar here and there and farther eastward toward [the] lake, [a] tamarack swamp most of which was dead, only the bare poles standing over large areas, forming a scene most desolate."[25] This bleak wildland was part of the basin of Glacial Lake Agassiz.

The three bird collectors were accompanied by a local man, E. L. Brown, another of Roberts's cadre of observers and a well-known outdoors man in the small hamlet of Warren. Brown served as a guide not only to the wildland east of town but also to the isolated community of Warren, from whom the collecting party rented horses and a big, heavy wagon with which to haul supplies.

The midsummer weather of northwestern Minnesota was not hospitable. It was remarkably cold; at the end of the first stormy day, in a town without even a rude hotel, they slept on hay in a barn, next to the horses. The journey across the prairie had been interesting, though. The party had crossed the old Pembina trail, the route of the Métis with their oxcarts, cutting through groves of poplar, winding north to Winnipeg. Forty years after the Métis, Roberts was intrigued to find the trail still well marked and clearly defined.[26]

They reached Thief Lake on the second day, "just in time to get caught in a drenching rain storm," pitching the heavy canvas tent "in a perfect deluge of water and with an accompaniment of flash after flash of lightning and crash after crash of thunder." The storm thoroughly soaked the men and their equipment, but in this first test of wilderness camping, the party proved resilient. "All worked good naturedly and we put up the awning in the storm and then the stove (it had become jammed in some way and required a good deal of tinkering before it would go together) and soon had hot coffee and a good supper. I went with [the] team to a farm 1½ miles away and got a wagon full of hay, also milk and eggs and all this helped very much to make the night fairly comfortable after a drenching."[27]

Though the storms continued intermittently, Roberts set about the task at hand: recording the bird life, collecting specimens for documentation, and noting the habitat. With Dart, he encountered a small colony of Brewer's Blackbirds and the nest of a Traill's Flycatcher, as well as Clay-colored Sparrows, kingbirds, and Purple Martins. In one of the many tamarack swamps, they discovered the nest of a Broad-winged Hawk with three nestlings, and a week later, Roberts went back to photograph it:

[We] spent some hours trying to photograph the . . . hawk . . . she
was very shy and we waited over two hours before she returned
to the nest. Altogether we secured two exposures at the nest with
the concealed camera and two with the reflex on adjourning dead
tamaracks. I had left a dummy consisting of green focusing cloth
over some branches on camera stand in tree and my coat hanging
on limb at place (100 ft. distant) where it would be necessary to sit
in order to make exposures. This plan helped matters. The cloth and
coat were in position some days through all the storms we had.[28]

Hawk eggs hatch on consecutive days, resulting in nestlings of varying
sizes. The close watch of the nest allowed Roberts to observe how these
unevenly sized nestlings handled a large garter snake brought to the nest by
the mother bird. "She left the young to tear it up themselves. This the largest [nestling] proceeded to do, standing on it and tearing the head . . . off
first . . . the younger [did not seem] to get any share of the food."[29]

Possibly to promote the survival of all three nestlings, Roberts took the
oldest bird back to camp. There, it quickly became tame and readily ate the
bits of meat and other choice treats it was offered. Its presence only enhanced
the general masculine bonhomie of the rough and ready camp, with the big
canvas tent draped over a ridgepole, a kerosene lantern hung from a tree limb,
the heavy cast-iron cookstove, pairs of lace-up leather field boots tucked in
corners, and makeshift tables at which to skin dead birds and put up skins.

A story was told that on this trip or the return visit in 1901, Roberts and
Dart were called upon to use their medical skills unexpectedly. Though he
did not record the incident in his journal, apparently he and Dart got lost
while out collecting and stopped at a farm to ask directions. They found the
farm wife very ill with what they suspected to be severe appendicitis. Placing
her on the kitchen table and using the scalpel and forceps employed in putting up bird skins, they performed a successful appendectomy.[30]

If true—and the relater of the tale is generally reliable—it was not the
only case of appendicitis associated with Marshall County and the collecting expedition. Two weeks into the 1900 trip, in the remote northeastern
corner of the county, Roberts himself was stricken with apparent appendicitis. He prepared to leave immediately for Warren to catch the train home.
Suffering from abdominal pain, he endured a rough two days in a springless

farm wagon to get back to civilization.[31] This dire situation should have been a warning, but it was not.

In November 1901, as he prepared to leave home for the American Ornithologists' Union meeting in New York City, he again experienced severe abdominal pain. This time, he opted for an appendectomy. The procedure was still considered dangerous, with high risk of potentially fatal infection. Jennie sent a cable to the assembled ornithologists, first to inform them of the impending procedure and soon after to report he had survived the operation.

Many of the birdmen immediately wrote letters of concern and sympathy, but once Roberts was on the mend, William Brewster's assessment was common: "It must be a source of lasting comfort to know that one's appendix has been removed for sooner or later appendicitis comes to strike about every other man one knows and then thoughts of the danger of its occurrence when one is off in the wood beyond hope of medical or rather surgical aid is not pleasant to contemplate."[32]

In 1902, the entire Roberts family and John Nordquist spent the summer at Itasca State Park in north-central Minnesota. The children were ages thirteen, twelve, and ten, old enough to go on hikes and picnics and to help with fieldwork.

The land around the headwaters of the Mississippi River was declared Minnesota's first state park in 1891, but its protection was a slow, arduous process. Much of the land within park boundaries was privately owned and consisted of magnificent red and white pine stands. Although the federal government deeded over nearly seven thousand acres of forest, including ten miles of shoreline, to the new park, prominent lumbermen such as John S. and Charles A. Pillsbury and Frederick Weyerhaeuser demanded full compensation for the timber on lands within the park.[33] The state legislature only reluctantly agreed to provide funds for land acquisition.

A romantic aura surrounded the wellspring of the mighty river. The long search for the Mississippi's source inflamed the public's imagination, and despite a lack of roads and accommodations, 364 hearty tourists visited Itasca State Park in 1900.[34] At the time, there was a commissioner's residence, an elegant white frame house with gables and a mansard roof; several other two-story houses; and a small compound owned by Theodore Wegmann, situated on the east arm of Lake Itasca. Wegmann operated a store, which also housed the post office, and a couple of log cabins (one sporting a set of moose antlers over the entrance) that were grandly labeled a "hotel." Outside the store were several rough rocking chairs for tourists who wished to take in the view. The Wegmanns provided meals and lodging to park visitors. There were six miles of roads in the park and a saddle trail leading to the headwaters of the Mississippi River.

Postmaster and hotelier Wegmann wore many hats. He also served as game warden in the park and was busy, because poaching was rampant. Hunting and logging within park boundaries were banned from the onset, but the law was flagrantly ignored.

There were other indications of abused and misused land. Beavers, trapped in previous decades into obliteration, were gone. In 1901, three animals were brought in from Algonquin Provincial Park in Ontario and released on Schoolcraft Island, and they had survived. Park signs suffered from vandalism, an indication of local opposition to the park itself. But perhaps the greatest threat to the park, besides the pine logging, was that of a dam that had been constructed on the tiny Mississippi a half mile from its outlet. The flowage created by the dam threatened the pine forests on Lake Itasca's shores and would be the cause of a showdown between the park commissioner and the dam operators in 1903.[35]

Roberts brought his collector's shotgun, for which he would have needed a permit, and his camera. He photographed the red pines on "Preacher's Hill," Chamber's Creek, the nascent Mississippi, a small, rough bridge spanning its width, and farther downriver the effects of the dam on its flow. The Roberts children were captured dressed in hiking boots and brimmed hats, wearing sturdy jackets, riding in rowboats, and posing beside recently erected geological markers that attempted to impose order on the wilderness. Jennie, too, can be seen in photos, always wearing a fashionable hat, tilted at an angle, and stylish outfits.

As he methodically moved toward his lifelong goal of assembling a definitive account of Minnesota bird life, Roberts collected from each of the state's major ecosystems: the prairie and its wetlands (Heron Lake and surrounds), the boreal forest (Lake Vermilion), the aspen parklands of northwestern Minnesota (Marshall County), the mixed woods of north-central

Minnesota (Itasca), and the oak savannah and Big Woods remnants skirting Minneapolis and St. Paul. He also sent trusted ornithologists out to other areas: Frank Benner and Bert Gleason collected on the prairie of Lincoln County in 1897; Dart surveyed the Duluth harbor in winter 1900. In 1905, William Dutcher of the Audubon Societies inquired about the advisability of creating a sanctuary for the gull colony at Isle Royale in Lake Superior. Roberts sent Dart to assess the site.

Dart played another crucial and unique role in Roberts's bird work. In 1903, upon completion of his residency at St. Barnabas Hospital, he set up his medical practice at 1603 Fourth Avenue South, working out of Roberts's office and acting as his partner. That summer of 1903, Roberts was on the Mississippi and its tributaries, collecting and photographing. Dart remained in Minneapolis and saw Roberts's patients, most likely because he had not yet had time to build up his own patient population. Jennie and the children were also at home, just a hallway away from the office, and Dart often asked her whether sick patients needed a visit.[36] During the weeks Roberts was gone, Dart posted daily missives updating the physician on the status of his patients: a very sick patient had died; another was improving; the parents of a colicky baby did not trust the new doctor, and Dart felt hard-pressed to deal with the mother's "explosive nervous make-up."

In one letter, Dart closed with, "Mr. Kilgore will be glad to respond to a call from you at anytime and is anxious to join you."[37] Will Kilgore was a twenty-four-year-old clerk, son of a local lawyer, living at home and already possessing a keen interest in and knowledge of birds. He had met Roberts years before, as a student, when he had brought a dead hawk to the physician to identify. In summer 1903, the slim young man accompanied Roberts in and out of creek valleys in southeastern Minnesota, learning technique and helping in photography. He would mature into a trusted colleague in the decades to come.

For four field seasons, Roberts traveled to the southeastern corner of the state. Lake City was often his residential location, where he took a room at Brook Lodge. These were the years when Dart based his own practice at Roberts's office and covered for him when the older man was out on bird work. In 1907, when Dart moved his office to the Masonic Temple downtown, Roberts no longer took long weeks away from his medical practice.

After 1907, his medical records show his attendance at the delivery of many obstetric patients in June and July, the heart of the bird nesting season, an indication that he felt increasingly responsible to his obstetric cases.

As early as 1898, he had already pinpointed obstetric work as his true ball and chain in medicine. In a letter to a fellow photographer, he wrote, "I am hoping to be able to devote all of next June to bird photography, but if it is like most years, a few 'baby cases' that cannot be deserted will loom up before long and my hopes will be dashed. I am a general family practitioner that does by having 50% of my practice among personal friends." To this same sympathetic correspondent, he wrote late one night, when the house was quiet and the rest of the family slumbered, "I am now so desperately busy into professional work I haven't had time to eat or sleep. I do all my bird work at night—normally between 11:30 and 1 o'clock. It is now 'the small hours' and I shall have to [leave off] to prepare for a busy day tomorrow." In a third letter, he admitted to becoming "a bit discouraged." "I have been too busy of late to do more than dream of birds and photography, but am always looking for an 'empty day.' "[38]

~

CHAPTER 10

A Florida Interlude

> The Redstart is imbued with a spirit of unceasing
> activity.
>
> — *The Birds of Minnesota*, 2: 291

D r. Roberts leaned on the gunwale of the *Hildebret* and watched with delight as a large flock of Magnificent Frigatebirds dipped and rose over the silvery waters of Barnes Sound at the very tip of Florida. The enormous birds sailed above the mangroves, descended to the water's surface to pluck out unsuspecting fish, then lofted to ride the gentle breezes brushing the coastal expanse. The day before, he had admired a stunning flock of White Ibis, whose snowy feathers had gleamed under the subtropical sun as they wheeled in formation overhead. He and his companion, Jim Bell, had tried to photograph the exotic-looking birds but had only succeeded in shooting—with a gun, not a camera—two of them, which the physician had promptly turned into skins. The taxidermic effort had provided a bit of entertainment at just about the cocktail hour: "Skinned one of the ibises with an audience and assistance of our trained nurse between five and six o'clock," he later noted in his journal.[1]

Roberts was on medical duty on the yacht anchored off the coast of the Everglades. His patient, James Stroud Bell, the chief executive of Minneapolis's premier flour miller, the Washburn-Crosby Company, was in ill health. It seemed likely that a winter spent in Florida's sun and mild climate would be beneficial, but he was reluctant to leave his personal physician for months at a time. When the subject was broached, Roberts was amenable to leaving his practice during the snowy months of January, February, and March to accompany the Bells on their private yacht, and, when not working, to enjoy the astonishing avifauna of the Everglades.

The little party left Miami January 21, 1914. The Minnesotans on board were Bell and his wife, who had married the widowed Bell just two years earlier; her maid, Burrige; Bell's son, James Ford Bell; Stella Tennyson, the private nurse, who often assisted Roberts in his obstetrics work; and the good doctor. There were also an eight-man crew and a local guide, who would prove to have a colorful and unsavory past.

A chief amusement of the expedition was fishing. One quarry was the Spanish mackerel, for which they used crawfish or clawless lobster as bait. (The bait also provided a convenient lunch for the party the first day out, which Roberts pronounced as "excellent.") That day, they saw grouper and mullets and a shark. Brown Pelicans, cormorants, gulls, and terns winged overhead. Put-putting up Angel Creek in the rain, they encountered Little Blue and Louisiana Herons and a school of porpoises. A few days later, Roberts wrote in his journal that "the sea about the yacht last night was full of incandescent small creatures of some kind which flashed and twinkled like aquatic fireflies."[2]

Of the bird life, the pelicans were especially captivating. Big, boldly colored, and bizarre, the birds commanded the attention of all on board. "The pelicans when flying, with alternate flappings and sailings close over the water, carry their bills nearly in a line with their body with necks drawn in. . . . We have all found much entertainment in watching these huge birds which are always with us wherever we are," Roberts noted. At a fishing resort on Long Key, where the *Hildebret* docked to take on supplies, a young pelican "was so tame that it came fearlessly on the dock in answer to our call of 'Bill, Bill' accompanied by the display of a fish or white object resembling a fish. It permitted itself to be stroked or taken by the bill and waddled up and down the dock among the men and boats in a most fearless and comical manner. An amusing sight was to see it sitting contentedly but expectantly on the side of the dock close to someone fishing, waiting in the hope that the fish was to be turned over to him. . . . These birds are so grotesque and ungainly that there is a never ending fascination in watching them. As Mrs. B says, 'They have such long noses.' "[3]

Florida's unique avifauna, its mangroves and cypresses, palmettos and verdant keys were eye-opening to Roberts, who celebrated his fifty-sixth birthday on board the yacht. He had traveled very little—mostly to the American Ornithologists' Union meetings held in the big cities on the East Coast, and to Philadelphia to visit relatives. He had spent a month in Bermuda the year before, recuperating from overwork, and some years before that, had vacationed in Gulf Port, Mississippi, again as an antidote to stress, but had never gone to Europe and had seen little of the western national parks. Though his friends both at home and in the American Ornithologists' Union spent appreciable amounts of time vacationing in sunny climes, Roberts had never been able to pull himself away from the work that anchored him in Minnesota.

One night in the Keys, the men went fishing for tarpon, a prize game fish that gives anglers a thrilling fight as it is reeled in. The moon was out and lent the water a glistening sheen. Everyone was anxious that the ill Bell catch a tarpon, and he obliged them by hauling in a beautiful twenty-eight pounder. Jim Bell hooked one but lost it. Alas, Roberts caught only a small gray snapper. He later reflected, "It was a strange, weird way of fishing in this going back and forth over a course, dragging an invisible line right in the silvery path of the moonlight going away from the moon. The tarpon put up a good fight and it was an exciting time all in the semi-darkness, with a dim lantern flashed on the scene just at the finish."[4]

The group on board the *Hildebret* was convivial. When the seas were rough and the weather was windy or squally, they stayed on board, reading or writing letters. When they docked to take on supplies and pick up mail and stayed overnight, they often went out to the movies. At Key West, they took a stroll around town. The fastidious and proper Roberts was not impressed, describing it as "a very dirty, decayed and generally unsightly place outside government grounds . . . a southern, almost foreign look. [I] hear Spanish (Cuban) everywhere on streets."[5] The leisurely pace was perhaps too sedate for the young nurse, who confided in a postcard sent to a fellow nurse back home, "I wish you were along to keep me company. Dr. R. is fine company, but he is busy with the men most of the time."[6]

Leaving Key West, the *Hildebret* crossed a choppy Florida Bay with an aim to fish the inland waterway of the west coast. Almost immediately, Roberts commented on a dearth of birds in his journal—and on the mosquitoes, which "descended upon the yacht at sundown and were a great annoyance. They are little fellows but bite and behave just like their larger brethren."[7]

Disappointed in the poor fishing, they left Ten Thousand Islands for East Cape Sable. This was the infamous region in which a warden hired by the Audubon Societies to protect a bird sanctuary was murdered by a plume hunter only nine years earlier, in 1905. Roberts related the story, as told to him by the local guide, Joe. Joe "sympathized with [the poacher] saying the warden had the 'big head' . . . and that . . . the [poacher] shot in self defense." Roberts was skeptical of this account and scribbled a reminder to himself in the journal to "look up evidence at time." He added in the journal, "Joe . . . is 'one of them.' His brother is a plume hunter and his brother-in-law had a pair of wings of a Roseate Spoonbill killed only a few days before in the boat in which we were fishing."[8]

To a bird lover, this brief encounter with Florida Bay's bloody recent past must have been an indescribable experience. Roberts had been intimately involved from the earliest days with the Association of Audubon Societies, had seen the graphic photos of piles of dead birds, birds killed by the tens of thousands for their frilly, showy, or colorful feathers, and personally knew the people who had hired the unfortunate warden who became a martyr to the cause. Nonetheless, when Joe left them a week later, his term of service over, the Bells and Roberts were sorry to see him go. He had been a knowledgeable and observant guide, providing a bit of insight into a way of life that was truly exotic to the northerners.

With the departure of the guide, the focus on board changed from sport fishing to socializing. Roberts had celebrated his birthday at Miami by going to the movies in the evening with the younger Bells and Mrs. Stroud Bell—Roberts's patient had not been well enough to leave the yacht. Then, the *Hildebret* hauled anchor and made her way to Palm Beach, where the entire party spent two weeks in the Royal Poinciana Hotel, the gargantuan resort built on Lake Worth as a winter retreat for America's wealthy in the Gilded Age. The six-story, Georgian-style hotel had greenhouses and porticos, rooms to accommodate two thousand guests, and three miles of hallway, down which bellhops rode bicycles to deliver messages. The grounds were lush with palms and showy gardens.

When the Bell party disembarked for their fortnight, the Royal Poinciana was in its heyday. They met other Minneapolitans in residence—the Franklin Crosbys, the John Crosbys, and Charles Pillsbury, among others. Yet, these two weeks were perhaps Roberts's least favorite. He ceased his journal entries and wrote a terse postcard to his son Tom: "[The Royal Poinciana is] a memorable place to look on and see idle humanity trying how to 'outdo others.' No place for the serious mind or one who cannot play its game with skill and finesse. . . . [Money] goes at a pretty quick pace here. So the shekels fly." His next sentence reveals the unspoken social gap between patient and doctor: "Mr. Bell seems at home here and different, saying more than anything I have [seen] thus far."[9]

Roberts did make one comment on Lake Worth, the great shallow lagoon on which the Royal Poinciana was built: its surface was covered with migratory scaup!

When the party reboarded the yacht, they headed north of Palm Beach, into the country of the famous Indian River. The birding was good on the shoals of the river, and Roberts resumed his journal, recording hundreds of scaup, cormorants, and ospreys, kingfishers and pelicans, and four species of heron—which must have been particularly gratifying, since it was the herons that had been especially targeted for their feathers, and many species had been at the brink of extinction. The landscape on the east coast was different from the Everglades. There were small live oaks and what he termed "cabbage palmettos," a stocky native palm, and few mangroves. He and Jim Bell took a dingy and poked about the backwaters for an hour, encountering a number of "snake birds" (anhingas) and long-braked clams on the shore.

Farther north, the *Hildebret* docked at Ormond, where Roberts met up with Frank Chapman, on vacation from the American Museum of Natural History in New York. Chapman and his wife vacationed in Ormond each winter, and Roberts and Chapman had arranged to spend a few days together. Roberts allowed his friend to show him the sights: the golf course (where he saw John D. Rockefeller playing the links); a palmetto scrub, where they caught sight of a pair of "famous" Florida Jays; and another good birding area, where they racked up a nice little list of songbirds. Jim Bell and Roberts spent some time with the movie camera, too, making motion pictures of Laughing and Bonaparte's Gulls. They took turns, one man throwing bread into the air to entice the gulls in to them, the other cranking away, recording the action on film.

At Jacksonville, they reentered the jarring commotion and bustle of an urban area, after two months of what Roberts termed the "more secluded civilization" of the southern coast. Jacksonville enjoyed a booming lumber trade, with extensive yards and wharves, as opportunists homed in on the valuable big cypress stands.

Beyond Jacksonville were numerous orange groves that enchanted the northerners. Roberts wrote, "All [were] in full blossom just now, present[ing] a feature of special pleasure as we went along and the delightful fragrance filled the air over the course we followed. The entire boat inside and out was thus filled with this sweet odor." Here, too, they passed long stretches of logged-over swampland, described by Roberts: "All this country was once the site of extensive cypress grove swamps, but it has been timbered over long ago and all the large trees cut out so that only the smaller ones and recent growth remain."[10]

As March wore on, the first signs of spring appeared. Shad were running in the streams, and fishermen seined them, securing thousands in a day. Roberts detected the first frog chorus. The cypress trees showed pale green, feathery leaves, and the oaks seemed brighter, despite the festoons of hanging moss. The ubiquitous cabbage palms, however, had become "wearisome to look at, they remind one of great disorderly mops standing upside down on their handles."[11] Bell was not much improved, having good days and bad days, sometimes able to venture out to explore the small towns they passed, sometimes too ill to leave his bed.

In mid-April, the Florida sojourn was over. The elder Bells remained in Virginia with the nurse, and Roberts took the train home. He arrived with only a month to settle in before marrying off his daughter to Joseph Seybold. Catharine was the first child to leave the nest.

It would seem to have been the natural time for Roberts to make the leap into another life after his time in Florida. He had successfully been away from his practice for three and a half months, and stars had not fallen from the sky. His children were grown and anticipating the future. He had perhaps worked out a satisfactory arrangement with the Bells as a physician held on retainer. The spring field season loomed in front of him—indeed, he thought he detected a change in the avifauna during those last days in Florida—the birds were already winging their way north to Minnesota's forests.

But it did not happen. He and Jennie hosted a wedding, yes, but he then went back to his practice, delivering seven babies in the months remaining in 1914 and drawing consternation from a few friends in the American Ornithologists' Union, who had fully expected him to "retire" from medical work and were dismayed to learn that the stork had, once again, upset his plans.

In 1915, however, the stars aligned. He had managed to not take on any more obstetric cases and delivered his last baby in May of that year. Bell died in April—perhaps that was a release for the conscientious physician, as well—and by August, he had a new work address in Millard Hall at the University of Minnesota. He and Jennie moved out of the big house and medical office at 1603 Fourth Avenue South, where they had lived for twenty-five years, bought a duplex at 2303 Pleasant Avenue in south Minneapolis, and moved into the comfortable upper apartment—a home that did not have, and would never have, an exam room.

CHAPTER 11

The Associate Curator

> In form and general appearance Franklin's Gull closely
> resembles Bonaparte's Gull, but on closer inspection
> it will be found to be possessed of an exquisite beauty
> all its own.
>
> — *The Birds of Minnesota*, 1: 550

Thomas Roberts was ready to tear his hair out. In the August heat of 1915, he stood in a storage room in Pillsbury Hall on the University of Minnesota campus. The air was heavy with dust and humidity, and insect pests fluttered all around, signifying disaster. The Dall sheep skins collected by Jim Bell were infested with bugs feasting on their skin and hair, and someone had left open the box containing them. Winged creatures had escaped and were attacking the bird skins and other mounted specimens in the room. The scourge was everywhere—in every box Roberts had opened, chewing on every feathered object mounted for display in glass cases. Someone had ineffectually tried to contain the infestation by strewing about a few mothballs, but, as Roberts grimly noted, the loathsome creatures were enjoying the joke.

This was to have been the week when he moved into his new office on the second floor of Millard Hall—temporary digs in the medical school, awaiting the completion of the new Animal Biology Building. Arriving home from Lake of the Woods after a summer's research trip, he had thought about the office, his new place of work at the University of Minnesota, about setting up his library, making space for his bird movies, organizing a desk. Now it would all have to be delayed while he tackled the bugs. It would take a week, working with an assistant and laboring every day, to disinfect every skin and hermetically seal every box and case. It was, he assured his friend and new boss Henry Nachtrieb, "a big and nasty job" but absolutely necessary to save the skins.

Thank goodness his own bird skins, all six thousand of them, were not anywhere near Pillsbury Hall! He had been renting space for his collection, and Frank Benner's, too, in Emma's Handicraft Guild Building downtown, since the collections had become too large to keep at home. He was waiting for space in the new building—space he could oversee and guard from the kind of sloppy oversight that had led to the sprawling mess that August.

He was fifty-seven years old. Had he made the right decision to close his medical practice and throw his lot with the Natural History Survey at the university? His American Ornithologists' Union friends thought so. "This is great news, and I am sure that you will never regret the step it called for," an exuberant Frank Chapman wrote from the American Museum of Natural History in New York. Chapman must have been privy to Roberts's doubts, for his comments were written to buoy his friend's spirits: "This is not retiring; it's [a] change of occupation. Now you will have an opportunity to do a fine thing for your state both curatorially and as an author. I rejoice with you in the opportunities which now on every hand invite you."[1]

Roberts's American Ornithologists' Union traveling companion, Ruthven Deane of Chicago, always a source of bird-world gossip, also had his ear to the Minnesota grapevine: "I hear you have now resigned from your medical practice, entered the University of Minnesota, as Professor of Zoology, and can now devote your time to ornithology, finish up the 'Birds of Minnesota,' go duck shooting, play golf and [have] a good time generally—I hope this is all true and I should be glad to have you O.K. it."[2]

But such gleeful missives were sent before the infestation in the bird room. The mess was a stark contrast to his tidy, orderly medical office, and it must have caused Roberts further misgivings, for a week later, he received a consoling letter from Chapman: "I can fully understand the twinge which must accompany the change from old to new conditions, but once you are fully established I am sure you will not regret a single step which you have taken."[3]

Roberts could not have made the unconventional transfer from a medical practice to an academic position but for the cordial, genuine friendships that he had cultivated over years. Nachtrieb, head of the Zoological Division of the Minnesota Natural History Survey and de facto curator of the natural history museum, had long considered him Minnesota's foremost bird authority. Nachtrieb also wore the hat of chairman of the Department of Animal Biology, the department that Roberts would join.

Many years had intervened since Roberts and Nachtrieb had worked together as land examiners. They had been young bucks in their twenties then, camping out and enduring the rigors of fieldwork together. The two had maintained a warm friendship in the decades since.

Nachtrieb's boss, university president George Vincent, knew Roberts, too. Roberts had taught at the medical school in the first few years of Vincent's tenure as president. Vincent received a letter of support for the addition of Roberts to the Natural History Survey staff from Dr. Will Mayo, a university regent, who also knew the physician personally.

A crucial part of the timing for Nachtrieb and Roberts was the promise of a new building to house the zoology department and the museum. Nachtrieb knew of the doctor's vision and wanted him to have input in the design and the space needed to house an expanding bird collection.[4] The incipient new building, more than any other single event, probably dictated when Roberts left his practice.

But there was another consideration, one that perhaps Roberts did not share with even his closest friends: he felt the clock was ticking. The men in the Roberts family—his grandfather, his uncle, his own father—did not live much past seventy; he expected to be like them.[5] He was nearing sixty. There were not many years left in which to make his mark in the bird world and produce his comprehensive book on Minnesota birds. Soon after his birthday, he spoke with Nachtrieb, and Nachtrieb started the wheels turning that would lead to Roberts's joining the Department of Animal Biology at the university.

Finding money to support Roberts's fieldwork and collection efforts proved to be the greatest hurdle for him to overcome in making the switch. The board of regents unanimously elected him as professor of ornithology in the Department of Animal Biology and as associate curator of the Zoological Museum in May 1915, but they failed to attach a salary to the positions.[6] Instead, they promised they would make "every effort" two years hence to make the positions paid ones.

It was Roberts's wealthy friends who stepped forward to foot the bill for his work at the nascent museum and, the next year, solicited funding for his collection trip in northern Minnesota. Chief among these donors was James Ford Bell, whose generosity and deep interest in Minnesota natural history had previously led him to fund research trips for other professors.

To underwrite Roberts's summer collection trips, another friend, George Partridge of the dry goods firm Wyman-Partridge, sent letters out to twenty prominent businessmen, asking the majority to contribute $100 and a core group to donate $250 (the Mayos of Rochester were included in the latter. The brothers contributed, adding that they would make a "strenuous effort to have the next legislature continue the work in the proper manner").[7] Most contributed to the "Dr. Thomas Roberts Zoological, or ornithological, or whatever ological fund it is," as one backer put it, enclosing his check.[8] Partridge wrote to Roberts, who was already at work in the field at Heron Lake, that he had secured $2,500 for that field season, and remarked on Roberts's wealth of "strong friendships." Nearly everyone "expressed their admiration for what is termed your 'rather eccentric makeup.'"[9] But the funding was given to further the museum and its collection—Roberts would work without a salary for the first four years.

The year 1915 was a watershed for Roberts. In the spring, he closed his medical practice, reserving as patients only a few special families that kept him on retainer; in summer, after the field season, he moved his office to the university and assumed curatorial duties; in the fall, he took what Bell termed "the final step" and sold the big, sprawling house and medical office at 1603 Fourth Avenue South.[10] He and Jennie bought a duplex home on fashionable Pleasant Avenue in south Minneapolis. Their near neighbors included Amos Abbott, Thomas's medical mentor in his youth, and his wife. The Robertses, with their two grown sons, moved into the upper apartment, which was spacious and included living quarters for domestic help. The lower apartment was rented out, providing income they could rely on in the first uncertain years that Roberts was at the university and not drawing a salary.

In November 1915, his daughter, Catharine, added to the shifting status of the elder Robertses by making them grandparents. Catharine Lyon Seybold was born on November 10, at home, a few blocks from 2303 Pleasant Avenue. Dr. Roberts was not the attending physician.

In the next few years, his married children would move several times but always to homes within walking distance of 2303 Pleasant, which became a hub of familial activity, as the house on South Fourth had been. Emma Roberts, too, remained intimately involved with the clan. Never married, trained as a watercolorist under Childe Hassam in New York, and established as a

Minneapolis artist, Emma became the supervisor of drawing for the Minneapolis public schools in the early 1900s. Her real recognition, though, came with her formation of the Handicraft Guild, an organization supporting the Arts and Crafts movement that became nationally known—and whose building harbored Roberts's valuable bird skins. So immersed was she in the Arts and Crafts movement, that years before Roberts's move to south Minneapolis, she built a house on the outer edges of the city, near Minnehaha Creek, that showcased the guild's artists. But it was only a streetcar ride to the busy Roberts household, where she was present for celebrations and outings.

The move to 2303 Pleasant Avenue was at once symbolic and practical. As an embodiment of his new life, it was the first family home that did not have a medical exam room in it; practically, this meant that would-be patients could no longer come to him—he had no office. He would be the one deciding how much he would work as a physician and how much he would pursue his lifelong love affair with birds.

The University of Minnesota that Roberts returned to in 1915 was flourishing under the ministrations of an excellent president, George Edgar Vincent. Brilliant, energetic, and likable, Vincent had taken the presidential reins from the venerable Cyrus Northrop, who had served as president for twenty-seven years (still the longest-serving president in the history of the school). At the time, enrollment at the university was six thousand students, and though it did not increase much in his tenure, the graduate school nearly tripled in size. Vincent abolished the requirement of daily chapel attendance, reworked the university budget, and reformed most of the colleges, including the law and medical schools.

When Vincent arrived on campus, the heart of the university was the Knoll, where Old Main had been erected and Roberts had taken undergraduate classes. The imposing Romanesque structure of Pillsbury Hall, housing the sciences, was twenty years old, but the mall was a mere twinkle in the board of regents' eye. Across the street from the fortress-like Armory—where the Bell Museum of Natural History would one day stand—was a military parade ground.

Already, though, the university was pushing south beyond Washington Avenue. Elliot Hospital, which Roberts had helped site, was admitting the sick, and Millard Hall was training medical doctors. The Animal Biology Building, a yawning hole with girders and rebar forming a skeletal frame in the summer of 1915, staked another claim of the university at the corner of Washington Avenue and Church Street, where streetcars clattered and clanged, carrying riders between Minneapolis and St. Paul. Frame houses, remnants of the residential neighborhood upon which the university was encroaching, stood between the new Animal Biology Building and Elliot. The school had plans to take over and demolish these, as opportunity presented itself.

Professor Roberts's quarters in Millard Hall were necessary, since the zoology department, housed on Pillsbury's third floor, had long ago outgrown its space. Small though it was, the office was Roberts's toehold on the university that first year. He initially felt uneasy that the medical school might renege on its loan of it and wrote to Nachtrieb that he would "fight to the finish" to keep the space and intended to "lie low" until the medical school was in session, for fear it would reclaim the space.[11]

To the professors and students who would soon occupy the new Animal Biology Building, it may have seemed that the building, so long hoped for, was the last hurrah of the prewar years. It had been an era of expansion and optimism, but by 1915, the European Great War had already cast its shadow over an America that was trying hard to stay out of it.

Nevertheless, with the building going up across Church Street, Associate Curator Roberts set about establishing a genuine natural history museum. One of his first acts was to hire a taxidermist, Jenness Richardson, who was highly recommended by Frank Chapman. Though only in his twenties, Richardson had worked at the up-and-coming natural history museum in Denver and at Chapman's American Museum of Natural History.[12] He had been on a collecting trip to Africa and had both field and photography experience. Jenness was about the age of the Robertses' own young adult sons, and Thomas and Jennie took the bachelor under their wing in his first months in Minneapolis, entertaining him and helping him get established.[13]

To do taxidermy, Richardson needed supplies. The associate curator put in requests for purchases of cotton, glue, peroxide, arsenic, alum, absolute alcohol, and beeswax. He ordered display cases to exhibit small groupings of birds in the new building. He investigated obtaining biological material from the estate sale of the venerable taxidermist Henry Howling of East Minneapolis, whose curiosity shop—previously owned by Howling's father, William—he had haunted as a teen. He tried to buy silk wire from a New York City firm that made artificial flowers but found they did not have the necessary filament. Glass eyes were hard to come by. The European war had caused shortages, because German eyes could not be imported. Luckily, a Denver firm was able to provide him with eyes for mountain sheep, deer, mountain goat, coyote, bobcat, and bald eagles.[14]

After obtaining permission from the board of regents, the new associate curator threw out a large part of what had formed the old museum, dead animals that had been badly prepared and poorly maintained. With fine alliteration, he considered them "pathetic and moth-eaten mockeries of Minnesota animals."[15]

The working museum's collection of bird skins, those that Roberts had personally collected and would soon house at the new building, was sizable. Now, Roberts turned his attention to a collection representing the state's mammals. He sought advice from Vernon Bailey, the chief naturalist for the federal Biological Survey of the U.S. Department of Agriculture in Washington, D.C. Bailey, hailing from Elk River, Minnesota, described the features of good small mammal traps, sent pamphlets on the basics of fieldwork to educate Roberts's cadre of incipient trappers, and offered to spend a few days in the field with them, to make sure the collection got properly established.

In addition to this start-up work, Roberts found time to write. His monograph "The Winter Bird-Life of Minnesota" appeared in the December 1915 issue of *Fins, Feathers and Fur,* the publication of the Minnesota Game and Fish Department. The report, illustrated with his own photographs, was the first compilation of bird records reported to him by his many observers from across the state. There was great demand for reprints, and he sent out dozens, if not hundreds of them, many requested by public school teachers.

In June 1916, while Roberts photographed birds at Heron Lake, the faculty of Animal Biology moved their bookcases, desks, and lab equipment out of Pillsbury Hall and into the spacious brick-and-stone building down the road, near the medical school. It was a glorious facility, with ample lab space, a herbarium on the south end of the basement level, and an aquarium running along the west side that could be viewed by the public from without.

The associate curator was given two office spaces, which he promptly filled with his bird collection. He also took control over the rooms allotted to the natural history museum.

Bell had helped plan the new building. Although he was already a top executive at Washburn-Crosby Company, he had accompanied Nachtrieb on visits to the University of Wisconsin's museum and the Field Museum in Chicago to garner ideas. The original plan dedicated the entire third floor to a natural history museum. Bell had previously written to Nachtrieb to advise that space be included for Roberts's bird collection and also that Roberts be formally appointed curator of birds—shrewdly observing to Nachtrieb that "Roberts has so many devoted friends who have money, the department will prosper with Roberts in it."[16] The Bell presence loomed so large in the planning, in fact, that President Vincent felt compelled to write a letter to the enthusiastic benefactor, stating explicitly that Animal Biology would be first and foremost an educational facility to serve the needs of the department.[17]

A professorial Dr. Roberts, wearing owlish spectacles and dressed formally in a three-piece, blue serge suit with a pocket watch's gold chain spanning his ample abdomen, pondered the woodland caribou. A large buck sporting a magnificent rack, his head lowered in an aggressive posture, confronts a young male with small antlers. Nearby, a doe and her fawn view the incipient contest. The Newfoundland spruce bog, in muted hues of moss and ochre, seems to murmur with a breath of air. A viewer might hear a snort or the rustle of dry grass as a heavy hoof stomps a warning. But these caribou, ensconced in a floor-to-ceiling glass display case, are frozen in combat forever and lit by electric light resembling diffuse sunlight.

The woodland caribou diorama was the first of several that Roberts had planned for the new museum. This debut exhibit was actually not new. The animals had been collected years earlier in Newfoundland by Bell, and the entire diorama displayed at Pillsbury Hall. When the new Animal Biology Building opened, the whole display had been carted down Church Street— the first of what would become several moves.

Now that there was actually space in a new hall, Roberts allowed himself to think big, and the big-game hunters on the Washburn-Crosby Company's executive board helped him in the effort. The Dall sheep exhibit got under way. The ram, ewe, and young had been collected in Alaska by Jim Bell, and he had given them to the university in memory of his father. A third exhibit, featuring white-tailed deer, went into the planning stage. Fred Atkinson, a vice president at Washburn-Crosby, became responsible for bringing in the animals; Charles Corwin, a nationally prominent muralist, signed on to paint the background. Roberts and taxidermist Richardson thought that beavers might make another suitable display and began considering black bear as well.

But Roberts also thought small. Even as the huge dioramas were being sketched out, he arranged for small groups of backyard birds to be displayed in cases that hung on the wall. He was a stickler for detail. In one display, he needed a section of a pine trunk for a display of Pine Grosbeaks. Specifically, he wanted a jack pine trunk, and he wanted it from east-central Minnesota, where the birds had been collected. He enlisted one of his observers to saw off a piece of a trunk and send it to the university on the train.[18]

Roberts never thought of himself as an artist imagining these scenes. Unlike Emma, he had never picked up a brush, had never fashioned a wax leaf or flower. He might have argued that the honest depiction of nature was artistry enough, and if he were true to that world, he and the general public, his audience, would find it pleasing. But the dioramas that followed would belie that modesty. Both the displays and his photographic work revealed an artistic eye that put him in league with artistic Emma.

In fall 1916, his second year at the museum, Roberts started up a program of Sunday afternoon movies at the museum, with the assistance of a new movie projector bought by Bell. A fan of Hollywood's silent films, Roberts knew how engaging they could be. The museum offerings were aimed at families and featured charismatic animals such as the Victoria penguin and the bull sea elephant. Roberts could not be on hand for the first viewing, so President Vincent was present to make introductory remarks. Later shows sometimes featured Roberts's own motion pictures, for by now he had added a motion picture camera to his field equipment. *Home Life of Minnesota Birds* was especially popular, and Roberts would travel to smaller communities around Minnesota, showing the films at public libraries and school auditoriums. Roberts's films were well crafted, and Jim Bell suggested that he consider selling them as a way to fund his museum work—since the university monies were not forthcoming.[19]

Dioramas, mounted birds set in native habitats, wildlife movies—the new natural history museum under Roberts's ministration was flourishing, but educational efforts are worthless unless the public knows about them. In spring 1917, Roberts mounted a publicity campaign to drum up enthusiasm for the museum. The university's newspaper, the *Minnesota Daily*, ran an article on what the new building along Washington Avenue had to offer, and in a glossy, sophisticated monthly magazine, *The Minnesotan*, Roberts's unique personal story of leaving his successful practice to work at the museum for no salary was highlighted, accompanied by striking black-and-white photos of a few of the displays and of the associate curator at work. In the article, he told the author, "We want the people of Minnesota to come to our new museum; we want it to be one of the sought-for sights of Minneapolis, like the American Museum of Natural History in New York and the Field Museum in Chicago."[20]

Emphasizing the common bond of nature and art between the Roberts siblings, that same issue of *The Minnesotan* featured photos of Emma Roberts's house, with its Arts and Crafts elements of a tiled landscape in the fireplace and an original watercolor of trees and water over the mantel. Brother and sister knew how to use the media to promote their causes.[21]

The March 1917 issue of *The Minnesotan* with articles on a natural history museum and an Arts and Crafts house is a poignant one, for on April 6, only a few weeks after the magazine hit the newsstands, the United States entered the Great War, which had been raging in Europe for over two years. Life changed forever. President Woodrow Wilson initiated the first military draft since the Civil War, taking young male Minnesotans away by the tens of thousands. The Roberts boys, Tom and Carroll, were twenty-eight and twenty-three, respectively. Tom enlisted in the army and served as a lieutenant, based on the East Coast near New York. Carroll, in the Chicago area at the time, was also based in the East. Neither would see action in France, a circumstance for which the elder Robertses must have been profoundly grateful, for 3,480 Minnesotans would never return from the war.[22]

Too old to enlist and not inclined toward outward display of patriotic fervor, Roberts nonetheless did his part for the war effort. Among other activities, he joined his friends and about a hundred other men for the "Tuesday Night Roll Call," rolling bandages for the Red Cross.

The war drained off men and funds from the university almost immediately. Like other museum curators, Roberts pared down his summer fieldwork. At Itasca State Park he banded birds and did some collecting with his 22-gauge rifle. Jennie joined him at Douglas Lodge for the summer, and for two weeks, they hosted Will Kilgore, who as a youth had collected with Roberts. The Robertses had known the shy introvert for many years. In 1917, he was in his late thirties and unmarried. When first invited to Itasca by the Robertses, Will demurred, writing it "would [not] be right," but later reconsidered. He had a memorable time assisting in fieldwork and tramping through the woods in his first visit to the park. In thanking them later, he wrote that he was glad he could visit "this historic place as I have somehow always connected your name with Itasca."[23]

Kilgore was correct in associating the Roberts family with Itasca State Park. For a number of years, it was a summer home to them. The plan to buy an island off Isle Royale never came to fruition. Instead, the Robertses made frequent use of a cabin at Douglas Lodge, and the red pines and the sparkling waters of the headwaters became one place on earth where Roberts could step outside the demands of his work life and relax.[24]

But of course, the line between work and play for Roberts was thin. In 1917, he had another interest at Itasca—the reintroduced beavers, whose numbers had expanded so prodigiously. Charles Corwin, the muralist who had done the caribou background, stayed at the new School of Forestry at the park in June and did preliminary sketches of the scenery and the beavers' dam on Nicollet Creek: a diorama of beavers was in the works. Later, young beavers from northern Minnesota were livetrapped and brought to the university and placed in the zoology building's aquarium, for the viewing pleasure of museum visitors. The playful little beavers were a hit with the public. The museum's secretary wrote to Roberts that "the beavers are having a good time and are certainly attracting much interest" and that they were "growing fast and get tamer every day."[25]

Museum secretary Clara Carney's newsy letters to her boss give a lively picture of life at the museum that first summer of war. Writing from Animal Biology, she related the presence of a "nice B. oriole's nest" just behind the building, informed him that the janitor let the captive sparrow hawks starve to death because he thought no one would pay for the food (that must have caused Roberts to gnash his teeth), and added that someone "brought a nice hoary bat to your office last week." She knew of a possible "observer" for Roberts in Traverse County, and her nest and egg inventory of museum holdings was coming along well.[26]

Soon after coming to the university, Roberts was called upon to perform the other job bestowed on him, that of "Professor of Ornithology." He was assigned to teach a class on birds and was not enthusiastic about the prospect. The thought of it made him feel used up, as if teaching was the last resort of a researcher no longer able to go into the field. Nachtrieb, his boss, who loved teaching, briskly replied (in his unique spelling): "Don't get so workt up about settling 'down to be a teacher' at yur time of life. My, but yu must hav felt old when yu rote that! Yu don't seem to know what an excellent teacher yu ar and how privilegd yu ar. There is no scheme that wil make yu only a teacher. I supposed a doctor, I mean a good doctor like yourself, always was quite a teacher."[27]

On the first Tuesday of spring term, February 3, 1916, Professor Roberts strode into the lecture hall and faced his new students—five women and a single man.[28] The class ran Tuesday and Thursday afternoons from two o'clock until five o'clock, lecture and lab in the "long room" that was the repository of anything avian—skins, mounted birds not being displayed, skeletons, feathers. Enrollment in the course was limited to ten, and in the early years, it was mostly coeds studying to be teachers who signed up. This was especially so in the war years, when men were scarce on campus. The first seventeen lectures covered the evolution of birds, a discussion of the fossil *Archaeopteryx*, the anatomy of feathers and skeleton, and a discourse on bird families—a standard course in ornithology.

But beginning in April, students were in the field every class period. In a three-hour time slot, they were limited in where they could go and utilized the streetcar. The young women headed out into the field dressed in nautical middy blouses and skirts and broad-brimmed hats, and binoculars hung around their necks. When birding near campus, they visited the river bluffs on the east bank of the Mississippi. Later, they tromped under the Lake Street Bridge and in Washburn Park, a large parcel of undeveloped land where the

present-day high school stands. Pearl Lake, now a park, and the Long Meadow
Gun Club were other favorites. One Saturday, the class went out to Frank and
Marie Commons's farm on Lake Minnetonka to observe their bird-banding
operation, to see what got caught in the traps and how a band was placed on
a tiny leg.[29] Nothing captivates a new bird-watcher more than being able to
actually hold a delicate, softly feathered creature in one's hand.

Half a century had flown by since Roberts had learned the birds in his favorite haunts on what was then the outskirts of the city. All but the gun club
had fallen to development and the rapid expansion of an urban population.
In the interim, he had had to find new spots to introduce a new generation
to the beauty of birds.

The small classes fostered an intimacy between the young women and
their professor. Jennie, too, was pulled into the circle, as she accompanied
the class on some of their outings. One can imagine the Robertses enjoying the company of young people, with their own children gone, at war, or
married with small children. That first year, even Emma became involved
in class activities. Her house near Minnehaha Creek was a perfect meeting
place, from which the class walked to Washburn Park, and from there to
Pearl Lake, and back to Emma's along the creek banks. The first time Roberts
planned such an outing, though, it started raining early on, and the class, instead, stayed indoors in the elegant Arts and Crafts house, reviewing thrush
study skins, eating supper, and then watching a slide show and listening to
a talk on migration—always the lecture up the sleeve in the event of rain.

After leaving the university for teaching posts all over Minnesota, many
students corresponded with their former teacher, asking for bird-related
teaching material, telling him of their efforts in forming after-school bird
clubs, and reminiscing fondly about the "family feeling" of their bird class.
They often held reunions, and some classes passed around a round-robin
letter. One former student, teaching in Idaho, had compared notes with a
friend who had taken Joseph Grinnell's class at Berkeley and told Roberts
that she felt her class under him was much better, specifically because of the
field experience.[30]

The war intensified in 1918. The draft, which in 1917 had applied to men
twenty-one to thirty years old, was extended to men eighteen to forty-five.
This created a huge influx, an overwhelming number too big to handle. Fort

Snelling was once again housing military men, and the university became the site of the Student Army Training Corps, based on the farm campus in St. Paul but swamping both campuses.

Minnesota had other disasters to manage. In September, the towns of Cloquet and Moose Lake transformed into a maelstrom of flames, as fire swept through the slash of clear-cuts, leaving fifty-two thousand people injured or without homes. The state had just begun to address the devastation caused by the fires when the deadly Spanish influenza struck in October. The virus seemed to affect young people most severely. The first cases broke out at the training corps at the university, and these were transported to Fort Snelling for care. Within two weeks, Minneapolis recorded ninety-nine deaths, and an additional seventy-five occurred in St. Paul.

Minneapolis city fathers took drastic measures to stem the flood of flu. Church services were all canceled; theaters, dance halls, and other meeting places were closed indefinitely. Roberts was the chairman of the Influenza Committee of the local Red Cross, and Jennie, too, was involved in the effort to prevent the spread of the deadly disease as a member of the Public Health Committee of the civic-minded Women's Club. But the doctor himself fell ill in mid-October, possibly from flu—at some point, the family contracted the illness. From October through December 1918, there were seventy-five thousand cases of influenza in Minnesota out of a population of about two million people. About one in ten died, the largest death rate in the history of the state, the only time period when deaths outstripped births.

In a month of turmoil in Minneapolis, Thomas and Jennie received their own personal tumultuous news: son Tom had married Dorothy Reaser of Yonkers, New York, in a ten-day, whirlwind courtship.[31] The elder Robertses were far too pressed to attend the wedding.

Then suddenly, the war was over, and almost as suddenly, soldiers began returning. The American Ornithologists' Union met that month, as always; it was a year in which Roberts did not attend. He was told he had not missed much: "too much peace in the air!"[32]

Although the world focused on the Great War and events in Europe, for bird-watchers and others concerned about nature, there was both great satisfaction and great anxiety at home on the domestic front during the war years.

Legislation protecting migratory songbirds finally became reality with

the ratification of the Migratory Bird Treaty Act of 1918, still the primary legislation protecting songbirds today. A treaty safeguarding North America's
migratory birds had been several years in the making and had survived after
legal challenge.[33] It was long overdue; songbirds were still routinely shot for
target practice.

It was not only songbirds that were beleaguered in that era. The Greater-
Prairie Chicken and Sharp-tailed Grouse were nearing extinction, and possibly the Wild Turkey as well. Roberts was called upon to document their
status in Minnesota and report on the decline.[34] All were popular game
birds. Nonetheless, on September 24, 1916, Roberts read a letter before the
hunting/private conservation society, the Game Protection League, many
of whom were his personal friends. In it, he advocated a closed season on
grouse and prairie chickens. He later reported dryly to state game commissioner Carlos Avery that the proposal was not well received.

To save bird populations in peril, both federal and state conservationists advocated the elimination of predators on young birds. It is not hard
to understand conservationists' anxiety. Imagine a young covey of the increasingly rare prairie chicken—downy little chicks picked off one by one
by numerous predators, including feral cats, a growing problem, and foxes,
weasels, goshawks, Sharp-shinned Hawks, and Great Horned owls. Some
states instituted bounties on the raptors and predatory mammals, but bounties were deemed not workable—not because predators had recognized
value but mostly because there were easy ways for people to scam the system. T. S. Palmer of the federal Bureau of Biological Survey wrote Roberts
that "the bounty system is a very expensive and ineffective way to destroy
noxious species."[35]

But closed seasons did work. A large section of forest in northern Minnesota's Arrowhead region had been made a federal reserve, the Superior
Refuge, by President Theodore Roosevelt in 1911, in which hunting and
trapping were not allowed. A decade later, a university researcher noted
that black bear, otter, beaver, and fisher had made "a distinct comeback."[36]
Wood Ducks were a prime example of a bird that had been driven nearly to
extinction from overhunting and habitat loss, but whose numbers quickly
rebounded when hunting was curtailed.[37]

But for every step forward, there seemed to be another backward, into
rapacious use of the state's resources. Even as federal biologists recognized

southern Minnesota's Swan Lake as a major waterfowl breeding lake, there were clamors to drain the shallow wetland for agriculture.[38] Despite protection in the Superior Refuge, moose populations were in serious decline: large-scale logging of northern pine forests had eliminated much of the animals' habitat.[39]

Roberts believed that the only long-term solution to safeguarding Minnesota's birds lay in education. Certainly, the entire focus of the natural history museum was on introducing the general populace to the wonders and beauty of the state's natural heritage. But other opportunities arose, and Roberts latched on to them.

A few years after setting up the museum and establishing himself in the classroom, Roberts was approached to participate in the Boy Scouts of America program. At first, he was involved only in giving one lecture a year, on the birds of Minnesota, to Minneapolis scouts, but soon he took part in the training of scoutmasters and then in running a two-week training camp at Itasca State Park, using the facilities of the Forestry School to house the scoutmasters. Roberts lectured and led bird walks, but he also was superintendent of the camp. In 1920, the program ran from August 2 through August 14 and included instruction in trees, birds, wildflowers, astronomy, signaling, and, of course, that Boy Scout signature activity, knots. It trained scoutmasters from Minneapolis and St. Paul, Duluth, Norwood, and Hibbing.

Each day began with a setting-up drill, followed by a dip in the lake and "chow." Then, a flag-raising ceremony and classes. Every night ended with a campfire. In between, there were inspections of beaver dams, cedar swamps, and hornet nests; hikes amid the jack pines; star talks; and water sports. It was an exuberant two weeks in the north woods, with Roberts, in his sixties as an elder statesman. On the last night, Superintendent Roberts hosted a dinner for all the well-trained scoutmasters.[40]

Boy Scout activities reached the men and boys, but Roberts was drawn into the bird world of genteel women when he became involved in the early life of a bird club organized by the Woman's Club of Minneapolis. A high-profile civic group to which his wife and sister and many of his female friends belonged, the Woman's Club formed the bird club in 1915 as an offshoot of their Conservation Committee. This club aligned with Audubon chapters in other states—the nascent National Audubon Society—and became the Minneapolis Audubon Society. It was the first Audubon chapter in Minnesota.[41] Roberts was the speaker at its first official meeting and later served on its executive board. One can imagine the impeccably dressed Roberts, in three-piece suit and those rounded glasses, delivering in his soft, persuasive way "The Homelife of Minnesota Birds" to Minneapolis's social elite.

There were other educational opportunities. In this same time period, he wrote a monograph on the waterbirds of Minnesota as part of the biennial report of the Game and Fish Commission for 1918, illustrated with photos taken by Jenness Richardson and himself. The report contained records from his observers stationed throughout the state, noting the last appearance of species now extirpated from Minnesota, like the Long-billed and Eskimo Curlews. Roberts also used the report to refute some of Philo Hatch's claims from his 1892 report, and he printed a photo of a drainage ditch cut through a northern Minnesota wetland, calling it "a powerful factor in contributing to the disappearance of water birds."[42]

In 1919, *A Review of the Ornithology of Minnesota* was released as a research publication of the University of Minnesota. An abbreviated version of the bird book Roberts had long envisioned, it included a checklist; a review of game laws; commentary on introduced, extirpated, and vanishing species; a list of Minnesota's recently established game refuges; and a bibliography of Minnesota's ornithological literature.

These two publications, along with his 1915 "Winter Birdlife of Minnesota," contributed more systematically to the documentation of Minnesota birds than anything prior. Roberts's immense vitality spilled over into all aspects of his new life, energy that seemed unceasing, even as he entered his seventh decade. The people around him witnessed his newfound joy. Charles Bovey, a close friend who had known him as a bird-crazy teenager, wrote, "I am glad to see you so happy in this work."[43]

Birds gave Roberts so much sheer pleasure. Bird-watching and teaching others while out in the field were social activities delighting the convivial Roberts's heart. Searching for nests or checking up on nestlings offered soothing solitude. But occasionally, birds offered a deeper dimension, as the following account of an outing shows.

Late on Thursday, May 9, 1919, Dr. Roberts and his oldest son drove out to Washburn Park. It was approaching the peak of the warbler migration, but it had been a dark, rainy day, and the bird class had not ventured outside.

Toward sunset, though, the rain had let up, and Tom had driven his father out to the park, possibly to see if any new migrants had arrived, possibly to see if it would be profitable for the class to visit the park on Sunday.

The small leaves and bare branches glistened with the afternoon's rain, and the birds were atwitter as they foraged in the woods. The men saw a Palm Warbler stalking the leaf litter, a Black-and-white Warbler circling a branch, looking for supper. White-throated Sparrows whistled from the treetops.

Tom had been home only a few days. Unlike one of his close friends, a fighter pilot who never returned, he had survived the war and could now look forward to a life of peace, a home life, a work life at Washburn-Crosby. He had returned safely to Minneapolis. His bride would arrive on Sunday, and the Roberts family circle would widen. The relationship of Thomas to this beloved first son, his namesake, though, would change.

How the woods of Washburn Park must have harbored shades that evening! Memories of small, blue-eyed Tommy, accompanying his father on jaunts as a child, helping him with fieldwork at Itasca; memories of Thomas, in the horse and buggy with his own father, looking for whatever flew up from the roadside or from tree to tree, sometimes in this very patch of forest.

The setting sun's rays streaked the underbrush with gold. There was a steady drip, drip as the woods righted itself after the stormy afternoon. The clatter of a streetcar was very distant. They saw a White-crowned Sparrow, a Blackpoll Warbler, a Song Sparrow. Somewhere nearby, a Veery sang.

CHAPTER 12

Gains and Losses

The native prairie is largely a thing of the past.
— *The Birds of Minnesota*, 1: 489

The April morning in 1926 was chill and dreary as Dr. Roberts passed under the arching stone entrance of the Great Northern Depot situated high above the rushing Mississippi. Spring was advancing in Minneapolis, and the grass had greened. Lake Calhoun was open. Ice-out had been April 17, a little later than usual, and now the waterfowl were coming through in great waves. The Saturday before, he and Will Kilgore had seen three to four hundred ducks on the Minnesota River below Fort Snelling.

That Saturday no birding trips were planned, so perhaps it was just as well that the weather was disagreeable. Today he was meeting Homer Dill's promising young taxidermist, the student from Iowa State, who was arriving on the 7:45 train from Marshalltown to interview. The young man came highly recommended, and Roberts valued Dill's opinion. Dill was curator of a very fine natural history museum in Ames and had two students with exceptional skill in museum preparatory work, but the student coming to Minneapolis that morning was the one who seemed the best match for the position open at the University of Minnesota.

The capacious waiting room of the depot bustled with travelers carrying satchels and grips. There were families and businessmen, shoppers coming into the city for the day, and salesmen heading out. Passengers on layover sat on the hard, dark wood benches, reading the *Minneapolis Tribune,* their bags at their feet. A large idyllic mural of a mountain landscape on the wall opposite the ticket counters advertised the charms of the scenery through which a Great Northern train would travel.

Roberts checked his watch. A train had just arrived; it appeared the overnight run from Marshalltown was on time. The trip from Ames with a transfer in Marshalltown would have taken nine hours. His museum candidate would be both hungry and tired. The plan was to take the young man home for some breakfast—surely a student would be in want of bacon and eggs on a Saturday morning after all night on the train—and then to take him to the museum to see the dioramas, especially the unfinished Pipestone group. Roberts hoped to be able to assess the would-be preparator's personality, to gauge how well he would work as part of a team, how inclined he would be to take orders from a boss. He knew he could not measure his skill, at least not this weekend. He would have to take Dill's word that this man was qualified.

Then after a tour of the museum, Roberts thought he would take him to the Campus Club for lunch. It was nearby, in Minnesota Union, and the Iowan could get a feel for the University of Minnesota. He would be a guest of the Robertses tonight, and if Saturday had been auspicious, perhaps he and Will Kilgore would take him out bird-watching around the lakes the next morning. Supposedly he was very keen on birds.

As people streamed by, Roberts looked around, not exactly sure what this young man would look like. Then suddenly, a small man with dark hair and a firm jaw appeared before him. Dressed in suit and tie, he had a nice smile and a confident air as he stuck out his hand and said, "Dr. Roberts? I'm Walter Breckenridge."

The post–Great War years had been busy ones for Roberts, who was then in his sixties, heavier and stiffer, with the usual aches and pains of advancing age. Bifocals had become a necessary new accessory, although he retained his preference for the outdated and somewhat formal three-button navy serge suits, plain blue ties, anchored by a pearl-studded stickpin, and crisp white pocket handkerchiefs. He dressed much as he had in his years as a full-time physician, and truthfully, it could seem as if the rhythm of his days now was not much different than it had been before leaving his practice.

He had agreed to retain some patients when he closed his private office. These numbered about twenty-five families, and he often began his days with a series of house calls to those who had requested a visit. Sometimes this involved no more than administering vaccines. His wealthy clientele who were headed for Florida in the winter months needed a sequential vaccine against typhoid. Their children were inoculated against smallpox, diphtheria, and scarlet fever. He still had no means by which to treat bacterial infection, and he was quick to call in another physician for consultation—or to accompany a patient to the Mayo Clinic on the train if he thought treatment there was warranted. Often while in Rochester, he would work in a lunch with Will Mayo, if their schedules meshed.

There were days free from medical calls. On those days, he arrived at the museum early. On others, he might have a lineup of five or six appointments. Some of these, like the Albert Crosbys, were near neighbors—he could walk across the alley or next door to call. But others, like Frank Heffelfinger or the Commonses, lived out at Lake Minnetonka much of the time, a forty-five-minute trip in the 1920s. He no longer took a streetcar out to the lake, though. Roads were excellent, and John Nordquist still served as chauffeur. A house call to Lake Minnetonka was expensive, five times the cost of an in-town visit, but many of the Minnetonka residents were older and had relied on their physician for decades. Sometimes Minnetonka residents saved themselves the expense by meeting their doctor at the Minneapolis Club in town, combining lunch and a medical visit over the noon hour. And truth to tell, many times Dr. Roberts did not charge them.

Not uncommonly, the morning's round of calls involved a visit to ailing grandchildren. Of course, Dr. Roberts did not charge them, either. He and Jennie now had four—Catharine and Joe's girls, Catharine, Jane, and Marjorie Seybold; and Tom and Dot's young sons, Tommy and later, in 1928, Willbur. Roberts treated the children for the usual illnesses of childhood: colds, sore throats, tonsillitis, and, more worrisome, measles. More than once, he had accompanied a grandchild to the hospital for appendicitis.

He had not given up professional medical contacts in his life at the museum, either. He maintained his membership in the Hennepin County Medical Society and attended evening dinner meetings of the state Academy of Medicine, of which he was a founding member. He kept current, too. When a seminar on the latest research in bacteriophages, then considered a possible way to treat bacterial infection, was offered at the medical school, he signed up.[1]

His ornithology course had matured over the years and now ran for two terms, beginning on the first day of winter term, immediately after the Christmas break, and continuing through spring term into the middle of June. In the 1920s, his students were still mainly women, training as teachers. Each class posed for its photograph at the end of the term, after a day of birding. The images of the young women gave silent witness to the rapid changes in American life. Where once the coeds wore long skirts with middy blouses having lace-trimmed wide collars, and broad-brimmed hats, by the 1920s they had traded sun hats for close-fitting cloches. Frocks were shorter, draped and waistless; a few of the more daring wore sporty jodhpurs—pants! On women! The few male students continued to dress in suits and ties, with fedoras. Professor Roberts, that natty dresser, included a pocket watch and chain and often a boutonniere in his lapel. And everyone, in every year, sported a pair of binoculars slung around his or her neck.

Many of the women became competent bird-watchers and would go on to teach biology, start high school bird clubs, and organize small natural history museums. Some became naturalists in summer camps. Others went on to graduate work. It was, perhaps, because of these intelligent female students—along with the expert women birders in the Minneapolis Audubon Society—that Roberts respected the skill and bird sightings of women. Many male birders did not, and it was not uncommon for bird clubs at the time to exclude females.

At the beginning of spring term in early April, lectures ceased—at least if the weather was favorable. Then, the class headed outside to the field. They traveled in automobiles now—usually some of the young men had cars, and if they needed another vehicle, Nordquist also drove. They visited Lakes Calhoun and Harriet for migrating ducks, grebes, gulls, and shorebirds and walked the bridle path between the two lakes in search of songbirds. Classes still birded the east-bank river bluffs—neither Coffman Union nor Comstock Hall had been built—aiming for the Lake Street bridge, or walked north toward the Soo line crossing. A nearby cattail marsh provided a colony of nesting Brewer's Blackbirds and other early arrivals.

The birding spots his classes visited over the years reveal what had been lost and retained in natural habitat as Minneapolis grew. One afternoon's trip headed toward Minnehaha Creek and included Washburn Park, a lovely little parcel of oak woods with an understory that was nibbled away as public schools were built on the site. Trips to the creek and Washburn Park also included Diamond Lake and adjacent Pearl Lake, a little marsh that often dried up in summer. Pearl Lake was a favorite with Roberts because it harbored a surprisingly diverse bird community. From a little knoll above the marsh, he and his class would sit quietly and observe the more elusive birds—bitterns and gallinules, Soras, and maybe a rare King Rail, which might slip out onto the small marsh's mudflats to forage.[2] One summer, students found a small population of Least Bitterns in a wetland adjacent to what is now called Lake Hiawatha, a startling discovery inside city limits in 1928. The "nimble little acrobats," as Roberts termed the bitterns, lost their breeding grounds by 1932, as Minneapolis incorporated the marsh into the city park system.[3]

The classes ventured into St. Paul, birding Como Park and the university's farm campus. These were short trips that delivered the students back on campus by four thirty. But sometimes they went farther afield, and the class period stretched into the evening.

One place they visited year after year was Frank and Marie Commons' intensive bird-banding operation on their farm, Tanager Hill, at Lake Minnetonka. The Commons property had a wide variety of habitats, including meadow, marsh, and lakeshore. The students could not have been exposed to a better demonstration of the scientific undertaking that was yielding so much valuable information on birds—the Commons were nationally recognized pioneers in the field. They were also uncommonly gracious hosts. One student, after carefully recording all the birds and the notable blooming plants encountered on their visit, also jotted down the supper menu: sandwiches, ice tea (without sugar), milk, fruit, cottage cheese; she ended with "home by 7:45."[4]

Other patients of Dr. Roberts's hosted the students. W. O. Winston of Lake Minnetonka was one. He had recently acquired a rare copy of Audubon's four-volume double elephant folio edition of *The Birds of America*, which the students eagerly paged through.[5] Later in the spring, the wandering birders usually visited Miss Edgar's cabin at Nine Mile Creek in Bloomington to see songbirds. One glorious June day, the class encountered there six male Scarlet Tanagers, a Black-billed Cuckoo, a Yellow-billed Cuckoo, and a nesting Louisiana Waterthrush, delighting the professor.[6]

An enduring favorite site was the Long Meadow Gun Club along the Minnesota River. As he had in childhood with his father, Roberts visited there several times a spring with his class. They looked for migrating ducks on the lake, shorebirds on the mudflats, and upland songbirds in the meadows and woods above the floodplain. Field trips to Long Meadow were often scheduled for Saturday. One trip in mid-May, begun early in the day, garnered fifty-two species, including eleven species of warblers, a Grinnell's Waterthrush, and a Bonaparte's Gull. The professor must have been reluctant to end the winning streak, because even though the class had brought lunch along, they did not break to eat until 4:15 P.M. One student scribbled a peevish complaint in her field notes: "Nearly starved by that time, but Dr. Roberts would not give in."[7]

Roberts established a tradition of hosting the entire class to a chicken dinner out at the gun club near the end of the term. On a day on the cusp of summer, the class began early with a few hours of bird-watching and ended at a table on the long, screened-in veranda overlooking the broad expanse of the Minnesota River. The class's field assistants, as well as their wives, were always included, and there were usually several others at the meal—perhaps a visiting sister of one of the students or a friend of Roberts's from the Audubon club who had helped with fieldwork. Jennie was there, anchoring one end of the table, while the professor presided over the other. The class photo snapped that day memorialized the term.

In the school year 1920–21, Dr. Roberts hired Will Kilgore as an assistant. Kilgore worked for Minneapolis General Electric for twenty years before finally moving into work aligned with his true passion, birds. (He missed seeing a Nashville Warbler's nest at Itasca once and wrote his mentor that he was "sick" over it.) He had first gone into the field with Roberts as a shy introvert of twenty-four, and his skill matured under Roberts's tutelage in the years following. As he grew into his job at the museum, he would later step in for Roberts to lecture to the bird class, lead field outings, work with students on bird skins, and conduct tours through the museum. As the years went on, Roberts came to rely heavily on him.

Kilgore's collecting trips with Roberts dated from 1903. There had been many junkets since then, and in 1924, Roberts included him on another, along with university botanist and all-round naturalist N. L. Huff and John Nordquist. They planned the collection trip to the western part of Minnesota with several goals in mind. Roberts wanted to determine the ranges of two western species that were extending eastward into the state, the Burrowing Owl and the "Arkansas Flycatcher," later to be called the Western Kingbird. He was also mulling over a "prairie group" for the museum and needed to get out among the sea of grass once more. At the beginning, he did not anticipate the bitter fruit the trip would yield.

Roberts's former medical secretary Mabel Densmore spent summers in

Grant County, in the small village of Herman, and they had kept in touch over the years. Now in her late forties, she remained an avid birder. In 1924, the Roberts party made Herman their first stop, to chase down Densmore's recent report of the nests of a Marbled Godwit and a Marsh Hawk and of the presence of Burrowing Owls. These were all birds on which Roberts wanted more information.

The three-week outing undoubtedly had a tinge of nostalgia to it, for Roberts had spent time in Herman as a youth. At twenty-one, he and Frank Benner had taken the train out to the town when it was no more than a rough assemblage of frame buildings clustered on the rail line, surrounded by open prairie for miles. What a glorious time that had been for the two young bucks and their shotguns! They had never found the white pelicans that they had sought, but the treasure trove of prairie birds had been thrilling. The Marbled Godwits, those chunky, cinnamon-colored birds with the long, long bills, had been so abundant and so noisy that they had actually been a nuisance. They found Upland Sandpipers, Chestnut-collared Longspurs, Lark Buntings—the latter two were high prairie birds that were new to them—and ducks, so many, many ducks. The men had shot and skinned hundreds of birds, collected eggs and nests, always labeling and dating them, and taken them all home, a sizable addition to their collections.

In 1924, Roberts and his companions approached Herman in an automobile, not a train. The car tore along at twenty miles per hour, a respectable speed. The road trip had a promising start: in Kandiyohi County, they had spied two Marbled Godwits by the side of the road, and Huff thought he also saw little godwit chicks. Roberts had not seen a live godwit since the trip with Benner. The tally of Upland Sandpipers and hawks was slimmer: one sandpiper and only three hawks—two Marsh Hawks and a kestrel. However, Roberts did not record dismay.

In Herman, Densmore and her friend, Vera Barrows, led the party to the godwit's nest, in a large section of virgin prairie. They took photographs, but the parent birds were wary and would not approach the nest while the party remained, so they made no movies. The next day and the day after, the collectors returned, made a blind, and got some good photos and eventually movies. There were four eggs in the nest, all pipped, but after several days, three of the eggs never hatched, apparently having gotten too hot in the June sun while the men made movies. The fourth egg hatched, and the

precocial chick took off into the prairie grass but was eventually found, captured, photographed—and skinned for the museum collection. Another
pair of godwits nested in the same prairie remnant, but they had hidden
their nest better, and it was never found. These were the only two nesting
pairs of Marbled Godwits near Herman that the party discovered. Later,
they would come upon a flock of twenty-four east of town on a mudflat, the
largest they would see the entire trip.[8]

Having exhausted the godwits in the area, the men turned their attention
to the Burrowing Owls that Densmore had discovered. The owls were nesting in a badger den north of town. This was unusual—Burrowing Owls in the
Dakotas nested in prairie dog runs, and Roberts was anxious to describe the
burrow, the nesting behavior, and the young. The burrow proved to be quite
an enterprise to dig out. The hole went five feet down and five feet back, at
the end of which the diggers discovered ten partly incubated eggs. Burrowing Owls were not uncommon in Grant County; across the road from this
excavated and now useless burrow was another, with the little bird "standing
sentry." The farmer of this field told the collectors that owls had nested there
for years, that he considered the sentry his "little pet," and he warned them
against harming the birds.[9]

There were some species found to be plentiful near Herman. Meadowlarks and Mourning Doves were "abundant," and Brewer's Blackbirds were
also very common, as were the Arkansas Flycatchers, whose range Roberts
had wanted to map. But the plaintive whistle of the Upland Sandpiper, once
heard everywhere, was rare, and nesting prairie chickens, though termed by
Roberts in his notes as "fairly common," were often destroyed when farmers
burned off the prairie fields. Jackrabbits bounding over the open fields were
conspicuous.

On Lake Patchen, east of Herman, the party was cheered to discover a
wealth of Ruddy Ducks, rounded reddish birds with their stiff little tails held
at a forty-five-degree angle to the water's surface, though the flock appeared
to be all males. On the small prairie ponds in the vicinity of the bigger lake,
they found Mallards, Blue-winged Teal, pintails, and Gadwalls—an unusual
number of Gadwalls, they thought. But no Canvasbacks or Redheads. Densmore told them that many of the smaller sloughs had dried up in the past
three or four years and were now meadows or mudflats.[10]

After a week of collecting specimens, it was time to move on. The foursome headed north into Otter Tail County and to Ten Mile Lake, where they were met with a dearth of waterfowl. "The ponds and sloughs are without ducks ... because the country around [Ten Mile Lake] does not offer us much of interest we decided to move on," Roberts scrawled in his journal.[11] The party left the next day. The land, except for the knolls and hogbacks, was all under cultivation.

This was also the case as they drove west from Herman to Wheaton—all under cultivation. And from Wheaton to Browns Valley—all under cultivation. And the same from Browns Valley to Big Stone Lake. The tallgrass prairie that had been so yawning when Roberts and Benner had visited in 1879, that they had described as a featureless bowl, that they had gotten lost on, was gone, converted to agricultural fields. It had vanished in Roberts's lifetime.

In Madison, in Lac qui Parle County, the men inquired at a drugstore if anyone in town was interested in birds. A Mr. Peterson replied that his son was interested in butterflies, and this young man became their guide. So absent was the native grassland that the ornithologists needed to be piloted out to a quarter section of virgin prairie that had not yet been touched by the plow. The remnant was close to the Coteau des Prairies, the rocky uplift in southwestern Minnesota, and this they explored, and Roberts described it in his journal. But it did not give them either the Chestnut-collared Longspur or the Lark Bunting as they had hoped.[12]

The party continued tallying Arkansas Flycatchers. It became apparent that the species had established itself firmly in the state. They noted the many Loggerhead Shrikes, which they termed "migrant shrikes." In Montevideo, they found a nest with very small nestlings and took movies. But Roberts often scrawled "saw no birds of special interest" in the journal at the end of many days.

Roberts summarized the trip in stiff-upper-lip, scientific terms: the Arkansas Flycatcher was now a common bird throughout the state, the Burrowing Owl was generally distributed throughout west-central Minnesota, and there were a few Marbled Godwits left, at least in Grant County. Prairie chickens were seen frequently throughout the trip. Upland Sandpipers were in limited numbers. The Lark Bunting and the Chestnut-collared Longspur, once so common, were gone.

Scientific language aside, the experience had seared Roberts. While in Herman, he had written a postcard to Frank Benner, whose presence had been palpable to Roberts as he surveyed the vast changes that had come upon the prairie. Benner, in Minneapolis and a neighbor on Pleasant Avenue, replied with nostalgia, recalling the troublesome mosquitoes and an uncomfortably hot summer evening in the Herman hotel spent frantically skinning birds and blowing eggs before their train departed around midnight. Benner no longer was on fire with a passion for birds and, though wistful, was more interested now in perennial flowers.

At home, Roberts was more explicit about the losses he had seen. Four times a year, he sent off a "Seasonal Report" from Minneapolis to be published in *Bird-Lore* magazine. In his September–October 1924 report, he related how he had found the former prairie to now be a vast, cultivated plain, the bits of virgin prairie "few and far between." The Long-billed Curlew, both Sandhill and Whooping Cranes, and Trumpeter Swans were gone, as well as McCown's Longspur, Sprague's Pipit, and Baird's Sparrow. He called the Upland Sandpiper's numbers a "pitiful remnant" and noted the greatly reduced numbers of ducks and Marbled Godwits.[13]

Frank Chapman, still the magazine's editor, replied to his old friend with a sympathetic letter. But the eastern-bred Chapman had not lived on a frontier in his childhood, and he had an incurably upbeat personality. Rather than grapple with the cosmic loss of an unique ecosystem, he chose to console Roberts with a "buck up" message: "While I deplore the change which brings irreparable loss as you do, I find that my regret is not fully shared by those who did not know the past as well as the present, and I conclude that you and I are mourning not only for the birds of our youth but for our youth as well." He pointed out that some birds, like the flicker, had once been rare and were now common.[14]

Still later, Roberts wrote to Herbert Gleason, who had collected at Lake Vermilion with him in 1894 and was now living in Boston, his fame as a nature photographer secure. Gleason, though raised in Massachusetts, had tromped over Minnesota's prairies and woods and relished those days. He had also spent years and years recording the splendor of America's wildlands on film and had seen the destruction wrought as the frontier advanced westward. This old friend fully appreciated the significance of the loss. "I am sorry to hear about the disappearance of the birds in western Minnesota," he replied to Roberts's letter. "It is too bad that civilization is such a foe to wildlife."[15]

Witnessing the decimation of the prairie and the concomitant disappearance of birds now lent some urgency to Roberts's life. Within months after the disturbing field season of 1924, he approached Mabel Densmore with a job offer. She had been very young when she had last been in his employ, but he knew she was a quick study, attentive to detail, and, not insignificantly, very adept at interpreting his spiky, often illegible handwriting. With her knowledge of birds, she was the perfect person to handle the task he had in mind. It was time to write his Minnesota bird book.

Densmore had, perhaps, a fair understanding of the work ahead: sifting through fifty years of migratory, breeding, and overwintering records of the more than three hundred species of Minnesota birds and compiling them into readable form; deciphering the curator's longhand manuscript and typing it up; and serving as a corresponding secretary as "The Book," as she and Roberts called it, took shape. He would come to call her his partner in crime. The phrase indicated that he considered her a full-fledged colleague in the endeavor and was evidence that he had taken to reading the murder mysteries that served as a bedtime ritual. But it is doubtful that she expected the job to occupy her for more than seven years.

Keeping her Red Wing home, she arranged her life around the rhythms of the museum. She lived at times with the Robertses and later, as Jennie's health worsened, in a south Minneapolis flat and embarked on the work of making *The Birds of Minnesota* a reality. "Mabel Densmore begins at the museum," Roberts scribbled into his little pocket diary on January 19, 1925, and assigned her work space in a corner of his office. In the years to come, Densmore's brisk, cheerful attitude set an optimistic tone to the undertaking: "My! But there's a vast amount of valuable material in these things, isn't there. And it's good to see the [bird] biographies coming along at the same time," she wrote to her boss in 1928. And later, in 1929, "I'll be along ready for good hard work and we'll make this business hum!" And still later in 1930, "I'll be back soon—probably Tuesday & ready for action."[16]

The main thrust of the museum in the 1920s was the construction of the large dioramas, what Roberts called "habitat groups." In 1922, the museum staff completed a diorama set at Heron Lake, that magical wetland where Roberts had shot his first footage of Franklin's Gulls in the 1890s. The funds for the diorama had come from Charles and Louise Koon Velie, patients of Roberts.

In 1925, a large grouping of black bears opened. Procuring the increasingly rare large mammals had occupied an entire fall for the taxidermist, Jenness Richardson, who spent a fruitless two months in northern Minnesota chasing leads from Beaver Bay to Lax Lake to International Falls. Bruce Horsfall, an impressionistic artist of growing acclaim, who had recently provided illustrations for Frank Chapman's *Warblers of North America,* was hired to paint the background mural. The diorama opened to enthusiastic reviews. Horsfall was pleased with the working relationship he and Richardson had forged and anticipated the next big project with him.[17]

That next project turned out to be a large diorama of the tallgrass prairie set at Pipestone. After the 1924 trip to western Minnesota, it was obvious that the prairie ecosystem in the state had been decimated by agricultural cultivation. Consequently, Roberts sent Richardson and his wife, who was also a preparator, to North Dakota to collect material for the display. The two shot avocets, Willets, godwits, and Chestnut-collared Longspurs; collected buffalo berry and prickly pear cactus; and wondered if they should bring back some prairie sod. "There's lots of wild prairie here . . . lots of buffalo berry . . . badgers are quite common. [But] haven't been able to locate . . . the curlew," Olive Richardson wrote.[18] They took birds not only for the Pipestone group but also for the small traveling displays intended for the schools.

The tone of Jenness Richardson's letters to his boss was brisk, courteous, and professional, but it masked an underlying tension that had been growing for many years. As early as 1920, Richardson had been reluctant to let wildlife movies that he had shot go out of his possession when Roberts, in the field at Itasca, wanted to view them. A few years later, Kilgore reported that he had been unable to look over the material the Richardsons had collected in North Dakota—they were keeping it under wraps. Rumors circulated that the couple worked behind closed doors, not even allowing their boss into the prep room. The inclination toward secrecy did not sit well with Roberts, who wanted the final say over quality control in museum projects.[19]

The conflict came to a head around the holidays in 1925. Apparently, Richardson leaked information and photographs to the local press on museum work that was still in progress, most likely the Pipestone exhibit, which had been occupying most of his time. Roberts was unpleasantly surprised by what he considered a breach in ethics but was unsure of his assessment. He wrote to heads of other museums, and one by one they answered, assuring him that such a matter would not happen in their institutions.[20] In late March 1926, Richardson resigned under pressure and immediately sought out the sympathetic student newspaper, the *Minnesota Daily*. Front-page headlines blared, "Taxidermist Here Leaves Faculty," airing the dispute in favorable terms toward Richardson and assigning the cause to "accumulated friction" between him and the museum's curator, Roberts.[21]

The *Daily* bolstered the prominent news story with an editorial supportive of the taxidermist.[22] The public airing of an intramuseum fracas must have made the private Roberts cringe. But the championing of Richardson by the student newspaper caused benefactor James Ford Bell to growl, "an explanation to [the *Daily*] would put an end to such foolishness."[23] Roberts, however, thought all involved should just lie low and the storm would blow over.

Amid the increasing strife in the studios and halls of the Zoology Building, Roberts embarked on yet another venture, one that would bring wide publicity to the museum: he went on the radio. He had always been creative in seeking the public eye for his museum, and in 1926, the opportunity arose to talk into the public ear, too. Once again, his prominent patients were involved, this time as board members of the radio station.

WCCO Radio, owned by the Washburn-Crosby Company (the call letters reflected this), went on the air in 1924. On February 8, 1926, Roberts found himself before a microphone in the "Gold Medal studio" housed downtown in the Nicollet Hotel. His talk was titled "The Winter Bird Life of Minnesota," a topic he had been speaking on since his teen years in the Young Naturalists' Society. He could have given such a speech in his sleep, and maybe it was chosen to ward off any nervousness that might have arisen when speaking for the first time to an audience of untold thousands. Radio was new to Minnesota, and those who had invested in the new technology had the dial tuned to 830.

His second radio talk, "The Migration of Minnesota Birds," was also delivered in the Gold Medal studio, but for the third broadcast, Roberts did not have to go downtown. He merely crossed Washington Avenue to the electrical engineering building on campus, where the new university radio station, WLB, was located on the third floor. A gift to the university from the Washburn-Crosby Company, WLB put the University of Minnesota into an elite class of schools that had their own radio broadcasting stations. Roberts's talk, this time on "April and May Bird-Lore in Minnesota," was part of a "University Hour" that included a talk on chemistry and musical performances by students. Later in the month, listeners tuned in to a debate featuring student leader Harold Stassen, and still later, a special "Engineers' Day" program, with *Minnesota Daily* student columnist Cedric Adams announcing.

Listeners could write for copies of the nature talks, and requests came into the museum from all over the state. Roberts kept a record of the requests, by county, and appreciated the widespread enthusiasm for birds among the populace. Surely this must have been cheering to the man who had been sharing his own enthusiasm for things feathered for years.

At the same time he prepared the third radio talk, Roberts was casting about for a man to replace the departed Richardson. With no taxidermist, the big Pipestone exhibit sat unfinished; the preparator's studio, vacant. Within the month, his inquiries prompted a letter from the Iowa State University at Ames:

Dear Dr. Roberts:

Prof Dill received your letter relative to the position you have open for a museum preparatory and discussed the matter with me this morning. The conditions at your museum were rather fully explained in your letter and the work seems to be exactly the kind in which I am interested.

I will be very glad to accept your offer to come up and go over the situation personally. . . .

Very sincerely yours,
W. J. Breckenridge [24]

The young man from Iowa was only twenty-three, one of Dill's best students at Iowa State's natural history museum. Small, strong, and self-possessed, he told Roberts in his interview that day in April 1926 that he thought he could step into Richardson's shoes and finish the huge Pipestone display. Roberts liked him and, with Kilgore, took him to bird the Minneapolis lakes the next morning. The migrating ducks were thick, and the trio saw also a number of Horned Larks. Perhaps by including Kilgore on the birding outing, Roberts was soliciting his assessment of the would-be taxidermist, but he and Kilgore did not confer long, for the curator offered Breckenridge the job that same weekend. Only later did Roberts realize that he had omitted obtaining some crucial information about the young man and wrote his new employee to get it. In reply, Breckenridge wrote: "I received your letter with the questions this afternoon. My full name is Walter John Breckenridge. I was born in Brooklyn, Iowa, March 22, 1903. I will receive the degree of Bachelor of Arts in June of this year from the College of Liberal Arts, having majored in Zoology. I hope this answers the questions satisfactorily."[25]

A month later, Roberts's new preparator was on his way to Minneapolis, driving a secondhand Model T Ford that he had bought from his father, ready for his new job. He later claimed that getting the job had fulfilled one of his life's ambitions: finding work in a place like Minnesota, where there was still some untouched land.[26] The Robertses offered to house the young man until he could find a place of his own, after the imminent field season. Jennie objected to the Ford, though, which she termed a "flivver." The Model T, she said flatly, had to be parked out of sight in the alley.[27]

Breckenridge, or "Breck" as he soon became known, enjoyed his weeks in the first-floor apartment at 2303 Pleasant Avenue. The Robertses had him to dinner frequently and played cribbage afterward. The son of a hardware store owner, Breck was the product of small-town middle America, and the domestic life of the upper-class Roberts was new to him. In particular, he was impressed at dinnertime, when Roberts used a little foot pedal to summon the housekeeper for the next course in the meal. No one had *that* in Brooklyn, Iowa.[28]

Roberts took Breckenridge out to southwestern Minnesota immediately upon his arrival at the university. Already mid-June, the field season was passing, and the curator was anxious not to lose a season on the Pipestone exhibit. The collecting party was gone for ten days, ample time for Roberts to become acquainted with Breck firsthand; to see how much he knew, how meticulous he was in collecting, labeling, and storing material; to find out how their personalities meshed. Neither one could have known in those hot days on the Pipestone prairie just how fortuitous was Roberts's decision to hire Breckenridge.

The remainder of the summer was passed in Minneapolis. Roberts dealt with the museum's administration, and Breckenridge settled down to work. Personal tragedy struck the Roberts family that summer: a baby granddaughter born to Tom and Dorothy died suddenly in July. An autopsy revealed no discernible cause. Weeks later, Roberts returned home one day to find Jennie ill. She had been in poor health the previous winter, when the Richardson conflict was swirling, and had spent several months in California, away from the rigors of a Minneapolis winter. But nothing could avert the progressing heart disease, which would incapacitate her for years before causing her death.

One more significant change occurred in Roberts's life in the eventful year of 1926. After the departure of Richardson, the arrival of Breckenridge, the death of a grandchild, and the debilitating illness of Jennie, in mid-November, John Nordquist became ill. He had been with Roberts since 1890, since John Roberts's death. Over thirty-five years, the two had switched from horse to automobile. Nordquist had accompanied collecting parties out to the prairie and up to Itasca; he had set up bird blinds, worked with the camera, participated in movie making, and hunted ducks. He had walked with the bird class on outings and in that time, like Densmore, had become a bird-watcher himself. On a May class day in which Roberts saw two easily recognizable male Scarlet Tanagers, Roberts noted, "John is with and sees the one female tanager,"[29] which the professor had undoubtedly wished the students to see, since its greenish hue was so unlike the male's.

Nordquist's illness contributed to a trying time. Jennie was confined to her bed, under the care of a private nurse, and Roberts himself was experiencing painful episodes of angina and suffering from a cold. Nordquist was his patient, and Roberts called daily. Then suddenly, one morning as Roberts attended, the driver showed signs of a pulmonary embolism and rapidly expired. His death was a shock, most unexpected. Nordquist was sixty-three, younger than Roberts. Roberts signed the death certificate, an act he rarely performed now.

It was not only the passing of a most-trusted employee, but the loss of another link to the sepia-toned past. Roberts and Nordquist had forged their friendship in the premotorized age; the doctor had delivered both Nordquist children. The families had been intertwined for decades. Nevertheless, the next day, Roberts, ever matter of fact, wrote in his diary: "Called on Mary Nordquist. Began with a new chauffeur today, Bernard Conner."[30]

Awash in loss—friends, family, employees, the birds, the habitats that had so thrilled him—Roberts commenced work on making his youthful dream of writing a bird book for Minnesota a reality. Maybe this would be a step toward restoring what had been destroyed.

CHAPTER 13

Writing the Book

The Wren has many devoted friends who are ready
and willing to defend it.

— *The Birds of Minnesota*, 2: 92

Thomas Roberts threaded his way through the household at 2303 Pleasant Avenue South en route to his study, the little room in the big duplex where he could sit and think. The children long gone, the flat itself was a quiet space, but in his study he had a desk, some books (though the bulk of his library was at the museum), and his father's chair, an antiquated, straight-backed piece brought from Philadelphia so long ago that reminded him of his childhood. The study was warm with the glow of golden light, light suffused with the color of the autumn leaves outside the window. In late September, the leaves were turning quickly and hung only tenuously to branches under the onslaught of a cold wind. Far off, the rhythmic clang of church bells echoed in the morning air: Sunday, a day he frequently spent at home, writing letters or a paper, catching up on reading.

He heard the fall of footsteps at the back of the house and then a murmur of voices, the nurse saying something to Jennie. For more than a year, Jennie had been housebound, essentially an invalid, incapacitated by a stroke in the waning summer of 1927. He had greatly curtailed his social life—their social life—in the wake of this devastating circumstance. A home that had entertained guests for dinner three or four times a week now saw only family. When he needed to be at the museum in the evening, he met friends at the Minneapolis Club for dinner. Visitors from out of town stayed at a local hotel, where once he would have invited them to stay in the empty first-floor apartment, linger over dinner, and share a smoke at the Robertses' hearth. Still, Roberts did not mind a quieter life, telling friends that he was "well and contented" and that "there is no reason why I should roam except . . . to see my friends [at an American Ornithologists' Union meeting]."[1]

He eased himself into his desk chair, contemplated the spread of papers, the bird lists, the unanswered letters. Tick tick tick. The clock in the front room paced off the time. He and Jennie were reaching the end, there was no denying it. Although he could still tromp about in the field, nearly as spry as in his youth, there were times when his seventy years rose up to remind him he had lived the biblical three score and ten. He had had spells of pain in his chest, just under the sternum, a great weight pressing on him. When he caught a cold, he took to his bed. When really ill, he called a nurse to spend the night, since Jennie could not attend to him.

Reduced conviviality made it easier for Roberts to sit down and work on the magnum opus he had been moving toward his entire life. Indeed, he felt increasing pressure to put pen to paper and get the job done. On February 16 of that year, 1928, he had turned seventy, the ominous age for the Roberts men. In addition to the decline and death of friends and the dwindling of birdlife in Minnesota, he had a personal reason to devote long hours to writing. All year, he had been slowly working his way through the various families: loons, ducks and geese, owls, and so on. This morning he would begin on the wrens.

He had a great deal of personal experience with the wren family, those bustling and noisy little brown birds of summer. House Wrens used to nest in the yard of his family home on Eighth Street sixty years ago. He had seen Winter Wrens on his trip to Duluth in 1878 with his father. His youthful self had called their long, intricate song "a wild, ecstatic bit of wood melody," still a pleasing and accurate description in his opinion. He had first come across Marsh Wrens while out in the field working on the land-examining crew under Nathan Butler. And his secretary Mabel Densmore had provided him with a detailed description of a rare Bewick's Wren nesting near Red Wing—a sighting that was a feather in her cap.

The wrens are in the family Troglodytidae, a humorous appellation. It refers to prehistoric cave dwellers and was no doubt tacked on them because of the wrens', at least House Wrens', preference for living in cavities—little cavemen. Roberts mused that there was much to like about wrens. They were chipper, confiding, amusing in their choice of nest sites. He had once discovered a nest in a mailbox that held a house key—the house remaining unlocked until the young had fledged. Yet, he had to admit they could be "tiny fiends." He had witnessed the destruction of Scarlet Tanager eggs by a busy wren; it was a trait of the birds to peck holes in eggs of other species, eliminating competitors. Some of his observers thought that wrens were indirectly responsible for the disappearance of other appealing species from an area.

Then he settled down, with pencil and paper, and began to write:

> The Wrens constitute a large natural group of some 165 species, only fifteen of which are found in the Old World. They are most numerous within the American Tropics. Ridgeway ("Birds of North and Middle America," part 3, p. 475) states that while superficially the Wrens most resemble the Mockers (Mimidae), they are more like the Creepers and titmice in the degree of cohesion between the anterior toes.[2]

Miss Densmore could type it up later.

Roberts had planned his book to be a comprehensive authority on the birds of the state, of use to both the amateur sitting at a kitchen table in rural Minnesota and the professional bending over a study skin, pondering a subspecies. As such, it had to be at once complete and readable, a sizable undertaking. The book he planned had several parts. The introduction would cover everything from the geologic history of the region to its climate, vegetation, and faunal communities. In this section, he would include the effect of winter on birds, bird migration, and the changes in birdlife due to human settlement. He wanted to compile a history of past ornithologists in Minnesota and discuss the conservation of birds in state law. Lastly, he thought something should be mentioned about the promise of new research, such as that involving bird-banding, to solve certain unknown aspects of bird biology. The introduction would be illustrated with anatomical drawings of wings and feathers.

The bulk of the book would be given over to a systematic description of each phylogenetic bird order, beginning with the Gaviiformes, the loons. Each species in the state had its own section containing facts, dates, sightings, biology, and even stories that Roberts pulled from his considerable past with his acute memory. These sections were illustrated with line drawings of beaks or feet, and photographs, often of nests with eggs, to illustrate key points.

One section would feature a key to the birds—a scientific aid to help people identify birds in hand. This was a feature not necessarily found in a state bird book, but it illustrated Roberts's teaching orientation. He imagined a bird enthusiast, far from any good library with a beautiful dead bird she had found, wondering what it was. Paging through several hundred pages of words would be futile, and illustrations cannot show all the possibilities of plumage. A key, though—what natural history students use to identify everything from fish to twigs—would be a reliable guide.

The use of a key is a bit of a game, something like Twenty Questions. Roberts's key begins: does the bird have three toes, or does it have four? The hopeful identifier selects the appropriate choice and then comes to the next set of options: Are the toes fully webbed, or are they not fully webbed? The choices become more and more detailed, as the user scrutinizes tail feathers, eye position, bill shape, and so on, until an order is settled upon. Then the user starts at the next level and identifies the bird as a member of a particular avian family and, lastly, makes the right choices in the key to arrive at a scientific name, which was given not in Latin, but English, a custom ornithologists hold, contrary to other biologists.

Roberts began work on the key in 1926, but he did not start de novo. He had been writing and perfecting keys for his bird classes for ten years. He claimed "entire satisfaction to pupil and instructor."[3] The key was amply illustrated with drawings by young Breckenridge, who had proved to possess immense talent as an artist as well as a taxidermist. The tiny pen-and-ink pictures bore labels: "Foot of Virginia Rail," for example, or "Bill of Great Horned Owl: nostril opening on edge of cere," or even "Face of Barn Owl." Details, details, details—as many as Roberts felt were needed to be of service to the reader.

The key to the warblers was written, or at least extensively revised, in 1927. It was crucial to get this key right, since the warblers were a large, complicated group with many different plumages. Bird enthusiasts were intensely interested in these challenging migratory birds and would likely use the key extensively. Once it was completed, Roberts sent the key off to Frederick Lincoln of the Biological Survey in Washington, D.C., who in turn handed his wife a tray of stuffed warblers and gave her Roberts's manuscript. She reported it worked very well.

While Roberts devoted hours to the key, Densmore methodically compiled the observer notes for each species. This was a gargantuan task, given the number of observers (at least 161) and the years covered, 1874 through 1931. The data for the Dickcissel, a small bunting of open meadows, illustrated the intricate information: the earliest spring migration date for the bird was May 5, 1898, in Faribault, Rice County, for southern Minnesota. The average of sixteen spring migration dates, May 5–27, was May 18. A similar calculation was made for earliest dates of fall migration, and not only for southern Minnesota but also for the north. Nesting date: June 21, 1930, a nest with four eggs was found at Frontenac in Goodhue County by Risser (a bird class student). Six other dates of nests at various stages were also enumerated. Food sources were listed; Roberts noted that the Dickcissel was "an exceedingly valuable bird, especially in regard to its grasshopper diet."[4] It may seem odd that a label of "valuable"—valuable to humans, of course—was applied in this strictly scientific work, but Roberts was anxious to hammer home the point to a society that had only recently been compelled to give up shooting songbirds. Readers would recall the severe economic losses from the grasshopper plagues fifty years ago. Bird conservationists all over the country took pains to point out that birds offered excellent insect control. The little Dickcissel "of trim, natty appearance and funny little song" was certainly among the least offensive when it came to encroaching on agricultural profit.[5] This level of detail—and certainly in greater depth for some birds that were far more common than the Dickcissel—was repeated for each of the 327 species covered in *The Birds of Minnesota*.

After enumerating the "facts" as compiled by Densmore, there followed a longer section of text in which Roberts discussed in less terse language the biology of the various birds. These he called "bird biographies," and they invariably contained vignettes of his experiences with each one over his long life. For example, he recalled the flock of American Goldeneye Ducks that used to spend the winter on the open Mississippi River at the foot of St. Anthony Falls, before an apron was built over the cataract to protect it, and before the milling district grew to such noisy proportions.[6] And he recalled the screech owl that was accustomed to roosting on the overhead light fixture in the vestibule of Pillsbury Hall at the university.[7] Calling himself "the writer," Roberts related in "The Vireos" section a most charming story of a nesting Red-eyed Vireo, on which he was keeping an eye, taming it to the point that he could visit the site and actually touch the bird without her flying off the nest. One evening at dusk, he approached the nest to find the bird "fast asleep . . . sunk low in the nest, tail standing up at a sharp angle, wings and side-feathers fluffed out as in brooding, and the head resting sidewise on the rim of the nest, eyes tightly closed. With face only eight or ten inches from the sleeping bird [the writer] discovered that she was making a little noise with each inspiration—actually snoring! She did not awake, and was left to her peaceful slumbers."[8]

The bird biographies comprised the bulk of the text, and Roberts saved Densmore a good deal of trouble by dictating many of them exactly as he would dictate letters. Most of these were completed in 1929 and took up the major part of his time that year. He worked at the museum, he worked at home, he even worked in a hotel room during unscheduled times while away at the American Ornithologists' Union convention in Philadelphia that year,[9] all the while conducting his bird class in the winter and spring and seeing patients in their homes on morning house calls. His health was good that year, though Jennie's continued its downward spiral. He cut back his normal workload only by relinquishing tours through the museum and speaking engagements to various groups. These he turned over to the ever-capable Kilgore.

As the saying goes, though, a picture is worth a thousand words, and it was the illustrations that made up the fourth and most expensive section of *The Birds of Minnesota*. In the end, six artists would contribute paintings to the book, but this is not what Roberts had originally envisioned for his cherished tome. The leading bird artist of the 1920s was Louis Agassiz Fuertes, a charming, accomplished man at Cornell University in Ithaca, New York. A fixture at the American Ornithologists' Union meetings, Fuertes had provided illustrations for dozens of major books both for the amateur birder and the professional. He had illustrated the *Birds of New York*, published in 1910, and the three-volume *Birds of Massachusetts*, the first volume of which came out in 1925. Frank Chapman had worked with him extensively at the American Museum of Natural History, and Roberts considered Fuertes a personal friend. It was a given that he would do the paintings for the Minnesota book.[10]

Then, on a Sunday in August 1927, after spending a day in the Catskills with Chapman, Fuertes was killed when his car was struck by an oncoming train at a railroad crossing. The sudden, stunning loss was felt throughout the East Coast birding community and half a continent away in Minneapolis, the possibility of the wonderful artist turning his brush on Minnesota's birdlife vanished. Only one of his illustrations would make it into the book, a plate of a covey of Bobwhite Quail that Roberts owned.

Fuertes died without finishing illustrations for the third volume of *Birds of Massachusetts.* The publisher brought in another painter, Allan Brooks, to complete the work, and it was to him that Roberts turned when he was ready to hire an illustrator in 1929.

Major Allan Brooks was a contemporary of Fuertes, a Canadian educated in England and especially conversant with the bird fauna of the Northumberland moors. He had earned the military title as a hero of the Canadian army in the Great War and had recently completed illustrations for *Birds of Western Canada.* A self-taught artist and knowledgeable natural historian in his fifties, he worked out of a studio in British Columbia with a large bird skin collection but traveled to Canada's east coast for occasional painting trips.

Roberts did not hand him the entire project, though. Something unexpected had evolved between 1927, when Roberts had thought to engage Fuertes, and 1929, when he approached Brooks: Breckenridge's artistic skill had blossomed. Roberts informed Brooks that Breck would do "the major part of [the illustrations], but both he and I feel that it would be desirable to have a few illustrations from you."[11] He then asked him to do a plate of an American Goldeneye (duck), male and female, and three other species of ducks that might look similar in the field and be found in the same habitat.

Roberts had no idea how much such a plate might cost. This request was his first venture into the artistic realm. He was concerned about the expense, because he was using his own savings for these first few paintings—at least, he would pay from his own pocket until he got a good idea of the overall cost of commissioning a plate, having it reproduced by a lithographer, and printing it off. And he had no clear idea of how many plates the book would require, but he was sure he wanted most, if not all, the birds of the state represented. How else could the book serve as a useful identification guide?

Brooks wrote back that he charged fifty dollars for a fourteen-inch-by-ten-inch painting of one or two birds; additional birds in the picture would cost ten dollars each.[12] This seemed reasonable to Roberts, and so the work was begun. The wraps on the goldeneye painting, sent through the mail, were taken off at the museum in Minneapolis on April 16, and Roberts and his staff were thrilled. "We are all very much pleased with it. It is not only entirely satisfactory as to the birds but a pleasing picture," he wrote later that day to Brooks.[13] But Brooks's straightforward, yet masterful, work made Breckenridge's youthful lack of expertise more obvious, especially in background work. In the end, the older artist would take on the majority of the plates for the book.

The same day Roberts approached Brooks, he also wrote a letter to another highly regarded bird artist, George Miksch Sutton, asking him if he would be interested in doing a few paintings for the Minnesota bird book. Sutton, thirty-six at the time, was a protégé of Fuertes and would go on to earn a doctorate in ornithology from Cornell University and enjoy a distinguished academic career. In 1926, though, he was the state ornithologist for Pennsylvania, and Roberts knew he was planning a summer trip to Canada, so his time was limited. Roberts suggested only a few plates for him to consider: the flycatchers, the Ruffed Grouse, and the "Canada Spruce Partridge" (Spruce Grouse).[14]

The Spruce Grouse proved the charm in engaging Sutton. "I have for years wanted to do a male and female Spruce Partridge for somebody and it looks as though the opportunity has come at last!" he exulted to Roberts by return mail and accepted the invitation to contribute to the book. In the end, the Spruce Grouse painting was not so felicitous an opportunity. Sutton claimed it was one of the most difficult assignments he had ever taken on. The birds' plumage was so intricate and the scale so small—the brushwork required was "microscopic"—that he was not entirely pleased. Upon learning this, Roberts apologized for the "nervous strain" Sutton had suffered in making the plate.[15]

A few more plates were done, but by summer 1929, Roberts had decided he could spend no more of his own money on the paintings. His home finances—possibly the cost of full-time private nursing for Jennie for an indefinite amount of time—constrained him. He wrote to Sutton that he was not going to go ahead with more plates.[16] In that same letter, he told the artist that he had given the grouse painting and one of Brooks's to a lithographic firm in Minneapolis to get an idea of the cost and quality of reproduction.

Roberts was caught between two cherished ideals. On the one hand, he wanted the illustrations to accurately reflect the natural bird, but this was going to take money to do. The book might become too costly to produce. If it ever saw the light of day, only the very rich would be able to buy it. And on the other hand, the book just had to be affordable to all. The beauty of birds was not only for the wealthy. Indeed, it would be a travesty if his own observers in the small towns in Minnesota, his patients of modest means, and his former students, mostly schoolteachers, could not buy the book.

Many authors of state bird books had skimped on the quality of the illustrations, yet the book would be of little use if the illustrations were poor. Color in birds was extremely important; identification of closely related species might hinge on subtle shading. The pursuit of perfection ran through Roberts like a fine gold thread. It was what made him an exemplary medical student, a sterling diagnostician, a crackerjack ornithologist, and an exacting boss, who had surrounded himself with coworkers—Densmore, Kilgore, and Breckenridge—with the same excessive concern for details.

There were people who appreciated this quality in him and who shared the same high-minded value of the common good: his wealthy patients. So Roberts turned, once again, to them to support his endeavors. One Sunday in September 1929, he had lunch out at Lake Minnetonka with Jim Bell. When the luncheon was over, Bell had pledged ten thousand dollars toward the publication of the book.[17] Other donors followed. Roberts approached some of them. But they also took the initiative of soliciting each other.[18] Roberts had delivered some of their children. He had known others since boyhood. In the end, there were twenty-four in all, all former or present patients. The funds were raised within a few weeks in the fall leading up to and immediately following the crash of the stock market that marked the onset of the Great Depression. Their contributions became the Thomas S. Roberts Fund, to be used initially for the publication of *The Birds of Minnesota* and later as a permanent trust for the natural history museum. The trust was established in agreement with the University of Minnesota Board of Regents, and the contract specified that if Roberts should die before the book was finished, Kilgore and Breckenridge would finish the work.[19]

With funding secured, Roberts felt free to plan the rest of the plates. He wrote to Brooks to paint the "Ruby-throated Hummingbird, male and female and young male with the spotted throat." Brooks should include in the picture "the Spotted Jewel-weed, . . . a blue aster and a bit of boltonia or something of that kind."[20] The flowers, which bloom in September, anchor the picture in autumn, appropriate because of the presence of the immature male bird with the spotted throat feathers. Roberts was very specific and soon wished he had been more specific on the painting of the Bald Eagle and the Fish Hawk (Osprey). When that arrived at the museum, the eagle was posed crouching over a freshly killed male goldeneye duck. Brooks had painted what he saw in British Columbia, but Minnesota eagles rarely killed birds. They lived mostly on carrion or fish, often fish snatched away from Osprey. The painting was not accurate, and worse, Roberts worried that it would further incite the ire of duck hunters against the regal bird. He had been working hard to convince sportsmen that eagles deserved and needed protection, that they were not competitors with the shotgun. This was not the image he wished to promote. Still, he told Brooks, "The picture is very attractive and the duck is a beauty so perhaps we had better let it go."[21] The illustration remained in the book.

In December, Francis Lee Jaques—Lee to his friends—an artist on staff at the American Museum of Natural History and with Minnesota connections, made plans to visit Roberts at the museum. Well-known for his stunning backgrounds at the American Museum, Jaques's artistic eye appreciated birds relating to their environment. For this reason, he gravitated toward the bigger birds—ducks and loons, for example. He was said to have commented that "the difference between warblers and no warblers is very slight."[22] A hunter and natural historian, Jaques had provided observations for "The Book" from his earlier days in Minnesota, though his communication was mostly with Kilgore, who was about his age. Roberts sought Brooks's opinion on soliciting Jaques for a few plates. Brooks wrote back immediately, urging him to do so: "[Jaques] stands alone in America in making a bird picture."[23]

Jaques was very interested in the assignment. Breckenridge, who was finishing up the shorebirds and beginning the owls, suggested that Jaques be given the remaining large birds, which he did so well: herons, cranes, pelicans, and cormorants, a happy coincidence, since at the time, Jaques was in the American South and had been observing those species daily. Before the artist began on those species, though, Roberts requested that he do three plates that they had previously agreed upon: one with prairie chickens, one with the pheasant and Hungarian partridge, and one with the Passenger

Pigeon and the Mourning Dove. But within months, Jaques was asked to illustrate *Florida Bird Life,* and soon the artist would be very pressed for time.

At this time, Roberts approached one other artist to do some work on
the book, Walter Alois Weber, who was employed by the Field Museum
in Chicago. Weber was very young, only twenty-four, but Brooks considered him "a second Fuertes" and added, "Dr. Chapman's endorsement [of
Weber] also speaks volumes."[24] Weber was off on assignment for the Field
Museum in Bermuda. When he got back to Chicago, he began work on his
allotment, the *Zonotrichia* sparrows—Harris's, the White-throated, and the
White-crowned. Roberts loved Weber's depiction of those small birds and
immediately assigned him the rest of the sparrows, a big job, ten plates or
more. The young artist agreed but put in a request: "May I ask if the Jays
and Blackbird groups for your book are done? Of the perching birds these
are my special pets . . . and [giving them to me] would be greeted with great
welcome."[25] Roberts was reluctant, thinking the young man might be biting
off more than he could chew, but in the end, Weber painted both groups,
trading away the warblers to Brooks to get them.[26]

In April 1930, Weber drove out to British Columbia to work under Brooks,
although the older artist was initially reluctant to take on any student. He
considered it presumptuous, since he himself had never had any instruction.[27] Roberts may have been a bit uneasy entrusting any work to a twenty-
four-year-old. Brooks assured him he would oversee the paintings and
that Weber's birds were "well-balanced & graceful and his detail work very
good."[28] A year later, in summer 1931, Breckenridge went out to Brooks's studio both to collect and to study Brooks's technique. Breckenridge thought
the time spent in British Columbia was beneficial but confidently told
Roberts that "hard work on my part is the main thing and I'm sure that
after I get back [to Minnesota] I can continue to improve after this work
with Brooks."[29]

The following days were exciting at the museum as bird plate after bird
plate arrived. Roberts, Kilgore, Breckenridge, and Densmore eagerly viewed
each one, thrilled with the grebes, the gulls and terns, the pheasants and par-
tridges. Jaques's plate of the extinct Passenger Pigeon painted in muted gray-
greens was elegiac, heart-stopping. Jaques considered it "the best bird portrait
he ha[d] ever done,"[30] and Roberts declared it "artistically and in every way the
best thing that we have had thus far."[31]

Only two plates failed to get rave reviews, those of warblers done by Brooks. Roberts did not know how to express his dismay. "I am much distressed and embarrassed to have to say that they are not quite up to my expectations," he wrote. "Pardon me for saying, but . . . the prothonotary, Cape May (adults) and one or two others are too plump." He went on to a long list of problems: the relative size was off, the wing bars were wrong, color was not good. Brooks graciously took the criticism and made the changes but also offered a defense and invoked the name of the now-sainted Fuertes: "Fuertes was the only man who ever agreed with me that the birds of this group were often well-rounded."[32]

As the artists painted the plates in British Columbia, New York City, Harrisburg, Chicago, and Minneapolis, Roberts pursued lithographic firms to reproduce their work. The company producing the best work turned out to be right in Minneapolis. The McGill Company, located downtown at 501 Seventh Avenue South, had been in business in various forms in Minneapolis since the 1880s. Lithographers with the firm experimented with the industry-standard four-color offset process but found that a seven-color offset gave far superior results, and printing the image on high-quality art paper preserved the true color of the original painting. It was expensive, but the trust fund allowed Roberts to pursue the best. McGill's wanted to garner more work in this area and gave Roberts a price break. In what Roberts called "an acid test," they agreed to let the artist pass judgment on the quality of each reproduction. If it did not meet his expectations, there was no charge until the plate was acceptable. The firm so believed in the project that its president, Charles McGill, became a financial backer in the trust fund.

The University of Minnesota Press, which would publish the book, did not have its own printing plant, and McGill's later was awarded the contract to print the text, too. In this, they were not the lowest bidder, and the Press wanted to give the contract to a Chicago firm. Roberts would absolutely not hear of it. Two years into work with McGill's, he had come to appreciate their reliability and emphasis on quality, and he valued the ability to drop in and supervise the progress—something he would be unable to do with an out-of-state printer. Furthermore, his financial backers, all Minnesotans, wished to see their money and the employment stay within the state at the nadir of the Great Depression. They solidly backed Roberts up.[33]

The University of Minnesota Press was young. It had issued its first book in 1927, a biography of the university's second president, Cyrus Northrop. The Press had been established for the express purpose of publishing the work of university scholars. The director, Margaret S. Harding, had been at the helm since its inception and was the first woman in the nation to hold such a position. Smart, steely, and educated, Harding had whipped the infant Press into economic shape in a matter of months. A woman in a man's field, she was an activist for women's rights and headed up a largely female staff.

Despite this, rather than because of it, Roberts inclined naturally to the Press as a publisher. Loyal to a fault to things Minnesotan, Roberts looked no farther than this local institution to issue his precious masterpiece. He *was* a university scholar, and the work *was* intended for academic use, but he also targeted a nonintellectual, even noneducated, user. In accepting the book, the Press ventured into uncharted territory.

By 1931, the many strands of the book were finally being woven together. The lengthy manuscript had been more or less completed by September 1930. The printers set type, and Roberts received the first galleys in September a year later. From early spring, it seemed like he was running down to McGill's nearly every day. It became a habit to swing by the firm in the morning before arriving at the museum.

He became a frequent visitor to the University of Minnesota Press, based on campus on the first floor of Wesbrook Hall, as well. The meetings with Harding, who also served as the book's editor, were not always pleasant. He did not enjoy smooth dealings with her. They locked horns on a few editorial changes to the manuscript, some as basic as the use of *which* and *that,* but overall changes to the text were minor. The two disagreed on the expected sales of the book. Harding set the first run at 1,000 copies and predicted these would last for many months.[34] This was the upper limit of customary practice. The Press usually printed 250 to 1,000 copies in a first run.[35]

Roberts was not closemouthed about the unpleasant encounters. His staff and old friends, at least, heard about them and sympathized. Out of town, Breckenridge wrote that he hoped Harding was "calming down." Densmore, on vacation, wished, "May Mrs. Harding extend her stay in Colorado!"[36] One friend, himself a former publisher of a milling magazine, passed on to Roberts that he had heard chatter through the grapevine that the University of Minnesota Press "[doesn't] know the first principles of book making." He added, "These people are getting a fine reputation for themselves."[37]

Jennie suffered another stroke that rendered her temporarily unable to speak, and Roberts arranged to remain close to home. That summer, there were no collecting trips, no vacation in the north woods. Both Catharine and Tom owned summer homes on Christmas Lake west of Minneapolis, though, and Sundays were usually spent out there with the grandchildren, Jennie remaining home with the nurse. It had been years since they had gone out together for anything more than a short drive in the car.

Then the galley proofs arrived, and the proofreading began. All fall he read proof, Densmore read proof, Kilgore read proof. Roberts read at the office, he read at home, he read after medical calls and before social calls. He managed to take in the annual American Ornithologists' Union meetings in Detroit, taking Breckenridge with him, and he stopped in at McGill's hours before he left, and hours after returning. *The Birds of Minnesota* consumed him.

On April 5, 1932, McGill's commenced printing the two-volume book, occupying four of their presses. Five weeks later, Roberts held the first volume in his hands and purchased twenty copies, to "pay obligations." Densmore closed up her desk and headed home to Red Wing, after nearly seven years of work. Roberts wrote in his journal: "A big job finished." The second volume was completed and bound one week after that. "The end of a long, long trail," he noted.[38]

The *Minneapolis Tribune* sent a reporter to the museum to interview Minnesota's "bird man," and ran a high-profile article in the Sunday paper. Bird enthusiasts had anticipated the book for years, and even before the pages rolled off the presses, had been sending in their checks, requesting copies. The book was released June 6. Within three days, all one thousand copies were sold, to the glee of Roberts and his staff. The next one thousand were sold by mid-July, and the third thousand were half-promised. "Apparently we did a good job," Roberts wrote to Densmore. "What has Mrs. Harding to say now about the selling qualities of certain bird books, I wonder?" she answered in reply.[39]

These "merry" sales (Roberts's adjective) occurred before the appearance of reviews in *The Auk* and *Bird-Lore*. Both Witmer Stone and Frank

Chapman had kind words for Roberts's life work. "One must study the work at first hand to realize the vast amount of information that it contains as it is impossible to do it justice in a short [review]," Stone wrote in *The Auk*. Stone liked the fact that many artists were employed, commenting on the "Japanese quality" of Jaques's herons, which was "original and appealing," and adding that "Breckenridge's shore birds give promise of excellent work in this field."[40] Chapman called the two volumes "splendid," considered the illustrations of "exceptional beauty," and appreciated, too, the many artists, since each had given their own unique take on the birds they had rendered.[41] *The Birds of Minnesota* also snared a brief mention on an inside page in the *Saturday Review of Literature*.[42]

Roberts especially valued Chapman's opinion and read the review out loud to Jennie, who managed to pronounce him "a darling" for the wonderful review. From her bedroom, she had kept abreast of the success of the book, but the strokes had robbed her of the capacity for full understanding and pleasure.

In June and July, Roberts carried signed volumes out to Lake Minnetonka to his subscribers. Marie Commons—Frank had died the year before—received the first deluxe copy.[43] Jim Bell, John Crosby, and Charles Bovey, with whom Roberts was especially close, all received their copies on the Fourth of July. Roberts's siblings, Emma and Walter, both received early copies, as did his sister-in-law, Anna Cleveland, and his old high school chums Joe Kingman and Robert Williams. Edson Gaylord, a former fellow land examiner, also received one. Although Roberts got many requests for gratis copies, according to professional courtesy, he was able to grant none of the entreaties. The University of Minnesota Press required the profit from the sale of the first thousand books to finance the printing of the second thousand. With the United States now mired well and truly in economic depression, Chapman told Roberts, "How fortunate it is that the production of this work was assured when the world was brighter! It would, I imagine, be difficult to secure support for it now."[44]

Although he had enjoyed uncommonly good health all through the winter, spring, and summer of 1932 as McGill gave birth to *Birds,* Roberts now succumbed to several recurrent illnesses at once, as if he could finally let his guard down after the tremendous effort. In early September, he was again struck by abdominal pain that presented as appendicitis (which, lacking his appendix, was no longer possible). He took to his bed and promptly came down with an upper-respiratory infection as well. He lay in bed for most of the month, improving for a day or two, only to worsen.

While Roberts suffered from his various ailments, down the hall in her room, Jennie fell one day, apparently injuring a hip. However, an X-ray taken at the hospital showed worse: a neck fracture. Still, she lingered a few days more. Then, as the sun rose on a clear, mild October morning, Jane Cleveland Roberts passed from the world. Roberts was able to get out of bed to attend the funeral the next day but was too ill to be at the internment at Lakewood Cemetery several days after.

She had been part of his life for sixty years. Sick as she had been, a small, quiet presence, she had filled the house with such vitality that Roberts felt her sudden absence acutely. "Carroll moved in to live with me," he wrote forlornly in his journal a week after her death. "[He] took Mother's room."[45]

How does one recover from such a grievous loss? His bird book was published, a testimony to future generations of Minnesota's once-rich avifauna, but in other spheres Roberts's life at age seventy-four was falling away from him. The preceding decade had seen the deaths of Frank Commons, William Edgar, Charles Velie, and G. F. Ewe, all longtime patients and personal friends; Nathan Butler, his land examiner boss from long ago; Carroll Williams, his roommate in Philadelphia; Carlos Avery, his erstwhile ally in the state conservation department; and John Nordquist. "Are you not coming 'home' sometime?" he wrote Robert Williams, member of the Young Naturalists' Society of his teen years. "It would be a great pleasure to see you and talk over old times. Not many left who go back to the beginning of things."[46]

He mourned the disappearance of birds from western Minnesota, lost to the plow and the planting of grain. He mourned the absent birds of Minneapolis, their abundance, their brilliance, how they filled the skies, when everything was new to him. And it was true, as Chapman had observed, he was mourning his youth as well.

Old age was upon him. He now characterized himself as a "fat old man," who did not tromp up hills or through swamps with as much relish as he once had. Worse, for several years, he had been growing deaf and could no longer hear "most of the music of the woods."[47] To a birdman with so fine an ear that he urged others to learn the quality of the voice of a bird, rather than its specific song, the hearing loss must have been particularly devastating. Ever cognizant of the legacy of his Roberts ancestors, he frequently remarked to Emma, who herself was seventy-three, that they were both "living on borrowed time."[48]

Though he had confided to Chapman that he might retire when *The Birds of Minnesota* was completed, Roberts's natural buoyancy propelled him back into the mainstream of living after Jennie's death. He hosted two parties of houseguests in the first two months of his bereavement. He had company to dinner, people he owed—Densmore and his longtime nurse Caroline Rankiellour. He resumed house calls on patients and met friends for lunch at the Minneapolis Club. He went to the movies with Carroll. And for the first time in several years, he went out for New Year's Eve, ringing in 1933 at a dinner party hosted by the Charles Boveys.

CHAPTER 14

Building Mr. Bell's Museum

> [The White-breasted Nuthatch is] ever at home
> and busy among the shade trees of the city and the
> monarchs of the forest.
>
> —*The Birds of Minnesota*, 2: 82

The harried Thomas Roberts riffled through the papers on his desk. It was, as usual, a mess, strewn with journal articles, books, class lists, unanswered mail. He claimed that the disorganization was a holdover habit from his years as a physician, when he never had the luxury of a spare minute in which to straighten a desk, and it appeared that he had not become any less busy in these later years. It might have seemed odd that such an orderly mind was able to abide such a disorderly work space, but it was a habit he retained for his entire life.

A photograph of a young Clarence Herrick hung on one wall, a Clarence who would never grow old, reminding him of genius that had been cut down in its prime. At work in the untidy but productive office on the third floor of Zoology, Roberts could hear the clang of the streetcars passing on Washington Avenue and the muted grind of automobiles driving below on Church Street. The bulk of brown-bricked Jackson Hall filled the frame of his office window.

In the hallway, the clutter did not abate. By 1933, the museum had expanded to its limit. The large dioramas, the "super-star" displays, engulfed every possible wall space, and by default the museum staff was devoting its attention to the "small groups"—portable cases housing mounted songbirds, perched perhaps or with a nest. Walter Breckenridge lavished his taxidermist skills on these, and Roberts made agreements with local schools to display and rotate the groups between buildings, so the children were exposed to a variety of displays in the course of the academic year. His grandchildren eyed these with something like dread, for they knew that with the arrival of each new set to their school, they were likely to be called upon to opine with expertise on the stuffed birds. Breckenridge would eventually turn out 150 of the miniature scenes, which made their way to the elementary schools in Minneapolis, the state fair, and local sportsmen's fairs.

Tucked off from the corridors of the museum, the long, narrow "bird room" ran most of the length of the building, housing the study skins in shallow wooden trays stacked in cabinets against one wall. At a table overlooking the campus on the Mississippi, students sat on class days amid piles of feathered forms, pondering the plumages of immature hawks, the beaks of finches, and the conundrum of greenish fall warblers. This room, too, looked as if it were bursting at the seams.

The natural history museum needed more space. The original plans for the Zoology Building once included a wing stretching west on Washington Avenue. Roberts had given up hope that that would ever materialize. As early as 1924, people had tossed about the idea of a separate building. In fact, for a brief moment in 1931, it seemed like it might actually happen, when Jim Bell had offered $125,000 to build a new building, provided the state legislature would match the funds. But the legislature, in its wisdom, had passed up the offer. So Roberts was stymied in his dreams.

The newly bereaved museum director had many irons in the fire. The 1933 winter term began at the university, and his bird class roll listed twenty-two names. The class had doubled in size from the early days, when the professor and his small class of women could hop a streetcar to a birding site. Now, many of the students were men enrolled in a wildlife biology program based on the farm campus. Winter term consisted of lectures, given Monday and Wednesday afternoons.

The seventy-five-year-old physician continued seeing a sizable caseload of patients, making house calls on them before going into work at the museum. He was sitting for a portrait, painted by his daughter-in-law Dorothy's father, Willbur Reaser, an established portraitist. And he continued to accept a flurry of invitations to dinner, extended by his solicitous patients and friends. They kept a watchful eye on the widower, who now occupied the flat at 2303 Pleasant Avenue by himself. Noon dinner at the spare, elegant mansion of Mrs. George C. Christian overlooking Fair Oaks Park, recently carved from the site of the demolished Washburn mansion. Monday night supper at Mrs. Charles Velie's, herself adjusting to life without a mate. Supper at Emma's. Supper at daughter Catharine's. An evening with Tom and Dot and the boys. Through the wintry gales, the spates of snow and rain, the tear of wind, the treachery of slippery sidewalks, and the darkness of January mornings and evenings, Roberts soldiered on. The warmth of an evening with friends or family only magnified the emptiness as he opened the door to his apartment and silence engulfed him. "[Mrs. Roberts's] final illness was very sudden and brief and I am left lonely and restless," he had written to a friend.[1] He spent the late evenings alone with a book, reading into the wee hours of the morning. He read popular novels but favored mysteries. His reputation for reading a book a night was well known, and he would recommend good ones to his grandchildren.

Chronic bronchitis plagued him. He had battled the illness since before Jennie's death, and it had never completely cleared up. He periodically took to his bed for a day or two but did not seem to improve. Constant coughing weakened him. Finally, concern for his health propelled him to accept an offer extended by Charles and Kate Bovey and her sister, Josephine Velie, to accompany them to Chandler, Arizona, for a month's vacation. Perhaps the dry desert air would give him some relief. So, six weeks into winter term, he turned his lecture schedule over to Will Kilgore and headed south.

The Hotel San Marcos of Chandler would probably not have been Roberts's first choice of accommodation had the focus of the trip been bird study, and had he been footing the bill. A fashionable resort resplendent with palm trees, a swimming pool, a golf course, and acres of irrigated lawn amid the Sonoran desert, it was where the wealthy came to escape the rigors of a northern winter. Roberts hated the damp air of the sprinklers, the sudden drop in temperature of a desert winter night, and being displaced from his accustomed habitat. The Boveys had a cottage on the grounds, not rooms in the hotel; Roberts enjoyed sunshine on the patio and the sparkle of intelligent conversation. But he did not immediately improve, and he fretted about dumping the responsibility of the class on Kilgore, who had his own work to attend to.

Gradually, after weeks, the coughing lessened, and he felt himself getting stronger. He sought out a boy with an old Ford and hired him to drive into the surrounding desert in search of new birds. There amid the towering saguaros and blooming ocotillo, he began racking up a list. Roadrunners, a Crissal Thrasher, and brilliant Vermilion Flycatchers were exotic to a Minnesota birder. "This was the first time I have ever visited an entirely new locality. . . . I had an interesting time trying to identify birds with a field glass," he later wrote to a colleague. "This . . . is no easy job when the distinctions are not very evident." But to Kilgore, he groused, "There are several others that I cannot identify. O for a gun!"[2]

Roberts returned home in time to resume his teaching duties for spring term, when most class periods would be spent outdoors. The large class challenged the logistics established years before. "In the field we are like a moving army; six cars leave the building," he wrote to a former student.[3] Still, they traveled the countryside, from the Lake Harriet bridle path to Coon Creek in southern Anoka County, ending as always at the Edgar cabin on Nine Mile Creek in Bloomington.

One evening in July 1933, shortly before he was to go on vacation to the Lafayette Club on Lake Minnetonka, as a guest of Marie Commons, Roberts received an unexpected visit from Breckenridge. He was not alone. He was accompanied by an attractive brunette whom he had met a mere seven weeks before and whom he was now proposing to marry the very next day and take along with him on a two-month university expedition to Hudson Bay to study tularemia. Would Roberts, as his boss, consent to her going on the trip? Would he agree to be the best man at the wedding?

What could Roberts say? Breckenridge was neither impulsive nor reckless. The couple was already officially engaged. They were just fast-tracking the wedding. Within hours, he found himself in summer pinstripes, a rose pinned to his lapel, stepping in for "Dad Breckenridge" and witnessing the marriage vows of his assistant curator. "It was considered something of a romance," Roberts wrote later to Mabel Densmore, explaining how the event made the front page of the *Minneapolis Journal*. "It was a hurry up afternoon and Breck as usual was 20 minutes late. I kept Conner [Roberts's chauffeur] on hand and we rushed plenty at the last. There was a large delegation at the train to see the party off. The young lady went to work that day in St. Paul at 7 A.M., quit at 12 noon and was ready before Breck! So you see she can hustle. They are all back and seem still to be good friends."[4]

That year, there was another bird book in the works. The University of Minnesota Press's Harding wanted a much slimmer volume that featured the popular illustrations from *The Birds of Minnesota* with the text honed down to a single page opposite each picture, giving the bare facts about nests and eggs, range, and behavioral characteristics. McGill's ran twenty thousand copies of the original pictures. Roberts remained leery of the formidable Harding and fretted in a letter to Frank Chapman, "I can't find a name for the [new book]. It is no longer the birds of Minnesota and the Press rules out all references to any geographical area. I am worried what they will do to it. With the original work I had the whip hand but I have largely lost it now. I am so afraid that they will insist upon something that will be an embarrassment to me and make my ornithological friends smile. The Press thinks only in commercial terms."[5]

They settled on *Bird Portraits in Color,* presumably dignified enough to keep the ornithological friends straight-faced, and the trimmed-down version proved successful. The Press would sell out its twenty thousand copies by 1944.

In 1934, Roberts began revision of his monumental *The Birds of Minnesota.* He had discovered some errors in the first edition that wanted correcting, remarkably few, and felt he needed to update the nesting and range records. He extended the bibliography to 1936, when the second edition was released, and rewrote the general index, all with the editorial aid of Densmore, who would continue working periodically for him at the museum until the end of his life.

The Great Depression deepened. By 1932, General Mills had laid off half of its employees, and citywide thirty-five thousand people were out of work. Ten thousand Minneapolitans applied for relief that year.[6] Roberts, a minimally paid employee of the university, was somewhat immune from the worst financial losses, and he still had some income from his medical work. He worried, though, about losses he had taken on a corporate default on bonds and the financial drain of Jennie's long illness, when a private nurse had been in attendance almost around the clock. Later, as the Depression wore on, he would feel obligated to keep working, needing the income.

The 1930s were hard years for birds, as well. A deep, persistent drought gripped North America that decade. In the Everglades, site of the fierce fight to protect the region's wading birds from exploitation from the feather trade, wetlands shrank, concentrating the birds. This facilitated a renewed assault on them, as local residents, strapped for money and living close to the edge, once again turned to poaching as a source of black-market income.

In Minnesota, 1933 was an arid year that lowered lake levels and dried marshes. The drought extended into the winter, with January unusually warm and dry. Temperatures rose above freezing during the day, the freeze-thaw regime killing many of the native plants in the wildflower garden at Glenwood Park. What snow was on the ground disappeared, and the remaining winter months were brown ones. Roberts, not inclined to alarmism, wondered in a letter, "Is a desert ahead for this interior region?"[7] Worse, the May that followed in 1934 was the warmest on record, and a terrific dust storm wracked the state, with high winds that continued for thirty-six hours. The waterfowl migration, already under way, was "scanty and irregular."[8] Following the dust storm, it evened out but brought an unusual number of shorebirds: Hudsonian Godwits, Stilt Sandpipers, and Northern Phalaropes appeared in Minneapolis. Roberts attributed the odd phenomenon to strong west and northwest winds that blew the birds eastward.[9] On Memorial Day, the temperature reached 106 degrees. Under the relentless lack of rain, shallow Swan Lake in Nicollet County, a famous nesting place for ducks, shrank dramatically. Densmore, spending the hot summer in western Minnesota, reported that the marshes and lakes in the Herman area, where Roberts had looked in vain for prairie birds a decade before, had evaporated.[10] Lake Minnetonka was five and a half feet below normal, and Minneapolis city officials were pouring water into the city lakes to keep them presentable.[11]

The numbers of ducks and geese dropped precipitously as the drought ravaged the continent. Roberts agreed with the National Association of Audubon Societies that there should be a closed season on all waterfowl hunting for at least a year or two.[12] He thought that, as much as hunters liked to shoot ducks, they would understand the effect of the drought on populations and agree to a temporary hunting ban. But it did not happen. The head of the federal Biological Survey, Jay Norwood "Ding" Darling, opposed it.

As the drought lingered on through two more summers, Roberts grew disillusioned with hunters and sportsmen's organizations like Ducks Unlimited and the Izaak Walton League. Himself a hunter, he was generally not opposed to shooting ducks for sport and table and had spent many a fall day in a duck blind on the sloughs. But he now saw sportsmen as the chief offenders in the effort to preserve the ducks. "Most of them are against legislation that will curtail their hunting activities," he wrote a concerned citizen of southern Minnesota. "Some progress has been made in this direction but more drastic measures are needed. In my opinion nothing will save the waterfowl but the suppression of all hunting for a series of years. But the passing of such legislation seems impossible by the federal government or the state."[13]

Waterfowl were not the only birds suffering declining numbers. Birds of prey were also under assault, not from the drought but from persistent misunderstanding about their role as predators. For decades, people had labeled birds as "good" or "bad" with regard to the services that they provided to humans. Roberts himself took pains to point out the usefulness of birds in *The Birds of Minnesota*, as he aimed his book at a populace raised on the custom of shooting any kind of bird if it thwarted human activity—eating crop seedlings or excavating holes in telephone poles, for example.

Even men with training in conservation could be quick to condemn certain birds: "The Goshawk is a savage destroyer of small game and poultry," George Miksch Sutton, then working as a state game man, wrote in 1928. "His smaller cousins, the Sharp-shinned Hawk and Cooper's Hawk, are killers."[14] These three species together with the Great Horned Owl, were often singled out as particularly bloodthirsty and deserving of annihilation. Their "crime" was an appetite for domestic poultry, grouse, quail, and pheasant chicks—any game bird men might want to shoot themselves—and for the small, "defenseless" songbirds that people now enjoyed watching at their bird feeders. The Minnesota Legislature had passed a version of a law recommended by the National Association of Audubon Societies (NAAS) that protected most raptors, like Red-tailed Hawks and Osprey, a long time prior to this. Carlos Avery had been commissioner of Game and Fish at the time of its passage. Roberts regarded Avery as an ally, with a sane view of predators. But the commissioner then, as in present times, was a political appointment, and Avery was replaced in 1924 by a man with a less ecological bent. In February 1927, Avery had written to Roberts to tell him that he had recently received a letter from the NAAS, informing him that the Minnesota law had been changed, removing protection of all raptors, from little saw-whet owls and diminutive kestrels to Red-tailed Hawks, which dined mainly on mice.

How could such legislation slip past Roberts? Avery himself was flummoxed. "I wonder how in the world this came to be done and if there is any possibility of getting it corrected at the present session of the Legislature," he wrote in 1927. "It must be that someone was 'asleep at the switch.'"[15]

"The Fish and Game Department, the Izaak Walton League and all sportsmen's organizations are united against these birds. It is almost a hopeless fight as things stand," Roberts wrote to T. Gilbert Pearson, who in 1934 had been pressured out of his position as president of the NAAS over the issue. "Talking and writing do no good."[16] The issue of raptor protection gained national prominence, particularly on the East Coast. Some faulted the established leaders of the NAAS, like Pearson, for settling into complacency after the bloody fights to end the feather trade decades before. The NAAS was deemed not up to the crisis and as having gotten into bed with the munitions industry, which supplied hunters with shells and bullets. Led by Rosalie Edge, a wealthy New York ex-suffragette, activists formed the Emergency Conservation Committee (ECC) to address the slaughter of raptors and waterfowl. In particular, the committee acted, when the NAAS would not, to protect Hawk Mountain in Pennsylvania, a locale at which migrating raptors were funneled in great numbers every fall. Pennsylvania at this time had a bounty on hawks, and massive numbers of migrators were massacred along the ridge of Hawk Mountain.[17]

Roberts was a leading advocate of hawk and owl protection in Minnesota but was too much the old-fashioned gentleman to support the ECC's provocative language and pugnacious action. "I am not in sympathy with its methods of procedure," he told one of his observers, who had thought Roberts would sign on to the committee. Roberts was also staunchly loyal to those on the NAAS board when the ECC focused its attacks on them: "It is my very best friends that they are attacking." He was even more blunt with a young ornithologist seeking advice from him. He labeled the ECC's tactics "unfair and malicious," and he ended his commentary with, "Save me from Mrs. Edge and her kind." However, he told the NAAS that he did not think Audubon should be in "too close relationship with sportsmen's organizations and state game commissioners. Their ideas of conservation are not the same as the Association should have."[18]

In the 1930s, the NAAS tried each legislative session to introduce a bill protecting the beleaguered birds. The national group pinpointed Minnesota legislators who were key allies, used like-minded people on the Game and Fish Commission to speak for the bill, and called on Roberts to contact important players. Sharp-shinned and Cooper's Hawks and goshawks were always excluded; a reprieve for them would have been too hard for the public to swallow. But each time they failed to get protection, Roberts blamed great conflict between the governor and the legislature, and in one year ineptitude on the part of the Game and Fish Committee of the legislature, where the bill languished for want of a sponsor. "I might have gone down [to the capitol]," he wrote to T. Gilbert Pearson. "But I am no good at that sort of thing—fighting ignorant politicians."[19]

The drought and pervasive ignorance of ecosystem ecology—a science then in its infancy—exacerbated ill-conceived land practices. One enormous mistake that came to a head in 1933 involved an area of Minnesota that Roberts knew well and loved: Mud Lake, in eastern Marshall County, in the far northwest reaches of the state. Roberts and his intrepid party had been in the region in 1900 and 1901, collecting bird and plant specimens for the natural history survey. They had been entranced by its wild beauty. But in the intervening years, the vast, marshy land had been subjected to the largest public drainage project in the United States.[20] A million dollars had been spent trying to convert the wetlands to agricultural land, but the venture failed to make money. When the despoiled land was forfeited for want of tax payments, Marshall County, threatened with bankruptcy, turned to the state for help. The legislature, in turn, appealed to FDR's New Deal. Minnesota would bail out Marshall County if the federal government would buy the land for a wildlife refuge.

On July 5, 1934, Roberts received a telegram from the Migratory Waterfowl Program of the federal government, asking him if Mud Lake and the surrounding land would be desirable as a Wildfowl Refuge Restoration Project. Recalling "it was in fact a paradise," Roberts replied that "if it is possible to reclaim an area that has been 'dead' for many years, then I think it is an ideal place for such an experiment." He was less sanguine over the restoration prospect of another of his favorite places, Heron Lake. "It was formerly the greatest place for breeding and migrating waterfowl in the state," he wrote, but now "the shore line is almost entirely leased to gun clubs which might stand in the way [of government habitat restoration]." "The carp are a serious problem at Heron Lake," he added. "The former great growth of wild celery [a staple in waterfowl diet] has largely disappeared."[21]

With conflict over bird protection at home, it was a joy for Roberts to gather with like-minded friends, and the annual American Ornithologists' Union meetings, usually on the East Coast, provided the perfect opportunity to mix business and pleasure. He had missed a number of the meetings when Jennie had been bedridden; now he seemed determined to not miss a one, as long as his health held. During the 1933 convention in New York City, he not only took in all the meetings by day but also ran about town at night, attending dinners and receptions, one at Chapman's, the Radio City Music Hall production of *Little Women,* and the legendary Roxy Theatre. He saw his brother, Walter, in New Jersey and a favorite cousin in Baltimore. He paid a call to Carroll Williams Jr., the son of his roommate from his Philadelphia years, and he squired about the widowed Marie Commons, who was also in New York to attend the meetings.[22]

He also took the train to the American Ornithologists' Union meetings in Chicago in 1934, traveling with Kilgore, and in 1935, to meetings in Toronto. But by 1936, with Roberts at age seventy-eight, train travel had lost its appeal. Instead, he and Breckenridge headed down the highway to the meetings in Pittsburgh, Breckenridge driving Carroll Roberts's Ford coupe. Women in Roberts's life—Emma and Mabel Densmore—had undertaken long driving trips with a companion, but not he. Pittsburgh was his first road trip. The fact that the thirty-three-year-old Breckenridge would agree to undertake such a venture is a testimony to his affection for his boss and to Roberts's convivial nature.

The pair stopped at Madison, Wisconsin, the first night. The drive from Minneapolis was notable for the big flock of Canada Geese that flew overhead. They drove through the University of Wisconsin campus and later, in Chicago, went to the zoo. Evenings were often spent playing cribbage. Occasionally, they took in a movie. It took them four days to reach Pittsburgh, a nine-hundred-mile trip in all, and the elderly man reported being very weary in the evenings, but he wrote to Kilgore, tending the store at home and recovering from a severe heart attack, that Breckenridge was a good driver.[23]

Once at the meeting, of course, the gregarious Roberts came to life, greeting old chums, attending meetings, dining at banquets, and smoking fine cigars. Breckenridge showed some of the wildlife movies he had made— in color (and a full year before Hollywood released its first effort in color, *The Wizard of Oz*). On the return trip, Carroll Roberts met the pair in Cleveland and relieved Breckenridge of his passenger. Father and son then took a southern route home, stopping at the Mayo Clinic in Rochester so Dr. Roberts could see a very sick patient being treated at St. Mary's Hospital, one of "his babies" he had delivered decades ago. All in all, it was a successful trip, but back home, Roberts mused that an auto trip took too long and maybe next time he would take an airplane.

Next time, however, the 1937 American Ornithologists' Union meeting was scheduled to be held in Charleston, South Carolina. Roberts had attended a previous meeting there, in 1928, and had gotten rip-roaring sick with a respiratory infection that laid him low for a month. He attributed the severity in part to the extreme change in climate, being transported from a wintry Minnesota in mid-November to the balmy, summerlike warmth of the Deep South in a matter of hours.

He decided to pass on Charleston, but still feeling energetic and wanting to see friends and relatives, perhaps for the last time—one never knew at age seventy-nine!—he planned a trip to New York that included the American Museum of Natural History, a trip to his brother's (now seventy-four), and then to Philadelphia, his ancestral home. He still had first cousins in the city, and Marie Commons, who was remarried, had moved to a fashionable neighborhood there and would host him. He had no inkling how this trip would change his life.

In New York, he and Carroll settled in at the Sherman Square Hotel fairly close to the American Museum. He saw Chapman, who was in his mid-seventies, the next day. The two had remained close through letters despite demanding careers, and they had spent decades lamenting the inability to enjoy the other's company in person. He also spent a day with Walter and his wife in New Jersey, and attended a luncheon at the museum, connecting with Lee Jaques, another favorite person. He called on T. Gilbert Pearson, whom he greatly liked and admired for his stalwart stance on bird protection.[24]

Leaving the city, Roberts and Carroll followed the picturesque Delaware River valley south, the hard woods beginning, in late September, to kindle with the reds and golds of autumn. The highway ran directly through New Hope, Pennsylvania, home of his Philadelphia roommate, Carroll Williams, long dead. It was exactly the time of year that he had first come with Williams to the family's New Hope ancestral farm in 1883 as a medical student, a visit that had been marked by glorious fall weather and the gorgeous Bucks County landscape.

Roberts knew that Carroll's sister Agnes, whom he had not seen in years, was living in the family home by herself, twice widowed, and he and Carroll paid her a call before driving on to Philadelphia, another hour down the road. They were greeted by a tiny, trim woman, alert and birdlike, dressed in the subdued garb of a Quaker. She was seventy-seven.

Sometime in the next forty-eight hours, he decided to ask her to marry him. He would later claim that it was a marriage of companionship. It was evident she was lonely and, being childless, quite alone. He, too, was lonely. Five years after Jennie's death, he still anticipated coming home to her presence, only to be cruelly disappointed when he opened the door to an empty apartment. Maybe two lonely people could make life happier for each other. So, seizing the opportunity in a manner most uncharacteristic, he had Marie Commons drive him back to New Hope three days later, where he spent three hours with Agnes and made his case. "Proposed to her that she marry me . . . left for her to decide," he wrote that night in his diary.[25]

He gave her a week to weigh the pros and cons—a week that he spent mostly sick, battling yet another spell of bronchitis. Roberts hated inconveniencing his hosts and the fact that he was unable to see all the people he had hoped to see in Philadelphia. He wrote to Kilgore during this week of waiting and, maybe, of second-guessing: "You perhaps are wondering . . . what has become of me. I, too, feel sort of uncertain about myself."[26] He did not mention he might be bringing home a wife.

After a week, he took a taxi back to New Hope. Agnes said, "Yes," despite reservations that she had been leading a solitary life and her suitor was quite social. Together they went to the county seat to apply for a marriage license. Three days later, after a night of intense coughing and little sleep, Roberts again went to Bucks County. He and Agnes Williams Harley were married at the justice of the peace, then went to Philadelphia and caught the 2:08 Baltimore and Ohio train for Minneapolis. They phoned the other "children" in Chicago during a layover, after breakfast with son Carroll. That evening at ten o'clock when the train pulled into the station, the entire family formed a welcome party on the platform.[27] A granddaughter would later recall that Agnes, wearing a long, black dress, "charmed us all immediately."[28]

Had the newlyweds hoped to escape salacious gossip, they were sadly disabused of that idea when a *Minneapolis Tribune* reporter banged on the door the very next morning. An article appeared in Tuesday's paper of a "romance of 55 years" "bloom[ing]" between the "79 year-old director of the University of Minnesota Museum of Natural History" and a "smiling, demure woman" whom he had "bade goodby" "a half century ago."[29] It was the second time in five years that a wedding of the Museum of Natural History staff merited a newspaper article.

To Densmore, Roberts wrote a splendidly terse explanation. After opening a letter with several paragraphs discussing details of her next work spell with him, he switched topics: "You will be surprised I imagine to hear that I brought home with me my old friend Carroll Williams sister. I found her living all alone on a farm with no one in particular to care for her so we got married and she and I are now getting acquainted again. The children did not object so I guess it is all right."[30]

The marriage actually proved to be more than "all right." As Roberts had counted on, the two shared many interests: Agnes was a bird-watcher, an admirer of wildflowers, with a decent amount of knowledge about them, an avid gardener—and she played cribbage. Her Quaker roots harmonized with Roberts's. In a poignant way, their marriage brought Roberts full circle to his childhood in Germantown and his Philadelphia days. The pair had something more in common: they shared a birthday, February 16. The next year, on Valentine's Day, he wrote in his diary: "Birthday party for *us* at Minnich's."[31] He turned eighty; Agnes, seventy-eight.

In April 1938, Roberts paid a visit to Jim Bell's downtown office, presumably just to chat about life at the museum, Bell's vision for his property at Delta marsh in Manitoba, and other things of common interest. Suddenly, out of the blue, Bell asked, "How about the wolf group?" This was really a rhetorical question. There was no space to display the charismatic canids in the museum's current quarters. Bell had wanted to see a big diorama featuring timber wolves for years. In fact, Roberts had already acquired the specimens, which were very scarce, just in case he might have need of them. But on this day, Roberts answered as he had many times, that it would require the building of a new museum to house the group. "Well, why not?" Bell replied. Taken aback, Roberts asked him if he was truly serious about pursuing such a project. Bell was. And so the two embarked on one last undertaking to preserve and highlight Minnesota's natural heritage for its people.[32]

Bell had sought to build a separate building at the university to house the natural history museum in 1931, but the Minnesota Legislature had failed to provide matching funds to his offer of $125,000. In 1935, in a new twist to the ever-present rivalry between Minneapolis and St. Paul, the St. Paul Institute approached the Minneapolis-based milling magnate to fund a science museum, to be built on Kellogg Boulevard in the capital city. The institute had secured city council approval, engineers and architects, and a museum man to direct the new undertaking. They planned to apply for federal funding and were keenly interested in meeting with Bell.[33]

Bell, though, remained loyal to his alma mater and to Roberts. "I think that the University is the natural and proper ground for such a museum," he replied to the St. Paul petitioners, and he called Roberts one of the "outstanding ornithologists of this country."[34] To Roberts, Bell fumed, "Why don't our Regents wake up and secure some government assistance for the University?"[35]

Frustrated by the uninterest of the state legislature, this time Bell and the university sought a funding partner in the federal government. (Perhaps a bit ironic, since both Bell and Roberts were utterly staunch Republicans.) The Public Works Administration (PWA),[36] begun in 1933 as part of FDR's New Deal to underwrite large-scale public works, was in the midst of a second wave of funding in 1938. The projects involved private firms using skilled labor to build national infrastructure, like dams, bridges, schools, and hospitals. The university applied for PWA funding in the spring. By the end of July, the federal funds were secured. Roberts was jubilant and wrote to a student, "We are excited today because word came this morning from Washington that PWA had granted the money for a new museum building. This makes it a certainty and work will probably begin as soon as details can be completed. Next summer will see a grand moving bee and some moving it will be!! When we get a new building all by ourselves it will be a great day for me. I have been dreaming about it for years."[37]

In late August, Roberts, Breckenridge, and an architect from the venerable St. Paul firm of Clarence H. Johnston took the train to Chicago to study the displays in the Field Museum. Johnston had been the official architect of the University of Minnesota for many decades. He was dead by 1938; his son, Clarence H. Johnston Jr., designed the new museum. Johnston was at the time at work on a second major building on campus, Coffman Union, which would open six days after the dedication of the natural history museum. Another member of the firm was assigned to grapple with the complexities of designing the museum's interior, which the firm had never done. At the Field Museum, the trio scrutinized the display cases, their lighting, how reflections bounced off the glass cases, what type of molding was employed, and a thousand other tiny details. Stanley Field, the museum's president, joined the Minnesotans for lunch.

Back home in Minneapolis, Roberts described the jaunt in a letter to Chapman. "I suppose we should have gone on to the American Museum," he wrote, "but it looked like a long trip.... I wish [this project] had come sooner when I could have been more lively on the job."[38]

They broke ground that fall. A beautiful art deco building of Indiana limestone rose on the site at the corner of University Avenue and Church Street. Bell's son, Samuel, a New York City–based sculptor, designed bas-relief carvings of animals on the building facade, with an American bison positioned over the front entrance. The total cost of the building was $272,000, $150,000 of which came from Bell and the remainder from the PWA.[39]

Meanwhile, Roberts was thinking ahead to displays that would be possible in the new building. Lee and Florence Jaques were planning a trip to Minnesota in late September. Lee wanted to observe migrating ducks on the Mississippi Flyway, and the couple needed to be in Minneapolis for the release of their collaborative book *Canoe Country*, published by the University of Minnesota Press. Recalling the happy exchanges he had had with the Jaques while he worked on plates for *The Birds of Minnesota*, Roberts extended an invitation for the two to "bunk with us at our apartment."[40] The empty first-floor flat in the Robertses' duplex on Pleasant was open and perfect for a longer stay. They would have ample space, including their own kitchen. Although both Jaqueses were near fifty in 1938, Florence later recalled, "It was fun to live there, for we were treated like teen-agers. It was alright for us to go out to dinner, but if we went on Thursday Dr. Roberts liked to know by Monday, so that the chauffeur could be notified in good time and the maid would understand there would be two less for dinner."[41]

If dining in, the Jaqueses mounted the stairs to the upper flat and joined the Robertses in the dining room, Roberts manning the foot pedal to summon the food. Agnes was charming and gracious; Lee, somewhat diffident; and Florence, warm and vivacious. The quartet played many rounds of four-handed cribbage, boys against the girls. Roberts kept a running tally of the games in his little pocket diary, and in the next several years, as the Jaqueses made repeated trips to Minneapolis, they ran up quite a score, the Lee-Thomas team ending ahead of the Florence-Agnes team by one point.[42]

The couple left for their New York City apartment October 2 with no specific agreement that Lee Jaques would play any role in the displays that would be forthcoming in the new museum[43]—the university had yet to break ground for the building—but both the artist and the museum director were interested in collaboration. As soon as he had heard that a new museum would be a reality in Minnesota, Jaques had written Roberts about a possible position, strictly on the Q.T. because he was still under contract with the American Museum of Natural History in New York. Roberts had answered that letter within days of receiving it, telling the artist they could "have that talk you suggest. I shall be most receptive."[44]

A golden fall settled upon Minneapolis. As skeins of ducks and geese wound their way south along the Mississippi Flyway, the Robertses entertained more guests, friends of Agnes's from Pennsylvania, and then suddenly it was time for the two oldsters to also depart, like the migrating birds. The annual American Ornithologists' Union meeting was to be in Washington, D.C., this year. It was a long train trip for elderly people, but both were in good health, buoyed by the events in their lives, and interested in the chance to see dear friends and relatives, perhaps an opportunity never to repeat. Agnes had relatives in the D.C. area, and both had family in Baltimore. It would be Roberts's last American Ornithologists' Union meeting.

It was most fortunate that they decided to go, because the first day of the meeting, Roberts was awarded the Brewster Medal for *The Birds of Minnesota*. For one who had known William Brewster, for whom the medal was named, and most of the previous recipients, and who had felt he had lived on the periphery of the ornithological establishment as a Minnesotan, it was a great honor. The inclination to assume a modest attitude—even to himself—was strong. "Received award of Brewster Medal," he tersely scribbled in his diary. To a birding friend in Minneapolis, he joked, "I may pass [the medal] around for inspection among the chosen few. It was an agreeable surprise."[45]

In May 1939, the construction of the new museum well under way, the Robertses made a surprise appearance at the recently formed Minnesota Ornithologists' Union meeting in Duluth. It had been a busy spring for Roberts at age eighty-one. He had been out in the field every class day with his group of neophyte birders, visiting as usual all the old haunts: Lake Harriet's bridle path (he persisted in labeling it the "bridal path" in his diary), Coon Creek, and Long Meadow Lake. By late May, the weather in Minneapolis was warm and summery, lilacs and bridal wreath blooming. Not so in Duluth. He and Agnes encountered thick fog thirty-five miles south of the city and drove into a wet, clammy metropolis. Nonetheless, excitement hummed at the state teachers' college, where Minnesota's birding community was convening for the second time. The organizing meeting, uniting several local bird clubs, had taken place at the Zoology Building on the university campus the year before.[46] A full slate of speakers was on the program in 1939, including a report by Roberts's former bird student Olga Lakela, speaking on the nesting Piping Plovers at Minnesota Point.

One can imagine the buzz in the room increasing as the venerable eighty-one-year-old "Bird Man" and his dainty and equally ancient wife slowly made their way into the auditorium. Just the fact they had ridden the 150 miles up Highway 61 was remarkable. The vast, brooding presence of fog-shrouded Lake Superior must have called latent memories of the distant past to the old man's mind, for when invited to speak a few words, he began to reminisce about his earliest experiences with Superior: the trip at the end of high school undertaken with his father, visiting a Duluth that was raw and ungainly, a rough assemblage of frame buildings; the collecting trip to the Arrowhead for the Natural History Survey, when the party had been dropped far from Grand Marais's harbor onto open water and had rowed through the black night, longing for daybreak and the safety of its rocky shore. The younger set was entranced by the stories from sixty years before of a Minnesota that existed only in the pioneer past. They wanted to hear more and offered to publish any account in their journal, *The Flicker*.[47]

In June 1939, Roberts began a series of letters to the American Museum of Natural History to persuade them to loan Lee Jaques to the Natural History Museum for a number of weeks in early 1940. The Heron Lake background in the Zoology Building had been painted on a concrete base, not canvas, and Roberts thought they would need a new background for the group and wanted Jaques to do it. Hoping that Chapman would have some influence over the director of the American Museum, Roy Chapman Andrews, Roberts wrote to his friend first, then wrote to reassure Jaques, "I cannot understand why he should object to your coming to help us out, but there is no guessing what is in his mind," adding, "The walls are going up and it is beginning to look like a place. The contractor says it is going to be 'a little gem.'"[48] Jaques wrote back that both Chapman and Jaques's immediate supervisor, Dr. Clark, seemed inclined to let him go, though Chapman thought Jaques should use his vacation time to do the work in Minnesota.[49] As the months went on, it seemed like a done deal. At least, both Florence and Lee were hopeful, and the Robertses once again invited them to make use of their unoccupied apartment.

Then in mid-December, Roberts received an oh-so-polite letter from Roy Chapman Andrews: "Naturally we would like to do anything we could to help you out but your request for the loan of Jaques comes at a particularly bad time. . . . It would very seriously curtail our program if we should take him off in order to send him out to you. I am most awfully sorry."[50]

Roberts was devastated. "I am in sack cloth and ashes today—deep mourning," he wrote to Jaques. "From the tone of Dr. Chapman's last letter I was not prepared for such a decision. It was all settled in my mind that you were coming." The American Museum, feeling pressure from a benefactor to move its projects forward, had decided to send Jaques along on a trip to Polynesia—which Jaques was not keen on, since Florence could not accompany him. Beyond the loss of the premier artist for his cherished

museum, both Roberts and Agnes felt acute disappointment at being de-
nied a prolonged visit from the warm and engaging couple. "All your friends
were looking forward to your coming," Roberts wrote in closing.[51]

From his new office on the third floor of the Natural History Museum,
Roberts looked out and saw the rounded tower of the fortresslike Armory
across the street. The Stars and Stripes snapped in the January breeze atop
the peaked cap of the tower. Beyond the Armory lay brown-bricked Memorial Stadium, where the Golden Gophers had been entertaining enthusiastic
fans for almost a decade under Coach Bernie Bierman. Even Roberts, not
usually a football fan, had taken to listening to games on the radio on Saturday afternoons. In winter 1940, the campus was swathed in snow, but it
looked tidy and organized, everything in its place as it had been for years.

Alas, the same could not be said for the museum. The staff made the big
move from the Zoology Building to the new place in stages. Office furnishings, books, files, typewriters, and, of course, the tens of thousands of bird
and mammal skins were transferred early in December 1939. The headache
of transferring the "groups"—the caribou, the white-tailed deer, the Heron
Lake assemblage, the beavers, the black bears, the Dall sheep, and the Pipestone Prairie—was put off until the new year. In the end, the Heron Lake
background was successfully moved, using a technique suggested by the architect. All was chaos and confusion for many weeks, a circumstance that
distressed the orderly Roberts. The museum remained closed to the public
until May. Gradually, the disorder was put to right, and he wrote to Charles
Johnston, the architect, that the building was "a joy all around."[52]

Indeed, he hardly believed how elegant the place was. Sometimes when
by himself in the building, he stole out of his office to the elevator and took
it to the main floor, unlocked the door to the auditorium, and flipped on the
lights, just to be reassured that it was really as beautiful as his memory served
him. There it spread before him, the subtly striped sapeli wood paneling
from Africa, the fine upholstered seats, the pleasing rust color scheme—it
was all beyond what he had imagined it would be, and he was thrilled.

CHAPTER 15

The Cardinal Hour

> These fading woods and shortening days, and the
> chilling woods that make life hard and dangerous,
> warn [the Ovenbird] that it is time to hie
> himself away.
>
> — *The Birds of Minnesota,* 2: 248

The letter from his old friend Frank Chapman must have stung, rubbing salt into a wound still fresh from the blow that Roberts had been dealt before Christmas. Lee Jaques would not be coming to do any work at the new museum. "I can only hope that . . . you will find another Jaques in Minnesota and give him the opportunity for development that Jaques has found here," Chapman had written.[1] Had he meant to be kind? The line could be read as a subtle allusion to lore that long ago, at the start of Jaques's career, Roberts had passed over an opportunity to hire the unknown artist. Soon after, given the chance, Chapman signed on the painter and had chortled over his find for decades.[2]

It was also a disingenuous wish: Jaques had honed his craft for years. He was at his peak. No wildlife artist in the country could match his skill. Roberts was not going to find another Jaques anywhere.

Roberts was now an old man. Eighty-two on his next birthday, his hair was white, his mustache also, though a bit more tamed than in his younger days. His posture stooped, his belly ample, he no longer moved briskly, but the light in his eyes was still both keen and reflective. He scarcely had time to dwell on a tactless letter. The museum staff was in the thick of things, coping with the move into the new building. The dioramas from Zoology were in pieces, Kilgore confronted the skins in disarray, and Breckenridge was pulled in a thousand directions. Within days, Roberts sent an answer to Chapman that confounded in its own way: "Word has just come from Mr. Bell that 'Mr. Jaques's services will be available' and directing that I get in touch with you. What does this mean? I have no details. . . . Mr. Bell seems to have taken the matter in hand as he was very anxious for Jaques to do the background."[3]

Soon after, the American Museum's director, Roy Chapman Andrews, sent an official notification that "the situation has changed," but it was Chapman who wrote Roberts, in a second letter, that Bell had recently come to the American Museum to confer with him and Director Andrews. A third letter, this one from the benefactor himself, arrived at Roberts's desk: "I have the two sketches [for the proposed wolf group.] . . . I think one probably associates timber wolves with the winter more than any other time and, I would say, with heavy timber rather than open places. On the other hand, the open lakeshore scene appeals to me far more."[4] Like Roberts, Bell had dreams for the new museum.

Jaques arrived on April 7, conferred with Bell at his office, then went off with Breckenridge to the North Shore to do preliminary sketches. Within days, he was back at the museum and beginning to paint. The pinkish rhyolite cliffs of Palisade Head, a stormy Lake Superior lapping at its base, materialized under his brush as the artist painted with scant pause. Roberts enticed him out to the Cedar Avenue bridge one Sunday to observe migrating Tundra Swans (the Jaqueses were once again at home in the Robertses' lower apartment), and he took time off for an occasional Roberts dinner party. That May, the museum opened to the public, and people got a rare treat of watching the artist at work and a large group display come together.

By May's end, the wolf background was complete, and Jaques began a second, this one set on Lake Pepin in southern Minnesota. The diorama would eventually include migrating shorebirds, both mounted by Breckenridge in the foreground and painted in the background, a tricky challenge to proportion properly. Jaques exhibited his masterful eye in executing a near-seamless transition. A viewer might expect to see the mounted Caspian Tern take off and head out over the water. By the end of June, Jaques was cleaning his brushes, pleased with the whirlwind session. And despite the haste, his genius had not deserted him. Bell would later remark that of all the fine work in the new museum, the Lake Pepin background pleased him the most.[5]

It did not take long for the museum staff to settle into the new accommodations. A tradition sprang up in the sunny lunchroom adjacent to the main offices on the third floor. The staff gathered each day around a long table at noon to eat their sack lunches—Roberts was known for his jelly sandwiches—and chew the fat. The longtime staff, Roberts, Kilgore, and Breckenridge, ate alongside the young men who had been hired as assistants or as guides for school groups touring the museum. Young and old joined together to discuss research ideas, ponder ominous events in Europe, and everything else. Interaction with young people always energized Roberts. The "lunch club" became a highlight of his day.

It might have been these conversations that Kilgore and Breckenridge recalled when remembering their boss a few years later. They wrote of his "unwavering regard for the truth" and how if someone with fuzzy thinking spouted off unwarranted conclusions, Roberts's penetrating questions might not be too tactful. They agreed that it was sometimes difficult just to mull over a contentious topic. Roberts had made up his mind and was not amenable to another point of view. But, they observed, he was usually right.[6]

Surety of opinion carried over in his assessment of people. He rather quickly labeled those he met as "friends" or "not friends," and it took some doing to transfer from "not friends" to the favored category.[7] These prickly personality traits emerged only in his later years. As he grew increasingly isolated by the death of friends, hearing loss, and chronic ailments, letters coming off his pen became more irritable, especially if he felt the recipient had not dealt fairly with him. Only late in life was there some testiness though; earlier, his tone had been flawlessly polite. The idiosyncrasies of the old man must not have been offensive. Soon every young man at the lunch table would be leaving for faraway places, and nearly every one would write with nostalgia of the "lunch club."

Life had barely settled into routine in the new museum in 1940 when the dark shadows of impending war crept into daily life. William Abbott of Duluth, one of Roberts's longtime observers in St. Louis County, wrote of seeing a raven that "looked like a big black bomber sailing around," and he joked that if the bald eagles he had also observed had been "flying around with their claws full of arrows," he would have collected them for the museum.[8]

By 1941, even before the attack on Pearl Harbor, the young men gathered around the lunchroom table began receiving draft notices. One by one, they left for training. The largest camps were in the South; several of the young men trained in Louisiana or Florida and wrote letters back home that were read aloud to the lunchroom habitués. They often reported on birds they had seen while on long hikes, on the many interesting poisonous snakes, new to these northern boys, on the unfamiliar trees, and the pervasive damp of the Louisiana ground. They complained of wearing 1918 vintage wool uniforms in the southern heat and of training on machine guns used in the previous war.[9]

North in Manitoba, the manager at Bell's Delta Duck Station informed Roberts that Delta Marsh had been taken over by the air force and used for bombing practice since April. However, "there has been little disturbance to the ducks," he observed, adding, "heavy concentrations of birds used the bombed bays."[10] At the Mayo Clinic in Rochester, one of the "lunch bunch" doing medical research at the clinic complained that the defense industry had flooded the housing in the town, and he could not find anything to rent.[11]

After the December 7 attack, though, the tone of the letters changed. The grousing about living conditions ceased (though the bird sightings did not), and the young men described, as best they could, given the censor, what they were doing and where they were located.

Roberts himself felt a call to duty. "I am sorry that I am too old to be of some service for everyone that is able is surely needed. . . . Here [in Minneapolis] armed guards are patrolling all plants where war materials are being made. When I came by Honeywell Heat Regulator Company out on 4th Avenue South, late night before last, and saw armed men with rifles on their shoulders, walking all around the building with the thermometer at zero and a bitter wind blowing, it brought the situation right home," he wrote to an inductee.[12]

The government found a way for an octogenarian to serve. Roberts soon got a letter from the Emergency Medical Service, asking if he would be on the local emergency medical service of the defense council—as a physician. Roberts replied, "You probably know that I have long since retired from active practice and that I am not physically capable of engaging in any very active work. Still, if there is anything I could possibly do I should be willing to offer my services. It would probably have to be two or three hours a day of quite restricted service."[13] He was also asked to serve on the Minnesota committee on conservation of cultural resources. The National Archives in Washington, D.C., had assembled a plan to protect important material in case of attack. It pinpointed the new museum as having space in which to store artifacts that might need to be shipped out of the nation's capital.[14] On the domestic front, Agnes, a Quaker, generally pacifistic, threw herself into volunteer work with the American Red Cross, for which she would receive special recognition after the war.

By 1942, the lunch club was down to three—Roberts, Kilgore, and Breckenridge. The young men had scattered, to Europe and the Pacific theater. The bird class enrollment reduced to seven, small enough that the annual Decoration Day party was held at a private home on White Bear Lake. It was the last class not to be curtailed by the war, and the last class that Roberts taught in the field. The eighty-four-year-old went on every outing that spring. By 1943, gas rationing required the class of five to take streetcars on outings. Although Roberts appealed to the Gasoline Rationing Board for forty additional gallons, telling it that he used his personal car, a Buick Roadmaster getting twelve miles to the gallon, most trips were taken in town. In 1944, the bird class was canceled when only two students signed up. In 1945, with the nation on the verge of victory in Europe, enrollment was up again, and the eighty-seven-year-old professor gave every single lecture. But his knees had given out. Breckenridge took over all the field outings.

The campus became a beehive of military activity. Men marched in squads to and from classes, up and down Church Street. From his front office, Roberts took in the strains of military bands playing and detachments drilling on the field next to the Armory. The military commandeered the lecture rooms in the museum, including the lovely auditorium with the excellent acoustics, and used them for training.[15] Writing to a retired colleague, Roberts described the effect of five thousand servicemen on campus: The coeds at Sanford Hall had lost their dormitory to the military, so had all the frats on University Avenue. Augsburg College, too, had been swamped with soldiers and sailors. The old Men's Union (Nicholson Hall) had been rechristened the "S. S. America" and was run like a training ship at sea. Even from inside the museum, Roberts could hear recruits chanting and counting as they marched past. "Not much like the old peaceful days," he wrote in summary.[16]

The military also engaged Breckenridge to lecture on poisonous snakes of the world to a group of medical officers on campus. Breckenridge had only recently defended his doctoral thesis on the reptiles and amphibians of Minnesota and was the resident expert on herptiles in the museum. "Poisonous snakes of the world" was a pretty broad topic, but at least he did not have to opine on the effects of bites—an Army medical doctor covered that topic.[17]

Later that year, the army would approach Breckenridge to enlist in the Army Air Corps to work with experimental flights in high altitudes. He was forty at the time, with two children. A second lieutenant in the Civilian Defense Corp, he trained at Camp Ripley at intervals in the summer. Roberts discussed the matter with him and thought the offer appealed to Breckenridge. Privately, the older man wrote, "I will not say anything to influence him, but I feel that he should stay with his family unless a definite call comes. . . . I think he has become rather military-minded, and a commission in the Federal Forces urges him on rather strongly."[18] For various reasons, Breckenridge decided not to sign on.

Into this vigorous wartime atmosphere, the merry Jaques pair returned for another round of painting. Roberts's friends (and former patients) Charles and Kate Bovey had given money to assemble a group featuring Blue and Snow Geese. The birds would be shown at the peak of spring migration. In April 1942, Breckenridge, Jaques, and Martin Bovey, the Boveys' son, who was himself a naturalist, had collected the birds on an expedition to Lake Traverse on Minnesota's western border. The elderly doctor wistfully considered accompanying the party but instead lent his shotgun to Jaques—the Manhattan apartment dweller no longer had one.

Lee and Florence Jaques did not stay with the Robertses for the fall 1942 visit. Since the time they had last been in town, Carroll, the younger Roberts son, had suffered a debilitating stroke at age forty-eight. Carroll had left his work on the East Coast and moved back home, occupying the first-floor apartment. Instead, Florence happened upon a house exchange. A couple in Minneapolis would swap their little bungalow off of West River Road for the Upper West Side Jaques apartment in Manhattan. Florence was excited: the bungalow had a fireplace. "We were tempted to ask you and Mrs. Roberts if you'd drive by and look it over, but it seemed a shame to ask you to take responsibility—then you would have felt bad if anything turned out wrong," she wrote, as the couple arranged their upcoming stay.[19]

But Roberts did go look at it, immediately. He had his driver take him over to 3338 Edmund. No one was home, so he could only peek in the windows. He reported back to Florence that the place seemed attractively furnished and did indeed have a fireplace. The only drawback was that it was quite far from the museum, without a close streetcar line. With gas rationing, that might be an issue. Nonetheless, the Jaqueses made the swap.

The Blue Goose–Snow Goose group was set on Lake Traverse, where the birds had been collected, and was luminous with silvery blues of water and sky. Like the Lake Pepin group, it moved seamlessly from mounted birds in the foreground to painted birds on the background. Another masterpiece for Jaques.

Jaques barely had time to return to New York and settle in before Roberts wrote with another idea. "Breckenridge and I have now been wondering whether we could get Mr. Bell interested in a Sandhill Crane Group.... He wants big spectacular things and perhaps this could be made to meet his ideas. We have only one specimen suitable for the group but we could get what we needed the coming spring. The background could be made to show something of the so-called spring dance and that would make it a very striking display.... It is necessary to have something really big in order to arouse [Bell's] interest." Roberts added, "We [Agnes and he] miss you both very much and are already looking forward to a time when something may bring you back to visit with us again."[20]

That "something," though, was not a crane group—not yet. In 1943, the Jaqueses were approached by Harding of the University of Minnesota Press to do a companion book to *Canoe Country,* one set in the winter in the Boundary Waters. The Manhattan-based couple was uncertain where to locate to experience a snowy season in the north woods. They asked Roberts for suggestions, who, in turn, tapped his large social network. A former patient from Marine on St. Croix knew that Grace Nute of the Minnesota Historical Society had spent some time the previous winter at Gunflint Lodge, had done snowshoeing and dogsledding, and it had been very comfortable.[21] So, Gunflint Lodge it was!

While Florence Jaques gathered material for another book, her husband pondered how to best present a moose group for the museum. One was in the planning stages. Breckenridge would accompany state game wardens to collect a specimen in the upcoming fall. Roberts was hoping for both a cow and a bull, but the large mammals were very scarce. Since moose are inhabitants of the boreal forest, Gunflint Lake was a great place to be for the artist. From the piney north woods he wrote, "My impression of what the moose group ought to be is confirmed by what we've seen. Water in the foreground with these big beautifully colored lily pads with the stems traveling down to the bottom. It could be easily done with glass—no holes!"[22]

While the Jaqueses were up north, thinking about a future moose exhibit, the Natural History Museum lost a display, a priceless one. After the museum closing on a Friday, a thief entered the building and stole two precious Passenger Pigeons, which had been paired with a set of Mourning Doves. The extinct birds were irreplaceable. "Yes, we lost that fine pair of pigeons that Charlie Velie gave us several years ago," Roberts wrote to Bell, who had been out of town at the time. "They were in a small case on the balcony... had been there ever since we moved into this building. We are at a loss to understand how it was done. They were there one Friday at five o'clock because I, myself, was down there showing them to a visitor. The next morning about ten-thirty they were gone. The thief planned well. He removed the end glass and wrenched the birds from their stands. If it was done in the night it means a key to the building which we can't explain. If in the early morning it seems almost impossible that he could do it and avoid observation!"[23] University detectives were called, and a fingerprint man from the police department came over, but the birds were never returned.

The moose background was painted in the summer of 1944. As he had in 1940, Jaques painted two backgrounds in rapid succession. The background for a Swallow-tailed Kite display was small, but the donor of this display was George Miksch Sutton, a fellow artist and collaborator with Jaques on *The Birds of Minnesota*. Sutton had been based in Minneapolis the previous year, doing war work for the Army Air Force, housed in Northrop Auditorium, and had had a chance to renew ties with Roberts. The socializing had resulted in the kite group, which would be given in memory of his bird-loving mother, a Minnesota native.

The dramatic moose background, depicting Gunflint Lake, was set in the fall with turning leaves and a cow and calf. In the end, the Game and Fish Commission issued a permit to take only one animal. Breckenridge was on the expedition to get the moose, but he did not shoot it. He claimed later that he had seen that bull moose the day prior to it being shot, and passed on it, thinking it was too small. He found out otherwise when he had to figure out how to get the downed animal out of the swamp in which it was shot, and then to their camp, where he prepared it for shipping back to Minneapolis. Weighing the various pieces he had to take off, he estimated it as just over half a ton.[24]

Breckenridge and his crew had trouble fitting the huge animal into the display area, also. It was too tall for the six-foot case. Ever resourceful, Breckenridge finally cut off three of the feet, since the moose would be shown standing in the mud of a receding shoreline,[25] and the big rack had to be taken off for transport, as well. Roberts, looking on, later commented, "I was a little troubled by this myself but it went off very easily. The elk [a group in the planning stages] will probably go the same way."[26]

The Jacqueses spent the summer of 1944 as boarders at the Continuation Study Building just across the south lawn from the museum. They had no cooking facilities and spent many evening meals with the Robertses at 2303 Pleasant Avenue South, enjoying numerous rounds of four-handed cribbage afterward. The ravages of age, though, were telling more and more with the older couple. Both had been laid low for several months the previous winter from a virulent strain of flu, and even in the balm of summer, Agnes spent a week in bed from illness. Roberts began to notice more intense heart palpitations. Now, eighty-four and eighty-six, respectively, Robert and Agnes led lives that became increasingly curtailed. The Jacqueses were the only nonrelatives they entertained that summer.

But they maintained tight family ties. Roberts and Agnes had established a tradition of waffles for Sunday brunch and sometimes entertained grandchildren at the meal. Grandson Thomas Reaser Roberts, the oldest son of Tom, known to his grandfather as "Tommy," had married and was father to a son—Thomas Naus Roberts, a fourth Thomas Roberts. "Four Toms in a row," the oldest Thomas Roberts gleefully crowed to a friend.[27] Tommy was in the service, but he was home on leave that June and brought the baby over for inspection. Granddaughter Jane, who had married in 1942, also had a baby that summer, making Roberts a great-grandfather twice over.

More and more, Roberts seemed to refer to birds in the past tense. "I always found the Red-breasted Nuthatch a charming bird," he commented in one letter. There had been no bird class in 1944, so even had he been physically able, he had no students with whom to peer through binoculars. Like most long-lived people, Roberts viewed his youth and vigorous adult years with a certain luster. "I . . . cannot get about very far and have to limit my movements to my daily trips to and from the museum," he wrote to an editor. "One comes to live largely in memories of the past and with me I find no little pleasure in reviewing the experiences of the years gone by."[28] To Chapman, who had just turned eighty, he confided, "There is nothing especially wrong. I come to the Museum every day and do a few routine things but I can't just 'play the game' as I should like to do. This peaceful, quiet happy old age is not quite what it is cracked up to be. There is one recompense, however. My old friends and patients stand loyally by in more ways than one and this is a comfort and joy."[29]

Chapman sent back a poignant response: "I was delighted to hear from you this morning. One of the vital elements of friendship is time. Those we have known longest are apt to be dearest. The thought of you aroused a long chain of pleasant associations which are the background of our friendship. . . . Now I think of your home and Mrs. Roberts and the children and the 'Maxwell' and the early morning flights [of migrating ducks, viewed from a blind] all with . . . pleasure. . . . This summer . . . I sit out doors with the sky for a ceiling and the four winds for walls. . . . I've brought great numbers of Blue Jays, mockers, cardinals and red-bellied woodpeckers about me by feeding, and they make life. The lights are failing and the cardinals are coming. This is their hour."[30]

That summer, the sole bird Roberts was watching was a handsome, mottled-gray Common Nighthawk, which perched lengthwise on a tree limb outside his office window. It was his only avian sighting for the breeding season, save for the first robin appearing in the spring and an ill-fated pheasant that flew through the library window.

In October 1944, while at work in the museum, Roberts suffered a paralyzing stroke. He was eighty-six. The museum staff was greatly alarmed, but Roberts minimized it and would not call a doctor until he had reached home. There he experienced a second and then a third episode. Kilgore dashed off a letter to Jaques, and everyone prepared themselves for very bad news. A nurse was called, and Roberts spent the next five days in bed. On the sixth day, he got up and dressed. "Apparently all right," he scribbled in his diary.[31]

Twelve days after the attack, he was back keeping regular hours at the museum, and a week later, he voted optimistically for Thomas Dewey in the 1944 presidential election, only to see Franklin Roosevelt elected to a fourth term. His beloved state joined most of the nation in throwing its electoral college votes to the Democrat. However, Roberts could find some comfort in the election. A Republican, Edward John Thye, won the governor's race, defeating the first Democratic-Farmer-Labor Party candidate to run for the office.

Though he had claimed the previous year that his lecturing days were over, winter term 1945 found Roberts in front of the bird class once more. January 1945 was cold, but despite the weather, some illness, and the funerals of several friends—his old friend from the Young Naturalists' Society of his distant past, Robert Williams, was one—Roberts did not miss a single lecture the entire term. He also gave a short talk to the Minnetonka Garden Club, appeared at the evening extension bird class that Breckenridge and Kilgore ran, and celebrated his eighty-seventh birthday (along with Agnes, who turned eighty-five) at a party given by his sister, Emma, who was also eighty-five. "Many cards and flowers" he noted in his diary.[32]

Meanwhile, preparations were under way for yet another large diorama: the Sandhill Crane group. The ideas as outlined by Roberts and Breckenridge had appealed to Bell; furthermore, circumstances, sad ones, alas, had brought a donor for the group. The year before, a former assistant to Breckenridge, Russell Berthel, had died suddenly from an early heart attack while conducting a survey of prairie chickens in northwestern Minnesota. His family had agreed to fund the crane display in his memory. Excitement grew in the prep room of the museum as Breckenridge made plans to collect the birds. There was some uncertainty as to where to actually find Sandhill Cranes. The gawky, four-foot birds had more or less disappeared from Minnesota. Breckenridge and Roberts considered southern Manitoba, but the collectors ended up going to North Platte, Nebraska, where the birds still congregated in some numbers during spring migration. In March 1945, Breckenridge and his wife, Dorothy, headed out and met Lee and Florence Jaques there. The trip served more than one purpose. The artist wanted to absorb the ambiance of the migration, since the diorama would be set in the spring; Breckenridge toted his movie camera, hoping to get the dramatic courtship dance on film. He was only partially successful and wrote his boss, "I have never worked with birds more keen of vision or more suspicious."[33] They collected ten cranes.

After a trip to Ada, Minnesota, with Breckenridge to do preliminary sketches, Lee Jaques arrived in Minneapolis and commenced painting. That spring, as a prairie sky and cranes in flight took form under his brush, the broader canvas of the world also took shape. President Roosevelt died, Harry Truman took office, and the bloody war in Europe ended, which Roberts noted in his memorandum in bold letters, "V-E D." President Truman announced the victory on the radio at 8:00 A.M. on May 8, 1945. Later, the celebratory strains of the university's marching band could be heard from within the museum.

When the background was completed in mid-June, Jaques began new work on a series of transparencies that would be placed at the ends of the narrow galleries in the museum. For quite some time, Roberts had believed that he had been allowed to continue as director of the museum way past the retirement age—that summer he was eighty-seven—because he had contacts that could garner large amounts of money for the institution.[34] That assertion had proven true many times over, and in 1945, the veracity of the claim was again established when the Citizens Aid Society—consisting of several longtime patients—gave ten thousand dollars to the museum, with the stipulation that it be used in Roberts's lifetime. The sum was given personally to him, and he had exclusive say on how to spend it. He received word that the donation was coming while making a medical call—he was still practicing medicine in a limited way at age eighty-seven—to Mrs. George C. Christian, whose father-in-law had launched the endowed society in 1916, chiefly to care for people with tuberculosis. In an odd and subtle way, Roberts's life was again demonstrating the roundness of the world.

Roberts immediately wrote to Jaques. Having thought for years that he could die at any time,[35] the conditions of the donation electrified him. "[It has] to be spent *at once* . . . now while I am still alive! . . . After finishing up the Crane group background, can you take up residency here and settle down to this job? There should be some thousands of dollars left of the ten thousand and this will have to go into groups, the backgrounds of which will have to be painted. This would be for you, too."[36] Late in July 1945, Roberts secured an additional large donation for the museum, when the MacMillan family—again, patients—agreed to fund a large group highlighting an elk herd.

As August 1945 waned, Roberts engaged in a correspondence that would in retrospect signal the end of an era. A high-level executive at General Mills who was also widely recognized for his birding skill sent the museum director a list of birds seen in the Lake Itasca environs that summer. On the list were several species that Roberts questioned. He did not think the birds would be at Itasca at that time of year. Nettled, the birder supplied the details that Roberts had requested but added that "I use a pair of Bausch and Lomb 9 × 35 field glasses and that kind of field equipment gives one quite an advantage in studying birds, particularly when you are in the nesting region like northern Minnesota where you just do not have to depend upon a fleeting glance to identify a bird. I suspect that when better field equipment is available after the war, you will have a lot of unusual species reported because people are going to see and recognize species which they never were able to recognize before."[37] Roberts must have felt his advanced age acutely at this comment, remembering well a time in which keen eyesight and a shotgun sufficed.

It was not the first time in which Roberts's expertise might have been seen as outdated. In 1943, Bell had sent him a copy of the newsletter for the American Association of Museums (AAM). Bell apparently kept abreast of this professional organization, and Roberts, too, was already aware of the article. The author, Clark Wissler, president of the AAM, suggested that habitat dioramas, the very kind of expensive, elaborate displays that Bell and Roberts were pouring their resources into, were antiquated in their ability to convey scientific information. Dioramas were seriously flawed, Wissler contended, because visitors merely appreciated the artistic beauty of the scene and ignored the science. The trendiest museums had dismantled their habitat groups and were "presenting ideas" instead. Wissler also noted that these "ideas" exhibits might need to be changed frequently—the price museums must pay to entertain the public.[38]

To his credit, Roberts pondered the article and found it "illuminating and suggestive." He thought that Wissler was wrong. Roberts spent every third Sunday afternoon at the museum, alternating with Kilgore and Breckenridge, greeting museum goers and discussing displays. He had a good grasp of what visitors to his museum were learning. Still, Roberts replied to Bell, "Proper labeling and interesting personal talks do much to enhance [the diorama's] value," and "Every museum should have as large a corps of well informed and entertaining guides as circumstances will permit."[39] This last was a continuing bone of contention, as the university never gave

Roberts a blank check with which to hire staff. Roberts also pointed out that museums do not merely serve to entertain a demanding public but create what a public wants to see by serving up thoughtful, meaty fare—displays, lectures, and tours. In this, the Minnesota Natural History Museum was already "an active educational institution" that had "made for itself an important and worthwhile place in the community."

The extended stay in Minneapolis in summer 1945 gave Lee and Florence Jaques ample time to witness the decline of their friends at 2303 Pleasant Avenue South. Roberts suffered another stroke that left him temporarily with thickened speech and legs that felt weak and wobbly. He called it "slight." Agnes, who had been so active only a year before, rarely went anywhere, though she did gather her strength and go to the museum to see the completed background with the dancing Sandhill Cranes while the Jaqueses were still in town.

The Roberts hosted a farewell dinner for the Jaqueses the day after Agnes's museum visit. Roberts presided at the head of the table, as always, with the little foot pedal, and Agnes held up her end of the conversation at the other end. The evening included the obligatory game of four-handed cribbage. Lee and Florence were leaving the next day. The two had plans to return in the spring, when Lee would paint the background for the elk group. But as the Jaqueses made their way down the stairs and out into the dark August evening with cheery "Good-byes!" lingering on the warm, humid air, they must have wondered if they had seen their friends for the last time.

The Jaqueses departed as the first of the fall migrating birds, the warblers and orioles, swallows and grosbeaks, drained from the Minnesota woods. The days shortened with the onset of the fall equinox. Roberts learned that for the first time in many years, a small flock of Evening Grosbeaks had appeared along the bluffs of the Mississippi River, feeding on box elder seeds. He could not seem to recover the vitality that he had enjoyed for so long and confessed to "a growing weakness physically and mentally that is not at all to my liking."[40]

In October, as the Mississippi Flyway filled with scaup and teal clamoring noisily on the sloughs at Long Meadow, Roberts wrote to Lee Jaques, "Mrs. Roberts is not so well of late and is considerably restricted in her home activities. It isn't quite clear just what is ahead. . . . After you and Florence left there seemed to be a great void around here and it took some time to get adjusted to our normal routine. We are already looking forward to your return."[41]

Later that week, Agnes was rushed to Eitel Hospital with acute hemorrhaging. Her niece was sent for, but Agnes stabilized after surgery, and the family made plans for the long term at Franklin Hospital, just around the corner, walking distance, from Pleasant Avenue, since she was going to require complicated nursing care. Now, with snow flurries in the air, and the first snow buntings arriving in Minneapolis, Roberts traced a triangular route from home to the museum to the hospital for supper with Agnes.

As winter set in, Roberts felt unwell many days and stayed home in bed. On others, his old friends—mostly females; the men had died—stopped by to visit or invited him to dinner. Amid the spells of sickness, trips to visit the failing Agnes, and brief early snowfalls, he received a letter from Lee Jaques informing him of the death of Chapman on November 15.

Agnes residing at Franklin Hospital, Roberts once again lived a solitary life on Pleasant Avenue. He faithfully traced the home-museum-hospital triangle until falling ill himself on Christmas Eve. His visits to Agnes ceased. Christmas 1945 was snowy with heavy drifts blocking the roads. Sick in bed with the flu, he missed Christmas dinner with the family. He worried about Emma making it to the family holiday—he had always been there to look out for her—and was relieved that Tom battled the snow to her home to pick her up. He and grandson Bill had also been to see Agnes.

"My heart acting badly," Roberts recorded in his diary three days later.[42] His physician prescribed digitalis, used to treat atrial fibrillation, and it took effect. "Heart action better," he wrote the next day.

Roberts was moved downstairs to the lower apartment, where he did not have stairs to climb. His son Carroll, still suffering the effects of his own stroke and now overseeing the care of two sick octogenarians, braved the wintry weather to visit Agnes daily. On New Year's Eve, a clear, mild day, Roberts received a telegram relaying news of his sister-in-law Katie Roberts's death. Later in the day, he learned that his childhood friend and lawyer Joe Kingman had died that morning. He would be too ill to attend the funeral. On New Year's Day 1946, he wrote letters to his grieving brother, Walter, the newly widowed Mabel Kingman, and Agnes.

Winter term began. Clearly, he could not teach a class; still, Roberts was a creature of habit. On Monday, January 7, 1946, he went to work at the museum for the first time since before Christmas. At the end of the week, he was at the museum again to show the Berthels the finished Sandhill Crane display, the one that commemorated their son. Then, on January 12, he made an entry in his diary that was surely a difficult admission: "Not at museum. Yesterday was last day at museum."[43] He began to tie up loose ends.

When, in October, Roberts had felt increasingly unwell and unable to attend the evening meetings, he reluctantly resigned his active membership in the Minnesota Academy of Medicine, a group he had helped found in 1887 and of which he had always been proud.[44] It was the cutting of a professional tie that had defined him. He had one more to attend to.

Since Chapman had founded *Bird-Lore* magazine in 1899, Roberts had sent in regular accounts of bird activity in Minnesota. These seasonal reports, numbering 150, were a major reason that Roberts could claim 253 natural history publications but only seven medical titles. The reports were published quarterly in Chapman's magazine and continued when the publication adopted a new name, *Audubon Magazine*. Roberts persevered even after the sightings were not his own but were telephoned to him by his many friends and observers. Shortly after his eighty-eighth birthday and mostly bedridden, he relinquished the post and suggested to the magazine that George Rysgaard, one of his protégés, be given the position. In the past, he had fought against conceding to frailty, but now the forces of infirmity seemed to surge.

The calendar turned over to March, and a winter that had been relentless loosened its grip. When it became apparent that Roberts would not return to active life, visitors streamed into the little first-floor apartment on Pleasant Avenue: patients and the widows of patients; former students, home from the service; Emma, of course; Tom and Dorothy, Catharine and Joe; university vice presidents Willey and Middlebrook; university president Morrill. Breckenridge came and told him he was at work building the frame for the elk. Kilgore brought him news of the bird class. Caroline Rankiellour, the woman who had nursed Jennie through long illness and had served as the physician's obstetrics nurse when he delivered babies so long ago, called. Bell came one afternoon, on a good day, when Roberts was up and "fully dressed." Rysgaard dropped by with his first "Seasons" report for *Audubon*

Magazine. Granddaughter Jane brought her baby, Nicky. "Great grandchild," Roberts remarked in his diary.

Roberts wrote to his brother, Walter, half a continent away in New Jersey. The two had not been close geographically or emotionally for decades; Emma had been the sibling who had remained part of his life. The three had shared a childhood, though. They alone could remember their early days in Philadelphia, the courageous move to rough-hewn Minnesota, and the brave and cheerful parents who had raised them. Now that it appeared that a break in sibling ties was imminent, they could look back with something like joy that all three, in close contact with tuberculosis, had survived in good health into their eighties.

Later that week, Carroll came home from a visit to Franklin Hospital to report that Agnes had walked the length of a hallway in the hospital with the help of a nurse. But the effort had been too much. It was not likely she would do so again. "Final time," Roberts added in his diary entry for the day. Agnes would linger until July.

On April 17, Roberts, too, was taken to Eitel Hospital after suffering a heart attack. Eitel overlooked Loring Park, its bur oaks and its lake, a small patch of Minnesota protected from development. He had skated on its shimmering surface as a boy, both he and Minneapolis young and unformed. He remembered a time when it had been part of a vast wetland, yielding beautiful birds of wondrous form and color. He remembered when it all had been new.

Two days later, his great heart stopped beating. It was the evening of April 19, long past the time that the park's birds had taken cover for the night, even the cardinals, which forage at twilight, after the light has waned.

Epilogue

> It is feared that this wonderful bird is a thing of the
> past here in the north.
>
> — *The Birds of Minnesota*, 1: 301

Thomas Sadler Roberts rests in the Roberts family plot in Lakewood Cemetery, Minneapolis, next to his wife, Jennie. Many in the close-knit family that surrounded him soon followed him to the grave. Agnes Williams Roberts died in July 1946 at Franklin Hospital and was returned to the Williams family plot in New Hope, Pennsylvania, for burial. Son Carroll Roberts passed away less than two years later in February 1948; sister Emma Roberts, at age eighty-nine in December 1948; son Tom, in 1954; and Tom's sister Catharine, three weeks after. All rest in Lakewood Cemetery.

In the first decade after Roberts's passing, Will Kilgore Jr. also died, on Thanksgiving Day 1953 at age seventy-four.

Walter Breckenridge succeeded Roberts as director of the Museum of Natural History, and under his leadership the museum evolved into present form. Lee Jaques returned to paint several more backgrounds, including one with Tundra Swans, in memory of Roberts, and two "ecosystem" dioramas, one of Lake Waconia in Carver County and the other of Cascade Falls on the North Shore of Lake Superior. Breckenridge was at the helm when James Ford Bell's name was given to the Museum of Natural History, commemorating the man who so vigorously championed it.

Breckenridge retired in 1969 but enjoyed a remarkably long and active retirement, producing his best paintings, promoting Wood Duck conservation, courageously writing about the serious problem of human population pressure, and racking up numerous awards. He died in 2003 at one hundred years.

Lee and Florence Jaques retired to Minnesota and built a house in North Oaks, a St. Paul suburb.

Appropriately, much of Roberts's legacy can be found in protected nature reserves. In 1947, his name was attached to a small nature preserve on the southeastern shore of Lake Harriet. A tiny oasis in the middle of the city, the T. S. Roberts Wildlife Sanctuary is a stopover for migrating songbirds and a soothing retreat for humans.

Of the many places that Roberts studied over the course of his long life, perhaps none was as badly damaged by human activity as Heron Lake in southwestern Minnesota, in Jackson County, which exists as two parts connected by a wasplike waist. Drained, ditched, diked, and dammed, the surrounding watershed tiled and drained, the once-bountiful wetland is no longer the bird paradise it was in the 1880s. Much of the destruction happened in Roberts's lifetime. He would be pleased to know that the Nature Conservancy now owns two preserves, the Lindgren-Traeger Bird Sanctuary on North Heron Lake and the R. and J. Traeger Preserve on South Heron Lake, and is working with both private and public partners, including the Minnesota Department of Natural Resources, the U.S. Fish and Wildlife Service, and the Heron Lake Watershed District, to restore the wetland to some semblance of its former self.

The Thief Lake–Mud Lake wetland in Marshall County, northwestern Minnesota, fared somewhat better, perhaps because it came under protection earlier and more land was available to preserve. The Mud Lake Migratory Waterfowl Refuge was established in 1937, following recommendation by Roberts. Today it is known as the Agassiz National Wildlife Refuge, a huge, 61,500-acre preserve, with a 4,000-acre wilderness area in its heart. As at Heron Lake, a private-public partnership works to restore the wetland.

The bottomlands of the Mississippi in southeastern Minnesota that Roberts and Dart explored in 1898, chasing Prothonotary Warblers, have been protected as part of the Upper Mississippi River National Wildlife and Fish Refuge. It is long established that Prothonotary Warblers breed in Minnesota as far north as east-central Minnesota, but it is still a thrill to see one.

The land occupied by the Long Meadow Gun Club now forms a portion of the Minnesota Valley National Wildlife Refuge. The clubhouse no longer stands.

Hawks and owls gained protection from wanton killing in increments. In the autumn following Roberts's death, there was indiscriminate slaughter of birds migrating over Duluth's Hawk Ridge, despite Minnesota statutes that by 1945 apparently protected all raptors except Sharp-shinned and Cooper's

Hawks, Goshawks, and Great Horned Owls. The Duluth Bird Club (which had been organized by Roberts's student Olga Lakela) subsequently posted "no hunting" signs on what was then called "Hawk Hill" and insisted that city police enforce city ordinances regarding the discharge of firearms within city limits. Hunters claimed they would never stop shooting hawks, but the police did their job, and no birds were shot thereafter. By 1959, the remaining hawks were protected by state statute, but Great Horned Owls did not receive protection until 1972, when the U.S. Congress passed an amendment to a bird treaty with Mexico, granting the fierce birds protection.

The birds that Roberts took special interest in, those he studied or pursued in order to establish their range or occurrence in the state, have experienced a variety of fates. Prothonotary Warblers have continued to move northward, now breeding regularly along the St. Croix River. Burrowing Owls are still seen in low numbers in western Minnesota. Western Kingbirds, what Roberts called "Arkansas Flycatchers," are common in the western half of the state. Franklin's Gulls migrate through Heron Lake these days, but seldom nest there, because of widely fluctuating lake levels. Yellow-headed Blackbirds still frequent Long Meadow Lake but not in the numbers present in 1901.

Bald Eagles were very scarce in Roberts's adult years. He was alive when they came under protection of the Bald Eagle Protection Act of 1940. He would, I think, be amazed by the majestic birds' comeback from the brink of extinction, thanks to the Endangered Species Act of 1973. This law also saved the Peregrine Falcon, another species that was very rare in his lifetime, although in *The Birds of Minnesota*, he adds in the last paragraph of his section on peregrines a prescient observation that the birds are taking up winter residence in large cities with skyscrapers.

Roberts would be astounded by the large population of Canada Geese in Minnesota. In *Birds*, he wrote of its nesting in Minnesota in the past tense. Two photos of the ruination of their breeding grounds by drainage ditching accompany that section.

Roberts wrote of Trumpeter Swans: "The days of the Trumpeter Swan as a bird of Minnesota have long since passed." His "bird biography" of them in *Birds* is very short. The swan's comeback, thanks to patient, laborious attention, would gratify him.

Roberts also wrote of the breeding behavior of Sandhill Cranes in the past tense. He had found nests as a youth, but the birds had mostly disappeared by the time he was an adult. By 1911, a migrating flock passing overhead, witnessed by him and Frank Chapman at Heron Lake, was cause for excitement. In 1944, when he and Breckenridge cast about for a place to collect cranes for the museum exhibit, there was no place in the state to find them. Seventy years later, the crane population has slowly gained numbers, and the State of Minnesota is once more planning a hunting season for the leggy, graceful cranes. I cannot say what Roberts's response would be to this. He had confidence in the science of wildlife management, but in his later years, he grew disillusioned with the conservation ethic of most hunters.

Roberts and his friend Frank Benner went chasing after reports of nesting White Pelicans in Grant County in 1879 but came up empty-handed. That there are now twenty thousand pairs nesting in Minnesota would please him. Recently, a landowner went on a rampage and destroyed an entire colony of the big birds. This would have saddened but not surprised Roberts. That the Migratory Bird Treaty Act of 1918, legislation that he promoted so vigorously, was invoked to convict the ravager might have given him satisfaction, as well as made him marvel at the law's enduring effect.

The Bell Museum of Natural History still stands at the corner of University Avenue and Church Street on the University of Minnesota campus. It continues to draw thousands of Minnesota schoolchildren, who tour the dioramas and explore the natural world hands on in the Touch and See Room. The Bell also presents exhibits on contemporary environmental issues, such as sustainable housing. As I write this, the museum is displaying a lepidopteran collection titled "Flutter: Butterflies and Moths in Art and Science." Roberts would be pleased with the concept of uniting art and science.

These days the two-volume *The Birds of Minnesota* can be bought via the Internet for less than a hundred dollars. The 1936 second edition seems to be more available than the 1932 edition.

The Minnesota Ornithologists' Union established the Thomas S. Roberts award in 1963 to recognize outstanding contribution to Minnesota ornithology over a period of years. The first four recipients were personal friends of Roberts's and had provided observations of bird records for him. Many others felt the personal influence of Roberts, that influence extending to 1993, when one of his bird students, Gustav Swanson, was honored.

Over the five years of my research into Roberts's life, I have frequently been thankful that he is not alive to witness what is arguably the greatest threat to all birds: global warming. There was no menace on that scale in his day. The great midwestern dustbowl is the nearest approximation, and its manifestations alarmed him. As one to whom nature spoke "a various language," he could not have failed to hear the cries of distress.

Notes

1. A FLEDGLING START

1. John Roberts, journal, 14 June 1867, box 2, volume 2, Thomas S. Roberts and Family Papers, Minnesota Historical Society, St. Paul. Roberts refers to the steamer as the *Bay City*, but the *Key City* was the steamer running between Dubuque and St. Paul. His journal does not mention his daughter, Mary Emma, who was seven years old in 1867.

2. Ibid., 12 July 1867.

3. Ibid., 14 June 1867.

4. Lucile M. Kane, *The Falls of St. Anthony: The Waterfall That Built Minneapolis* (St. Paul: Minnesota Historical Society Press, 1987), 43.

5. *St. Paul Pioneer*, 15 June 1867.

6. Rev. W. T. Boutwell (1832), as quoted in *Schoolcraft's Expedition to Lake Itasca: The Discovery of the Source of the Mississippi*, ed. Philip P. Mason (East Lansing: Michigan State University Press, 1993), 338–39.

7. John Roberts, journal, 15 June 1867.

8. Ibid., 18 June 1867, and 28 June 1867.

9. Ibid., 20 June 1867.

10. Ibid., 2 July 1867.

11. Larry Millett, *Lost Twin Cities* (St. Paul: Minnesota Historical Society Press, 1992), 74.

12. John Roberts, journal, 25 June 1867.

13. *Minneapolis Morning Tribune*, 15 June 1867.

14. John Roberts, journal, 24 July 1867.

15. Ibid., 7 August 1867.

16. Ibid., 30 June 1867; emphasis in original.

17. Ibid., 25 August 1867, 10 November 1867, and 27 October 1867.

18. Ibid., 15 August 1867.

19. Ibid., 16 August 1867.

20. Ibid., 17 August 1867.

21. Ibid., 24 September 1867.

22. Ibid., 3 August 1867.

23. Millett, *Lost Twin Cities,* 84.

24. John Roberts, journal, 30 November 1867.

2. ACQUIRING AN EAGLE EYE

1. *Minneapolis Morning Tribune,* 7 March 1874.

2. This Powderhorn Lake is not present-day Powderhorn Lake. This pond lay between Twenty-Second and Twenty-Fourth Streets and Harriet and Lyndale Avenues and has long since disappeared. Charles Judson Herrick, "Clarence Luther Herrick: Pioneer Naturalist, Teacher, and Psychobiologist," *Transactions of the American Philosophical Society* 45, no. 1 (1955): 26.

3. Thomas S. Roberts, *Shotgun and Stethoscope: The Journals of Thomas Sadler Roberts,* edited and transcribed by Penelope Krosch (Minneapolis: James Ford Bell Museum of Natural History, University of Minnesota, 1991), 6 (1 April 1874 entry).

4. T. S. Roberts, "Rambles of a Bird Lover in Minnesota," *The Flicker,* 1 October 1944.

5. Roberts, *Shotgun and Stethoscope,* 6 (2 April 1874 entry).

6. Ibid., 6–7 (4 April 1874 entry).

7. Harry Woodworth, "Among Those We Know," *Golfer and Sportsman,* December 1938, 77.

8. Roberts, *Shotgun and Stethoscope,* 7 (14 April 1874 entry); emphasis in original.

9. Ibid., 6 (24 March 1874 entry).

10. Roberts, "Rambles of a Bird Lover."

11. Ibid.

12. Photo BR1031, Hennepin County Libraries, "Tepees on the West Bank of the Mississippi River about 1850."

13. Roberts, *Shotgun and Stethoscope,* 7 (15 April 1874 entry).

14. Thomas S. Roberts, *The Birds of Minnesota* (Minneapolis: University of Minnesota Press, 1932), 2: 222.

15. *Minneapolis Morning Tribune,* 19 April 1874.

16. Roberts, *Shotgun and Stethoscope,* 9 (30 May 1874 entry). Bartram's Sandpiper is called today the Upland Sandpiper. The Short-tailed Tern is today's Black Tern.

17. Roberts, *The Birds of Minnesota,* 1: 582.

18. Ibid.

19. Ibid., 1: 579.

20. O. Pettingill, *Ornithology in Laboratory and Field* (Minneapolis: Burgess Publishing Co., 1970), 422.

21. Roberts, *The Birds of Minnesota,* 1: 584.

22. Roberts, "Rambles of a Bird Lover."

23. Roberts, *Shotgun and Stethoscope,* 9 (3 June 1874 entry).

24. Ruth Bovey Stevens, *Just for Us* (Wayzata, Minn.: published by author, 1992).

25. Roberts, *Shotgun and Stethoscope,* 10 (13 June 1874 entry).

26. Ibid., 11 (30 June 1874 entry).

27. Roberts, *The Birds of Minnesota,* 1: 340.

28. Ibid., 1: 467.

29. Ibid.

30. Ibid., 1: 487. The Minneapolis, St. Paul and Sault Ste. Marie Railway later built a roundhouse to repair trains on Sandy Lake's shore, a facility that exists today as "Shoreham Yard." Sandy Lake disappeared in the 1920s. Shoreham Yard is contaminated with toxic chemicals in the shallow underlying aquifer.

31. Roberts, *Shotgun and Stethoscope,* 12 (27 July 1874 entry).

32. Ibid., 12 (31 July 1874 entry).

33. Ibid., 12 (6 August 1874 entry).

34. Roberts, *The Birds of Minnesota,* 1: 487.

35. Thomas S. Roberts to Franklin Benner, 27 September 1874, box 1, folder "Correspondence 1857–1876," Roberts and Family Papers. All subsequent quotations about this trip are from the 27 September 1874 letter.

36. Roberts to Benner, 18 October 1874, box 1, folder "Correspondence 1857–1876," Roberts and Family Papers.

37. Roberts to Benner, 11 December 1874, box 1, folder "Correspondence 1857–1876," Roberts and Family Papers. All subsequent quotations about the hunting trip are from the 11 December 1874 letter.

38. Roberts, *Shotgun and Stethoscope,* 15 (25 December 1874 entry).

3. THE YOUNG NATURALISTS' SOCIETY

1. Thomas S. Roberts, "Our Winter Birds," 15 March 1875, box 10, folder 46, Bell Museum of Natural History Records, University of Minnesota Archives.

2. Ibid.

3. Roberts, *Shotgun and Stethoscope,* 15 (20 February 1875 entry).

4. *Minneapolis Daily Tribune,* 12 March 1875.

5. Ibid., 11 March 1875.

6. Herrick, "Clarence Luther Herrick," 23–37.

7. Betty L. Engebretson, "Books for Pioneers," *Minnesota History,* March 1957, 222–32.

8. Audubon's book remains in the Athenaeum's collection, now housed on the

fourth floor of the Hennepin County Central Library, and is one of only two in the state. The other is owned by the Bell Museum of Natural History at the University of Minnesota.

9. Roberts, *Shotgun and Stethoscope*, 3.

10. Clarence Herrick, July 1875 report, box 10, folder 93, Bell Museum of Natural History Records.

11. Thomas S. Roberts report cards, box 10, folder 91, Bell Museum of Natural History Records.

12. Clarence Herrick, July 1875 report.

13. Herrick, "Clarence Luther Herrick," 31.

14. Thomas S. Roberts to Franklin Benner, 30 May 1875, box 1, Roberts and Family Papers.

15. Roberts, *Shotgun and Stethoscope*, 21 (14 June 1875 entry).

16. Ibid., 22 (19 June 1875 entry).

17. Thomas S. Roberts, "A Few Notes concerning the Breeding of the Hydrachlidon lariformis in Minnesota," box 10, folder 95, Bell Museum of Natural History Records.

18. Ibid.

19. Roberts, *The Birds of Minnesota*, 1: 6; Herrick, "Clarence Luther Herrick," 30.

20. Franklin Benner to Thomas S. Roberts, fall 1875, box 10, folder 95, Bell Museum of Natural History Records. Krosch dates this letter at August 25, 1875, but other documents put it more likely around October or November 1875.

21. Scott Weidensaul, *Of a Feather: A Brief History of American Birding* (New York: Harcourt, 2007), 134.

22. C. Judson Herrick, "The Young Naturalists' Society," *The Scientific Monthly* 54: 2.

23. Minutes to the Young Naturalists' Society, December 1875, box 10, folder 92, Bell Museum of Natural History Records.

24. Clarence Herrick, July 1875 report.

25. A breeding bird survey is under way.

26. Roberts, *The Birds of Minnesota*, 1: 5.

27. Thomas S. Roberts to Franklin Benner, 18 October 1874, box 1, folder "Correspondence 1857–1876," Roberts and Family Papers.

28. Roberts to Benner, 13 February 1875, box 1, folder "Correspondence 1857–1876," Roberts and Family Papers. The Blackburnian Warbler is now *Dendroica fusca*.

29. Thomas S. Roberts, 1877, "Strangers at Home," box 1, folder "Correspondence 1877–1880," Roberts and Family Papers.

30. Richard Scott to Thomas S. Roberts, 24 March 1879, box 10, folder 95, Bell Museum of Natural History Records.

4. COLLEGE BOY

1. Roberts, *Shotgun and Stethoscope*, 108 (28 April 1878 entry).

2. Ibid., 100 (29 January 1878 entry).

3. Ibid. (21 February 1878 entry).

4. Ibid., 108 (29 April 1878 entry).

5. Ibid., 109 (2 May 1878 entry).

6. Thomas S. Roberts to Franklin Benner, 11 March 1877, box 1, folder "Correspondence 1877–1880," Roberts and Family Papers.

7. Roberts to Benner, 19 August 1877, box 1, folder "Correspondence 1877–1880," Roberts and Family Papers.

8. Roberts, *Shotgun and Stethoscope*, 137 (25 May 1879 entry); the emphasis is Roberts's. The story was later published in *Forest and Stream* 12: 464.

9. Roberts to Benner, 23 December 1877, box 1, folder "Correspondence 1877–1880," Roberts and Family Papers.

10. Roberts to Benner, 24 March 1878, box 1, folder "Correspondence 1877–1880," Roberts and Family Papers.

11. Roberts, *Shotgun and Stethoscope*, 106 (18 April 1878 entry).

12. See Friends of Bassett Creek web site, http://www.mninter.net

13. Roberts, *Shotgun and Stethoscope*, 101 (25 February 1878 entry).

14. Ibid., 66 (17 March 1877 entry); ibid., 67 (4 April 1877 entry).

15. Roberts to Benner, 3 February 1878, box 1, folder "Correspondence 1877–1880," Roberts and Family Papers.

16. Roberts to Benner, 4 November 1877, box 1, folder "Correspondence 1877–1880," Roberts and Family Papers.

17. Roberts to Benner, 24 March 1878, box 1, folder "Correspondence 1877–1880," Roberts and Family Papers.

18. Roberts to Benner, 27 June 1878, box 1, folder "Correspondence 1877–1880," Roberts and Family Papers.

19. Roberts to Benner, 6 February 1876, box 1, folder "Correspondence 1857–1876," Roberts and Family Papers.

20. Roberts, *Shotgun and Stethoscope*, 120 (11 August 1878 entry).

21. Ibid., 129–30 (7 March 1879 entry).

22. Ibid., 138 (6 June 1879 entry).

23. Ibid., 147 (27 July 1879 entry).

24. Ibid.

25. Ibid., 148 (2 August 1879 entry).

26. Ibid.

27. Ibid., 151 (10 August, 11 August, and 12 August 1879 entries).

28. Ibid., 151 (14 August 1879 entry).

29. Ibid., 152–53 (18 September 1879 entry).

30. Ibid., 154 (25 October 1879 entry). Today, the City of Minneapolis impound lot, the former Irving Avenue Dump Site, and City of Minneapolis Linden Yard occupy this site. It has been assessed as a state Superfund site.

5. A GYPSY LIFE

1. Roberts, *Shotgun and Stethoscope,* 165.

2. Ibid., 166 (16 April 1880 entry).

3. Ibid., 166 (17 April 1880 entry).

4. Ibid., 166–67 (18 April 1880 entry).

5. Ibid., 170 (1 July 1880 entry)

6. Ibid., 170 (3 July 1880 entry). Young Roberts is observant. The plant is one of the hallmarks of the Anoka sand plain.

7. John Roberts to Thomas S. Roberts, 4 July 1880, box 1, folder "Correspondence 1877–1880," Roberts and Family Papers.

8. Roberts, *Shotgun and Stethoscope,* 170 (3 July 1880 entry).

9. Ibid., 173 (27 July 1880 entry).

10. Ibid., 175 (19 August 1880 entry).

11. Ibid., 175–76 (21 August 1880 entry).

12. Franklin Benner to Thomas S. Roberts, 8 October 1880, box 1, folder "Correspondence 1877–1880," Roberts and Family Papers.

13. Emma Roberts to Thomas S. Roberts, 24 July 1880, box 1, folder "Correspondence 1877–1880," Roberts and Family Papers.

14. Roberts, *Shotgun and Stethoscope,* 177 (10 September 1880 entry).

15. Ibid., 180 (2 October 1880 entry).

16. Thomas S. Roberts to Joe Kingman, 10 October 1880, box 1, folder "Correspondence 1877–1880," Roberts and Family Papers.

17. Roberts, *Shotgun and Stethoscope,* 182 (16–18 October 1880 entries).

18. Ibid., 182 (22 October 1880 entry).

19. Thomas S. Roberts to Franklin Benner, 14 November 1880, box 1, folder "Correspondence 1877–1880," Roberts and Family Papers.

20. Roberts, *Shotgun and Stethoscope,* 185 (15 November 1880 entry).

21. Ibid., 188 (11 May 1881 entry).

22. Ibid., 188 (28 May 1881 entry).

23. Ibid., 187 (5 May 1881 entry).

24. Ibid., 188 (27 May 1881 entry).

25. Ibid., 191 (16 June 1881 entry).

26. Thomas S. Roberts to John Roberts, 3 July 1881, box 1, folder "Correspondence 1881–1896," Roberts and Family Papers.

27. Ibid.

28. Ibid.

29. Roberts, *Shotgun and Stethoscope,* 17 August 1881 entry.

30. Ibid., 194 (3 August 1881 entry).

31. Thomas S. Roberts to John Roberts, 30 August 1881, box 1, folder "Correspondence 1881–1896," Roberts and Family Papers.

32. Ibid.

33. Roberts, *Shotgun and Stethoscope,* 197 (5 September 1881 entry).

6. THE MEDICAL STUDENT

1. John Roberts, journal, 28 December 1881, box 2, volume 3, Roberts and Family Papers.

2. Thomas S. Roberts to Franklin Benner, 23 January 1876, box 1, folder "Correspondence 1857–1876," Roberts and Family Papers.

3. Roberts, *Shotgun and Stethoscope,* 214 (23 December 1881 entry).

4. Ibid., 215 (10 January 1882 entry).

5. Ibid.

6. Thomas S. Roberts to Ralph Bailey, 21 August 1943, box 39, folder 40, Bell Museum of Natural History Records.

7. Roberts, *Shotgun and Stethoscope,* 226 (9 November 1883 entry).

8. Ibid., 233 (13 October 1883 entry).

9. Ibid., 227 (22 November 1883 entry).

10. Ibid., 226 (12 November 1883 entry).

11. Amos W. Abbott to Thomas S. Roberts, 4 January 1884, box 1, folder "Correspondence 1881–1896," Roberts and Family Papers.

12. Roberts, *Shotgun and Stethoscope,* 236 (26 February 1884 entry).

13. Ibid., 227–28 (23–26 November 1883 entry).

14. Woodworth, "Among Those We Know," 78.

15. C. Hart Merriam to Thomas S. Roberts, 28 September 1883, box 1, folder "Correspondence 1881–1896," Roberts and Family Papers.

16. W. J. Breckenridge and W. Kilgore, "Thomas Sadler Roberts (1858–1946)," *The Auk* 63 (1946): 77.

17. Thomas S. Roberts to Robert J. Hunter, 5 June 1940, box 38, folder 330, Bell Museum of Natural History Records. Osler went from Pennsylvania to Johns Hopkins Medical School, where he was one of the four founders of its modern program.

His advice to students included this: "Look wise, say nothing and grunt. Speech was given to conceal thought."

18. Development of the typewriter occurred over decades. The QWERTY keyboard was not set until 1874; the ribbon was first patented in 1886.

19. "125 Years of Service: A History of the Hennepin County Medical Society," *Bulletin of the Hennepin County Medical Society,* supplement to 51, no. 3 (June 1980).

20. Amos W. Abbott to Thomas S. Roberts, 12 July 1885, box 1, folder "Correspondence 1881–1896," Roberts and Family Papers.

21. D. Hayes Agnew, Alfred Stillé, Lewis P. Bush, Charles K. Mills, and Roland G. Curtin, *History and Reminiscences of the Philadelphia Almshouse and Philadelphia Hospital,* vol. 1 (Philadelphia: Detre and Blackburn, 1890).

22. Arthur Ames Bliss, *Blockley Days: Memories and Impressions of a Resident Physician, 1883–1884* (Springfield, Mass.: privately printed, 1916).

23. Ibid., 39.

24. Ibid., 78.

25. Ibid., 49.

26. Ibid., 40.

27. Ibid., 22.

28. American physicians were slow to embrace sterile techniques. See Candice Millard, *Destiny of the Republic: A Tale of Madness, Medicine, and the Murder of a President* (New York: Doubleday, 2011).

29. Ibid., 18.

30. Thomas S. Roberts to Robert J. Hunter, 5 June 1940, box 38, folder 330, Bell Museum of Natural History Records. Hunter, in Philadelphia, was collecting reminiscences to commemorate the late Dr. Osler in June 1940.

7. A FAMILY MAN

1. Joe Kingman to Thomas Sadler Roberts, 10 June 1885; and Harry Robinson to Roberts, 10 June 10 1885, both in box 10, folder 98, Bell Museum of Natural History Records.

2. Amos W. Abbott to Thomas Sadler Roberts, 22 July 1886, box 1, folder "Correspondence 1880–1896," Roberts and Family Papers.

3. D. W. Cathell, *The Physician Himself* (Baltimore: Cushings and Baily Press, 1882), 24.

4. John Roberts, journal, 15 May 1888.

5. Thomas S. Roberts, journal, 5 April 1888, box 4, folder 32, Bell Museum of Natural History Records.

6. John Roberts, journal, 11 May 1888.

7. Cathell, *The Physician Himself,* 21.

8. Jan Coombs, "Rural Medical Practice in the 1880s: A View from Central Wisconsin," *Bulletin of the History of Medicine* 64 (1990): 35–62.

9. Minutes to the January 5, 1889, meeting; and minutes to the April 5, 1890, meeting of the Minnesota Academy of Medicine, Minnesota Academy of Medicine Record Books, 1887–1956, Minnesota Historical Society.

10. John Roberts, journal, 20 May 1888.

11. Cathell, *The Physician Himself,* 15.

12. Kane, *The Falls of St. Anthony,* 115.

13. Davidson's *Minneapolis City Directory,* 1886.

14. *Minneapolis Tribune,* 6 May 1882, quoted in Kane, *The Falls of St. Anthony,* 114.

15. S. S. Kilvington, *Annual Report of the Board of Health, City of Minneapolis,* 1888, 30.

16. Ibid., 31.

17. A. J. Russell, *Loring Park Aspect* (Cedar Rapids, Iowa: Torch Press, 1919), 58. Thomas did, however, also observe a winterkill of the lake on April 5, 1880, prior to the sewer. Roberts, *Shotgun and Stethoscope,* 158.

18. Russell, *Loring Park Aspect,* 58.

19. John Roberts, journal, 27 June 1888.

20. Ibid., 21 August 1890.

21. Ibid., 26 April 1890.

22. Roberts, *The Birds of Minnesota,* 2: 419.

23. John Roberts, journal, 5 September 1888.

24. Ibid., 12 September 1890.

25. Clarence L. Herrick to Thomas S. Roberts, 29 July 1894, box 12, folder 130, Bell Museum of Natural History Records. In the ten years Herrick was in New Mexico, he served as president of the University of New Mexico from 1897 to 1901. He died at Socorro, New Mexico, September 15, 1904.

26. Thomas S. Roberts to Robert J. Hunter, 5 June 1940, box 38, folder 330, Bell Museum of Natural History Records.

27. Interstate 94 runs through the site of this house. Central Lutheran Church would have been a near neighbor.

28. Woodworth, "Among Those We Know," 77.

29. Jane C. Roberts to Thomas S. Roberts, 10 February 1913, box 6, folder 53, Bell Museum of Natural History Records.

30. Jane C. Roberts to Thomas S. Roberts, 2 March 1913, box 6, folder 53, Bell Museum of Natural History Records.

31. Jane C. Roberts to Thomas S. Roberts, 13 February 1913, box 6, folder 53, Bell Museum of Natural History Records.

8. THE BUSY PHYSICIAN

1. Woodworth, "Among Those We Know," 77.

2. Jane C. Roberts to Thomas S. Roberts, 13 February 1913, box 6, folder 53, Bell Museum of Natural History Records.

3. Woodworth, "Among Those We Know," 77. Roberts developed a taste for fine Cuban cigars.

4. Brenda Ueland, *Me* (St. Paul: North Central Publishing Co.; The Schubert Club, 1983), 7.

5. Woodworth, "Among Those We Know," 33.

6. Coombs, "Rural Medical Practice in the 1880s," 35–62.

7. *Annual Report of St. Barnabas Hospital,* 1901, Wangensteen Historical Library, University of Minnesota.

8. Roberts assumed the position in 1893, following Amos Abbott. St. Barnabas then closed from September 1, 1893, to November 1, 1894, while the old building was demolished. A new building was dedicated on All Saints Day, 1894, at 901 South Sixth Street.

9. *Annual Report of St. Barnabas Hospital,* 1897, Wangensteen Historical Library.

10. Minutes to the Annual Meeting of the St. Barnabas Hospital Staff, February 3, 1899, box 10, folder 99, Bell Museum of Natural History Records.

11. *Annual Report of St. Barnabas Hospital,* 1900, Wangensteen Historical Library.

12. Thomas S. Roberts to O. B. Warren, 8 September 1898, box 12, folder 135, Bell Museum of Natural History Records.

13. *Annual Report of St. Barnabas Hospital,* 1900, Wangensteen Historical Library.

14. Letters to Thomas S. Roberts: January 26, 1899; December 31, 1899; April 7, 1899; August 21, 1899; August 21, 1899; all in box 11, folder 100, Bell Museum of Natural History Records. I have omitted the names on letters from patients.

15. Ibid., July 35, [*sic*] 1898.

16. Ibid., March 13, 1899; March 15, 1900.

17. Clara Ueland to Thomas S. Roberts, undated, box 11, folder 102, Bell Museum of Natural History Records.

18. Breckenridge and Kilgore, "Thomas Sadler Roberts," 574–83.

19. City of Minneapolis Quarantine Officer (illegible signature) to Thomas S. Roberts, 3 July 1900, box 11, folder 104, Bell Museum of Natural History Records.

20. Frank Ryan, *The Forgotten Plague* (Boston: Little, Brown and Co., 1992), 10.

21. Thomas S. Roberts, "The Prophylaxis of Tuberculosis," *St. Paul Medical Journal* (1903): 96–111.

22. Leonard G. Wilson, *Medical Revolution in Minnesota: A History of the University of Minnesota Medical School* (St. Paul: Midewiwin Press, 1989), 112.

23. The building was demolished in 2011 in conjunction with major overhaul of nearby Northrop Auditorium.

24. The building that housed the walk-in clinic was also demolished in 2011, having been termed an "eyesore." It had recently housed Grandma's Saloon and Grill.

25. The gift of $120,000 was from the widow of Dr. Adolphus F. Elliot. It was supplemented by $40,000 from the state legislature. The bequest initiated the drive for a new overall campus layout, culminating in Cass Gilbert's design.

26. Wilson, *Medical Revolution in Minnesota*, 112.

27. Ibid., 119.

28. Jane C. Roberts to Thomas S. Roberts, 13 February 1913, box 6, folder 53, Bell Museum of Natural History Records.

29. Jane C. Roberts to Thomas S. Roberts, 2 March 1913, box 6, folder 53, Bell Museum of Natural History Records.

9. THE EMPTY DAY

1. Thomas Miller to Thomas S. Roberts, 28 May 1889, box 12, folder 126, Bell Museum of Natural History Records.

2. Henry Nachtrieb, *First Report of the State Zoologist Accompanied by Notes on the Birds of Minnesota by P.L. Hatch* (Minneapolis: Harrison and Smith, 1892).

3. Ibid., 2.

4. Henry F. Nachtrieb to Thomas S. Roberts, 28 March 1893, box 12, folder 129, Bell Museum of Natural History Records.

5. Roberts, *Shotgun and Stethoscope*, 242.

6. Ibid., 243 (11 June 1894 entry).

7. Ibid., 244 (15 June 1894 entry).

8. Ibid., 244 (15 June 1894 entry).

9. Ibid., 245 (16 June 1894 entry).

10. Ibid.

11. Ibid., 245 (18 June 1894 entry).

12. Ibid., 246 (19 June 1894 entry).

13. Chapman made a spectacular debut into the ornithological world in 1886 at age twenty-two when he took two afternoon forays down fashionable Fourteenth Street in New York City, counting the dead birds that adorned women's hats: 542 birds in the two counts.

14. Roberts, *Shotgun and Stethoscope*, 247 (27 May 1898 entry).

15. Ibid.

16. Thomas S. Roberts to O. B. Warren, 3 July 1898, box 12, folder 135, Bell Museum of Natural History Records.

17. Warren to Roberts, 6 July 1898, box 12, folder 135, Bell Museum of Natural History Records.

18. Thomas S. Roberts, "The Camera as an Aid in the Study of Birds," *Bird-Lore* 1, no. 2: 38.

19. Roberts to Warren, 25 August 1898, box 12, folder 135, Bell Museum of Natural History Records.

20. Frank M. Chapman to Thomas S. Roberts, 20 January 1899, box 13, folder 136, Bell Museum of Natural History Records.

21. Roberts, *The Birds of Minnesota*, 1: 550–52.

22. Walter Deane to Ruthven Deane, 19 November 1899, box 13, folder 136, Bell Museum of Natural History Records.

23. Woodworth, "Among Those We Know," 77.

24. Roberts, *The Birds of Minnesota*, 2: 299.

25. Roberts, *Shotgun and Stethoscope*, 250 (1 July 1900 entry).

26. Ibid., 250 (30 June 1900 entry).

27. Ibid., 251, (1 July 1900 entry).

28. Ibid., 252 (8 July 1900 entry).

29. Ibid., 253 (8 July 1900 entry).

30. W. J. Breckenridge, *My Life in Natural History*, compiled and edited by Barbara Breckenridge Franklin and John J. Moriarty (Minneapolis: Bell Museum of Natural History, 2009), 22.

31. Roberts, *Shotgun and Stethoscope*, 253. Roberts penciled this information in at a later date.

32. William Brewster to Thomas S. Roberts, 3 December 1901, box 13, folder 139, Bell Museum of Natural History Records.

33. John Dobie, *The Itasca Story* (Minneapolis: Ross and Haines, 1959), 73–74.

34. Ibid., 84.

35. Ibid., 89.

36. L. O. Dart to Thomas S. Roberts, 16 June 1903, box 11, folder 108, Bell Museum of Natural History Records.

37. Dart to Roberts, 18 June 1903, box 11, folder 108, Bell Museum of Natural History Records.

38. Roberts to Warren, 18 September 1898, 20 April 1898, 18 October 1898, all in box 12, folder 135, Bell Museum of Natural History Records.

10. A FLORIDA INTERLUDE

1. Thomas S. Roberts, journal, 28 January 1914, box 6, folder 56, Bell Museum of Natural History Records.

2. Ibid., 25 January 1914.

3. Ibid., 29 January 1914, and 30 January 1914.

4. Ibid., 31 January 1914.

5. Ibid., 4 February 1914.

6. Stella Tennyson to C. M. Rankiellour (undated), box 6, folder 58, Bell Museum of Natural History Records.

7. Roberts, journal, 6 February 1914.

8. Ibid., 10 February 1914.

9. Thomas S. Roberts to Thomas Cleveland Roberts, 21 February 1914, box 6, folder 58, Bell Museum of Natural History Records.

10. Roberts, journal, 25 March 1914, and 27 March 1914.

11. Ibid., 27 March 1914.

11. THE ASSOCIATE CURATOR

1. Frank M. Chapman to Thomas S. Roberts, 9 June 1915, box 14, folder 154, Bell Museum of Natural History Records.

2. Ruthven Deane to Thomas S. Roberts, 20 June 1915, box 14, folder 154, Bell Museum of Natural History Records.

3. Chapman to Roberts, 16 August 1915, box 14, folder 154, Bell Museum of Natural History Records.

4. Henry F. Nachtrieb to Thomas S. Roberts, 6 March 1915, and 19 June 1915, box 14, folder 155, Bell Museum of Natural History Records.

5. Woodworth, "Among Those We Know," 78.

6. George E. Vincent to Thomas S. Roberts, 6 May 1915, box 2, folder 25, Henry Francis Nachtrieb Papers, University of Minnesota Archives.

7. William J. Mayo and Charles H. Mayo to G. H. Partridge, 18 May 1916, box 14, folder 159, Bell Museum of Natural History Records.

8. E. C. Gale to G. H. Partridge, 5 June 1916, box 14, folder 157, Bell Museum of Natural History Records.

9. G. H. Partridge to Thomas S. Roberts, 6 June 1916, box 14, folder 159, Bell Museum of Natural History Records.

10. James Ford Bell to Thomas S. Roberts, 27 December 1915, box 14, folder 154, Bell Museum of Natural History Records.

11. Thomas S. Roberts to Henry F. Nachtrieb, 3 August 1915, box 2, folder 25, Nachtrieb Papers.

12. Jenness Richardson's late father had been the taxidermist for the American Museum of Natural History in New York City in the 1880s and had pioneered the crafting of dioramas.

13. William T. Hornaday to Thomas S. Roberts, 14 February 1916, box 14, folder 158, Bell Museum of Natural History Records.

14. Jonas Brothers Taxidermist and Furriers, Denver, to Thomas S. Roberts, 9 February 1916, box 14, folder 158, Bell Museum of Natural History Records.

15. Thomas S. Roberts, quoted in Caryl B. Storrs, "Minnesota's Wild-Life Museum," *The Minnesotan* 2, no. 9 (March 1917): 11.

16. James Ford Bell to Henry F. Nachtrieb, 22 December 1913, box 2, folder 23, Nachtrieb Papers.

17. George E. Vincent to James Ford Bell, 26 March 1914, box 2, folder 24, Nachtrieb Papers.

18. Lawrence Lofstrom to Thomas S. Roberts, 6 November 1916, box 14, folder 158, Bell Museum of Natural History Records.

19. James F. Bell to Thomas S. Roberts, fall 1917, box 15, folder 161, Bell Museum of Natural History Records.

20. Thomas S. Roberts, quoted in Storrs, "Minnesota's Wild-Life Museum."

21. *The Minnesotan* 2, no. 9 (March 1917): 31–33.

22. Theodore C. Blegen, *Minnesota: A History of the State* (Minneapolis: University of Minnesota Press, 1963), 474.

23. William Kilgore Jr. to Thomas S. Roberts, 12 July 1917, box 15, folder 163, Bell Museum of Natural History Records.

24. John A. Stillwell, superintendent at Itasca State Park, to Thomas S. Roberts, 22 October 1917, box 15 folder 164, Bell Museum of Natural History Records.

25. Clara K. Carney to Thomas S. Roberts, 1 September 1917, and 7 September 1917, box 15, folder 162, Bell Museum of Natural History Records.

26. Carney to Roberts, 3 July 1917, 12 July 1917, and 7 September 1917, box 15, folder 162, Bell Museum of Natural History Records.

27. Henry F. Nachtrieb to Thomas S. Roberts, 7 July 1917, box 15, folder 163, Bell Museum of Natural History Records. Nachtrieb was a vigorous proponent of phonetic—"fonetic"—spelling. Roberts's dissatisfaction with viewing himself as a teacher must have lasted awhile. By the time of Nachtrieb's letter, he had taught two terms.

28. Box 15, folder 165, Bell Museum of Natural History Records.

29. The Commonses did not use mist nets, as do today's banders, but devised traps and set them in various habitats. See Marie Commons, *The Log of Tanager Hill* (Baltimore: Williams and Wilkins Co., 1938).

30. Lynda Mueller to Thomas S. Roberts, 14 November 1919, box 16, folder 168, Bell Museum of Natural History Records.

31. Nancy C. Roberts, personal communication with author by e-mail, February 17, 2011.

32. Witmer Stone to Thomas S. Roberts, November 1918, box 15, folder 165, Bell Museum of Natural History Records.

33. The State of Missouri brought suit against a federal game warden who enforced the act in 1920, arguing in part that the treaty infringed on a state's sovereign rights. The Supreme Court upheld the law.

34. William T. Hornaday to Thomas S. Roberts, 3 March 1916, box 14, folder 158, Bell Museum of Natural History Records.

35. T. S. Palmer to Thomas S. Roberts, 25 September 1916, box 14, folder 159, Bell Museum of Natural History Records.

36. Charles Johnson, "Some Recent Observations on Wild Life Conditions in the Superior Game Refuge," *Fins, Feathers and Fur* 23 (1920): 1–4.

37. Thomas S. Roberts, *The Water Birds of Minnesota: Past and Present*, a biennial report to the Game and Fish Commission for 1918 (1918): 56–91.

38. H. C. Oberholser, "Swan Lake, Nicollet County, Minnesota as a Breeding Ground for Waterfowl," *Fins, Feathers and Fur* 13 (1918): 1.

39. Johnson, "Some Recent Observations on Wild Life Conditions," 1–4.

40. Report on the Training Course for Scout Leaders, Itasca Park, August 2 to 14, 1920, box 16, folder 197, Bell Museum of Natural History Records.

41. The chapter is still in existence, meeting monthly in south Minneapolis.

42. Roberts, *The Water Birds of Minnesota*, 56–91.

43. Charles Bovey to Thomas S. Roberts, 28 June 1916, box 14, folder 156, Bell Museum of Natural History Records.

12. GAINS AND LOSSES

1. Thomas S. Roberts, pocket diary, 27 November 1925, box 2, volume 8 (1925), Roberts and Family Papers.

2. Roberts, *The Birds of Minnesota*, 1: 444.

3. Ibid., 1: 192.

4. Bird notes of Mildred Mandel for 10 June 1920, box 42, folder 377, "Bird Class students' field notes," Bell Museum of Natural History Records.

5. The folio was donated to the university in 1928, even now one of only two or three in Minnesota.

6. Field notes by Thomas S. Roberts, 6 June 1918, box 42, folder 375, Museum of Natural History Records.

7. Bird notes of Mildred Mandel for 15 May 1920, box 42, folder 377, "Bird Class students' field notes," Bell Museum of Natural History Records.

8. Thomas S. Roberts, journal of trip to Herman, Grant County, June 1924, box 8, folder 79, Bell Museum of Natural History Records.

9. Ibid., 23 June 1924.

10. Ibid., 25 June 1924.

11. Ibid., 26–27 June 1924.

12. Ibid., 3 July 1924.

13. "The Seasons," *Bird-Lore,* September–October 1924, 340–42.

14. Frank M. Chapman to Thomas S. Roberts, 1 September 1924, box 18, folder 185, Bell Museum of Natural History Records.

15. Herbert W. Gleason to Thomas S. Roberts, 14 October 1924, box 18, folder 186, Bell Museum of Natural History Records.

16. Mabel Densmore to Thomas S. Roberts, 14 October 1928, box 21, folder 203; 17 October 1929, box 21, folder 206; and 2 January 1930, box 22, folder 212; Bell Museum of Natural History Records.

17. Bruce Horsfall to Thomas S. Roberts, 26 December 1925, box 19, folder 190, Bell Museum of Natural History Records.

18. Olive Peabody Richardson to Thomas S. Roberts, 18 June 1925, box 19, folder 192, Bell Museum of Natural History Records.

19. Breckenridge, *My Life in Natural History,* 21.

20. S. A. Barrett to Thomas S. Roberts, 14 January 1926, box 20, folder 197, Bell Museum of Natural History Records.

21. *Minnesota Daily,* 9 April 1926.

22. *Minnesota Daily,* 10 April 1926.

23. James F. Bell to Thomas S. Roberts, 23 April 1926, box 19, folder 193, Bell Museum of Natural History Records.

24. Walter J. Breckenridge to Thomas S. Roberts, 16 April 1926, box 19, folder 193, Bell Museum of Natural History Records.

25. Breckenridge to Roberts, 3 May 1926, box 19, folder 193, Bell Museum of Natural History Records.

26. Breckenridge, *My Life in Natural History,* 21.

27. Ibid., 22.

28. Ibid.

29. Thomas S. Roberts, bird notes, 11 May 1920, box 42, folder 375, Bell Museum of Natural History Records.

30. Thomas S. Roberts, pocket diary, 1 December 1926, box 2 (1926), volume 9, Roberts and Family Papers.

13. WRITING THE BOOK

1. Thomas S. Roberts to Herbert Stoddard, 15 August 1932, box 48, folder 434, Bell Museum of Natural History Records.

2. Roberts, *The Birds of Minnesota,* 2: 88–89.

3. Ibid., 2: 459.

4. Ibid., 2: 345.

5. Ibid., 2: 346.

6. Ibid., 1: 267.

7. Ibid., 1: 603.

8. Ibid., 2: 180.

9. Thomas S. Roberts, pocket diary, 26 October 1929, box 2, volume 13, Roberts Family Papers.

10. Thomas S. Roberts to Walter Alois Weber, 7 March 1931, box 49, folder 443, Bell Museum of Natural History Records.

11. Thomas S. Roberts to Major Allan Brooks, 5 March 1929, box 49, folder 440, Bell Museum of Natural History Records.

12. Brooks to Roberts, 12 March 1929, box 49, folder 440, Bell Museum of Natural History Records.

13. Roberts to Brooks, 16 April 1929, box 49, folder 440, Bell Museum of Natural History Records.

14. Thomas S. Roberts to George Miksch Sutton, 5 March 1929, box 49, folder 442, Bell Museum of Natural History Records.

15. Sutton to Roberts, 8 March 1929; Sutton to Roberts, 17 May 1929; Roberts to Sutton, 22 May 1929; box 49, folder 442; Bell Museum of Natural History Records.

16. Roberts to Sutton, 2 July 1929, box 49, folder 442, Bell Museum of Natural History Records.

17. Roberts, pocket diary, 22 September 1929, box 2, volume 13, Roberts and Family Papers.

18. Ruth Bovey Stevens, quoted in Patricia C. Johnston, ed., *The Shape of Things: The Art of Francis Lee Jaques* (Afton, Minn.: Afton Historical Society Press; Camden, S.C.: Live Oak Press, 1994), 120.

19. Contract between Thomas S. Roberts and the donors to the Thomas S. Roberts Fund, box 47, folder 424, Bell Museum of Natural History Records.

20. Roberts to Brooks, 7 October 1929, box 49, folder 440, Bell Museum of Natural History Records.

21. Roberts to Brooks, 30 October 1929, box 49, folder 440, Bell Museum of Natural History Records.

22. Roger Tory Peterson, foreword to *Francis Lee Jaques: Artist of the Wilderness World,* by Florence Jaques (New York: Doubleday and Co., 1973), xiv.

23. Brooks to Roberts, 11 December 1929, box 49, folder 440, Bell Museum of Natural History Records.

24. Ibid.

25. Walter Alois Weber to Thomas S. Roberts, 4 March 1930, box 49, folder 443, Bell Museum of Natural History Records.

26. Letters between Roberts and Weber, June 1930, box 49, folder 443, Bell Museum of Natural History Records.

27. Brooks to Roberts, 23 April 1929, box 49, folder 440, Bell Museum of Natural History Records.

28. Brooks to Roberts, 27 April 1930, box 49, folder 440, Bell Museum of Natural History Records.

29. Walter Breckenridge to Thomas S. Roberts, 2 August 1931, box 22, folder 215, Bell Museum of Natural History Records.

30. Florence Page Jaques to Thomas S. Roberts, 9 March 1930, box 49, folder 441, Bell Museum of Natural History Records.

31. Thomas S. Roberts to Francis Lee Jaques, 21 March 1930, box 49, folder 441, Bell Museum of Natural History Records.

32. Roberts to Brooks, 24 September 1930; and Brooks to Roberts, 2 October 1930; box 49, folder 440; Bell Museum of Natural History Records.

33. Thomas S. Roberts to W. T. Middlebrook, 24 July 1931, box 48, folder 430, Bell Museum of Natural History Records.

34. Thomas S. Roberts to William Abbott, 16 June 1932, box 48, folder 433, Bell Museum of Natural History Records.

35. *Minnesota Alumni Weekly,* February 7, 1931.

36. Mabel Densmore to Thomas S. Roberts, 3 September 1931, box 22, folder 216, Bell Museum of Natural History Records.

37. William C. Edgar to Thomas S. Roberts, 30 December 1931, box 22, folder 216, Bell Museum of Natural History Records.

38. Roberts, pocket diary, 20 May 1932, and 26 May 1932, box 2, volume 15, Roberts and Family Papers.

39. Roberts to Densmore, 15 July 1932; Densmore to Roberts, 17 July 1932; box 48, folder 432; Bell Museum of Natural History Records.

40. Witmer Stone, "Recent Literature," *The Auk* 49 (1932): 368–70.

41. F. M. Chapman, "Book New and Reviews," *Bird-Lore* 34 (July–August 1932): 282–83.

42. *Saturday Review of Literature,* November 26, 1932, 278.

43. A few copies were given a decorative binding and sold for $25. The price for standard-bound copies was $6. Roberts did not like this but acquiesced to the Press.

44. Frank Chapman to Thomas S. Roberts, 9 May 1932, box 48, folder 431, Bell Museum of Natural History Records.

45. Roberts, pocket diary, 13 October 1932, box 2, volume 15, Roberts and Family Papers.

46. Thomas S. Roberts to Robert S. Williams, 4 August 1932, box 48, folder 434, Bell Museum of Natural History Records.

47. Thomas S. Roberts to Dr. Alfred Lewy of Chicago, 2 August 1932, box 48, folder 434, Bell Museum of Natural History Records.

48. Woodworth, "Among Those We Know," 78.

14. BUILDING MR. BELL'S MUSEUM

1. Thomas S. Roberts to Mrs. C. E. Peterson, 19 October 1932, box 36, folder 314, Bell Museum of Natural History Records.

2. Thomas S. Roberts to W. E. Saunders, of London, Ontario, 18 April 1933, box 36, folder 315; Roberts to W. Kilgore, 15 March 1933, box 23, folder 225; Bell Museum of Natural History Records.

3. Thomas S. Roberts to I. Foster, 22 April 1933, box 36, folder 315, Bell Museum of Natural History Records.

4. Thomas S. Roberts to Mabel Densmore, 12 September 1933, box 36, folder 316, Bell Museum of Natural History Records.

5. Thomas S. Roberts to Frank Chapman, 23 February 1934, box 36, folder 317, Bell Museum of Natural History Records.

6. Annette Atkins, *Creating Minnesota: A History from the Inside Out* (St. Paul: Minnesota Historical Society Press, 2007), 172.

7. Thomas S. Roberts to Mrs. C. E. Peterson, 23 February 1934, box 36, folder 317, Bell Museum of Natural History Records.

8. Thomas S. Roberts to Elsie Chason, 10 May 1934, box 36, folder 317, Bell Museum of Natural History Records.

9. Roberts to Densmore; and Roberts to Peterson, 22 May 1934, box 36, folder 317; Bell Museum of Natural History Records.

10. Densmore to Roberts, 9 September 1934, box 24, folder 226, Bell Museum of Natural History Records.

11. Roberts to Peterson, 3 April 1934, box 36, folder 317, Bell Museum of Natural History Records.

12. Roberts to Peterson, 18 April 1935, box 36, folder 319, Bell Museum of Natural History Records.

13. Thomas S. Roberts to Miss Matilda Hummel, 11 March 1937, box 37, folder 322, Bell Museum of Natural History Records.

14. Weidensaul, *Of a Feather,* 167.

15. C. Avery to Thomas S. Roberts, 24 February 1927, box 20, folder 198, Bell Museum of Natural History Records.

16. Thomas S. Roberts to T. Gilbert Pearson, 27 December 1933, box 36, folder 316, Bell Museum of Natural History Records.

17. Weidensaul, *Of a Feather,* 170–74.

18. Thomas S. Roberts to F. L. Roberts, 26 June 1933, box 36, folder 315; Roberts to John Cochran, 6 July 1935, box 36, folder 320; Roberts to J. H. Baker, 5 December 1934, box 36, folder 318; Bell Museum of Natural History Records.

19. Roberts to Pearson, 8 May 1937, box 37, folder 324, Bell Museum of Natural History Records.

20. www.gorp.com/parks-guide.

21. Thomas S. Roberts to J. C. Salver, 6 July 1934, box 36, folder 315, Bell Museum of Natural History Records.

22. Thomas S. Roberts, pocket diary, 12–13 November 1933, box 2, volume 17, Roberts and Family Papers.

23. Thomas S. Roberts to W. K. Kilgore, 18 October 1936, box 25, folder 235, Bell Museum of Natural History Records.

24. Roberts, pocket diary, 20, 21, 22, and 24 September 1937, box 2, volume 21, Roberts and Family Papers.

25. Roberts, pocket diary, 29 September 1937, box 2, volume 21, Roberts and Family Papers.

26. Roberts to Kilgore, 5 October 1937, box 26, folder 240, Bell Museum of Natural History Records.

27. Roberts, pocket diary, 6–10 October 1937, box 2, volume 21, Roberts and Family Papers.

28. Marjorie Phillips, undated handwritten reminiscence, from Lane Phillips.

29. *Minneapolis Tribune,* October 12, 1937.

30. Roberts to Densmore, 21 October 1937, box 37, folder 324, Bell Museum of Natural History Records.

31. Roberts, pocket diary, 14 February 1938, box 2, volume 22, Roberts and Family Papers.

32. Roberts's account of the meeting given at a dinner for the University of Minnesota Board of Regents, hosted by James Ford Bell, September 28, 1940, box 40, folder 352, Bell Museum of Natural History Records.

33. Charles L. Peet to James Ford Bell, 3 April 1935, box 24, folder 230, Bell Museum of Natural History Records.

34. Bell to Peet, 5 April 1935, box 24, folder 230, Bell Museum of Natural History Records. The St. Paul Institute would eventually get their science museum. The effort in 1935 led only to an auditorium and an exhibition wing at the converted red sandstone mansion behind the state capitol that served as its home, but in 1999,

after a detour of several decades on Tenth Street, the Science Museum of Minnesota would finally settle into a permanent location on Kellogg Boulevard.

35. James F. Bell to Thomas S. Roberts, 5 April 1935, box 24, folder 230, Bell Museum of Natural History Records.

36. The PWA should not be confused with the Works Progress Administration (WPA).

37. Thomas S. Roberts to George Rysgaard, 28 July 1938, box 37, folder 326, Bell Museum of Natural History Records.

38. Roberts to Chapman, 25 August 1938, box 37, folder 326, Bell Museum of Natural History Records.

39. Thomas S. Roberts to L. C. Everard, 25 October 1939, box 37, folder 328, Bell Museum of Natural History Records.

40. Roberts to Francis Lee Jaques, 16 August 1938, box 37, folder 326, Bell Museum of Natural History Records.

41. Florence Page Jaques, *Francis Lee Jaques: Artist of the Wilderness World* (Garden City, N.Y.: Doubleday and Company, 1973), 88.

42. Roberts, pocket diary, 1941, box 2, volume 25, Roberts and Family Papers. Roberts kept tallies of his many cribbage partners on the back pages of the book.

43. Roberts to Chapman, 2 June 1939, box 37, folder 327, Bell Museum of Natural History Records.

44. Francis Lee Jaques to Roberts, 27 July 1938, box 26, folder 243; Roberts to Jaques, 1 August 1938, box 37, folder 327; Bell Museum of Natural History Records.

45. Roberts, pocket diary, 17 October 1938, box 2, volume 22, Roberts and Family Papers; Thomas S. Roberts to F. S. Davidson, 7 November 1938, box 37, folder 326, Bell Museum of Natural History Records.

46. Roberts, pocket diary, 14 April 1938, box 2, volume 22, Roberts and Family Papers. The meeting took place at the Museum of Natural History, then housed in Zoology.

47. Mary Elwell to Thomas S. Roberts, 24 November 1939, box 26, folder 245, Bell Museum of Natural History Records.

48. Roberts to Francis Lee Jaques, 2 June 1939, box 37, folder 327, Bell Museum of Natural History Records.

49. Jaques to Roberts, 14 June 1939, box 27, folder 247, Bell Museum of Natural History Records.

50. Roy Chapman Andrews to Thomas S. Roberts, 14 December 1939, box 26, folder 245, Bell Museum of Natural History Records.

51. Roberts to Jaques, 18 December 1939, box 37, folder 328, Bell Museum of Natural History Records.

52. Thomas S. Roberts to Charles H. Johnston Jr., 6 February 1940, box 38, folder 329, Bell Museum of Natural History Records.

15. THE CARDINAL HOUR

1. Frank M. Chapman to Thomas S. Roberts, 10 January 1940, box 27, folder 249, Bell Museum of Natural History Records.

2. Jaques approached Roberts in 1921 with an unusual request: he wanted to experiment retouching imperfect bird photos, and he asked if Roberts had any he could send him. Chapman had given Jaques Roberts's name. Roberts was not interested. (May 1, 1921, box 17, folder 175, D–M, 1921, Bell Museum of Natural History Records.) There are no records in the museum archived papers of a job request.

3. Roberts to Chapman, 19 January 1940, box 38, folder 329, Bell Museum of Natural History Records.

4. James F. Bell to Thomas S. Roberts, 16 February 1940, box 27, folder 249, Bell Museum of Natural History Records.

5. Thomas S. Roberts to Francis L. Jaques, 17 January 1941, box 38, folder 332, Bell Museum of Natural History Records.

6. Breckenridge and Kilgore, "Thomas Sadler Roberts," 574–83.

7. Ibid.

8. W. P. Abbott to Thomas S. Roberts, 1 April 1940, box 27, folder 249, Bell Museum of Natural History Records.

9. Robert Nord to Thomas S. Roberts, 23 April 1941, box 28, folder 255, Bell Museum of Natural History Records.

10. Albert Hochbaum to Thomas S. Roberts, 15 November 1941, box 28, folder 254, Bell Museum of Natural History Records.

11. Charles Evans to Thomas S. Roberts, 21 November 1941, box 28, folder 253, Bell Museum of Natural History Records.

12. Thomas S. Roberts to George Rysgaard, 13 December 1941, box 38, folder 334, Bell Museum of Natural History Records.

13. Thomas S. Roberts to the Emergency Medical Service, 5 June 1942, box 39, folder 336, Bell Museum of Natural History Records.

14. Collas G. Harris to Thomas S. Roberts, 12 February 1942, box 28, folder 259, Bell Museum of Natural History Records.

15. Thomas S. Roberts to Jerome Kuehn, 16 July 1943, box 39, folder 339, Bell Museum of Natural History Records.

16. Thomas S. Roberts to Charles Sigerfoos, 30 August 1943, box 39, folder 340, Bell Museum of Natural History Records.

17. Roberts to Rysgaard, 17 March 1943, box 39, folder 338, Bell Museum of Natural History Records.

18. Roberts to Rysgaard, 17 July 1943, box 39, folder 339, Bell Museum of Natural History Records.

19. Florence Page Jaques to Thomas S. Roberts, 6 August 1942, box 28, folder 259, Bell Museum of Natural History Records.

20. Thomas S. Roberts to Francis Lee Jaques, 8 January 1943, box 39, folder 338, Bell Museum of Natural History Records.

21. Marjorie Edgar to Thomas S. Roberts, 3 August 1943, box 29, folder 263, Bell Museum of Natural History Records.

22. Francis Lee Jaques to Roberts, undated, 1943, box 29, folder 263, Bell Museum of Natural History Records.

23. Thomas S. Roberts to James F. Bell, 15 December 1943, box 39, folder 340, Bell Museum of Natural History Records.

24. Breckenridge, *My Life in Natural History,* 26.

25. Ibid., 27.

26. Thomas S. Roberts to Charles Rief, 9 August 1945, box 40, folder 345, Bell Museum of Natural History Records.

27. Thomas S. Roberts to Charles Finley, 17 June 1944, box 39, folder 342, Bell Museum of Natural History Records.

28. Thomas S. Roberts to Edward Preble, 21 April 1944, box 39, folder 341, Bell Museum of Natural History Records.

29. Roberts to Chapman, 10 July 1944, box 39, folder 340, Bell Museum of Natural History Records.

30. Chapman to Roberts, 14 July 1944, box 30, folder 268, Bell Museum of Natural History Records.

31. Roberts, pocket diary, 26 October 1944, box 2, volume 28, Roberts and Family Papers.

32. Ibid., 16 February 1945, box 2, volume 29, Roberts and Family Papers.

33. W. J. Breckenridge to Thomas S. Roberts, 1 April 1945, box 30, folder 272, Bell Museum of Natural History Records.

34. Roberts to Chapman, 11 June 1942, box 39, folder 336, Bell Museum of Natural History Records.

35. Ibid.

36. Roberts to Francis Lee Jaques, 5 February 1945, box 40, folder 344, Bell Museum of Natural History Records.

37. W. Eastman to Thomas S. Roberts, 10 September 1945, box 30, folder 272, Bell Museum of Natural History Records.

38. Clark Wissler, *Museum News* (Journal of the American Association of Museums), 1 February 1943, from a paper read by Wissler at the AAM's annual meeting, 18–19 May 1942.

39. Roberts to Bell, 17 March 1943, box 39, folder 338, Bell Museum of Natural History Records.

40. Thomas S. Roberts to C. Judson Herrick, 28 August 1945, box 40, folder 345, Bell Museum of Natural History Records.

41. Roberts to Francis Lee Jaques, 11 October 1945, box 40, folder 345, Bell Museum of Natural History Records.

42. Roberts, pocket diary, 28 December 1945, box 2, volume 29, Roberts and Family Papers.

43. Ibid., 12 January 1946, box 2, volume 30, Roberts and Family Papers.

44. Thomas Sadler Roberts to John A. Lepak, secretary, Minnesota Academy of Medicine, 12 October 1945, box 40, folder 345, Bell Museum of Natural History Records.

Index

SUE LEAF is the author of *Potato City: Nature, History, and Community in the Age of Sprawl* and *The Bullhead Queen: A Year on Pioneer Lake* (Minnesota, 2009), a finalist for the Minnesota Book Awards. Trained as a zoologist, she now writes on environmental topics. She is president of the Wild River Audubon Society of east-central Minnesota.

Also Published by the University of Minnesota Press

A Wilderness Within: The Life of Sigurd F. Olson
David Backes

Hawk Ridge: Minnesota's Birds of Prey
Laura Erickson
Illustrations by Betsy Bowen

Twelve Owls
Laura Erickson
Illustrations by Betsy Bowen

Canoe Country and Snowshoe Country
Florence Page Jaques
Illustrations by Francis Lee Jaques

The Geese Fly High
Florence Page Jaques
Illustrations by Francis Lee Jaques

The Bullhead Queen: A Year on Pioneer Lake
Sue Leaf